IMAGES
of America

OLD TOWN

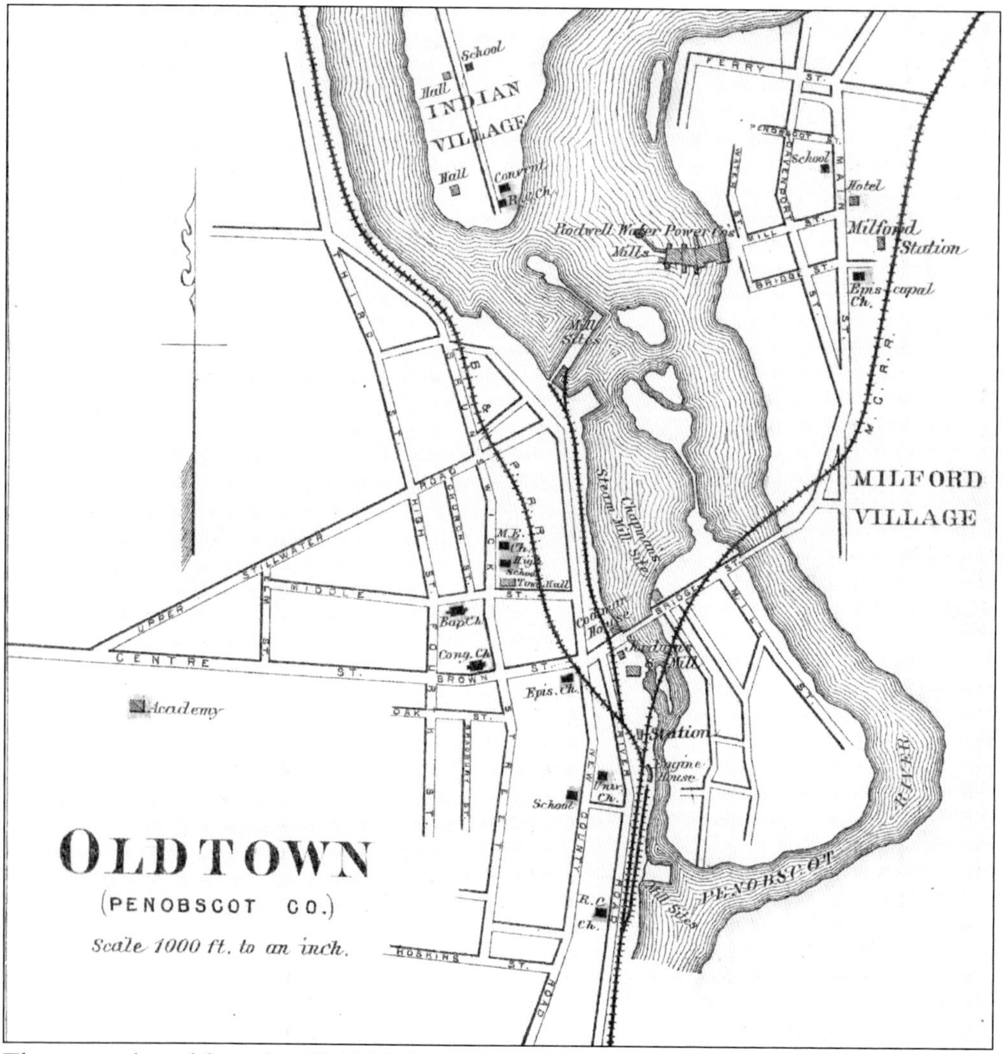

This map, adapted from the 1894 *J.H. Stuart State of Maine Atlas*, shows the central part of the city of Old Town, Maine, with the Penobscot Nation on Indian Island depicted at the top. Union Academy, an early secondary school, is located at the lower left of the map, below Center Street. (Author's collection.)

On the Cover: In this c. 1910 image, the W. Clement Mutty Pharmacy occupies a choice location in the Folsom Block at the intersection of Center and Main Streets in Old Town, once known as Folsom Square. A newsboy and his friend can be seen hawking the latest "Saturday Evening Post," most likely from the pharmacy. Printer C.W. Robbins, publisher of the *Old Town (Maine) Enterprise*, is located on the second story to their left. Joining these businesses are lawyer Clarence Scott, whose office was over the pharmacy; A.J. Goldsmith, clothiers; Dr. E.M. Marquis, who was also the city physician; Justin L. Keith's Old Town Shoe Store; and E.A. Blanchard's stove shop. Constructed in 1869, this building originally housed the pharmacy of Maj. Melville M. Folsom and his brothers Dr. Albion P. Folsom and Franklin W. Folsom. (Author's collection.)

IMAGES
of America

OLD TOWN

Peter R. Stowell

ARCADIA
PUBLISHING

ISBN 978-1-4671-2397-6

Published by Arcadia Publishing
Charleston, South Carolina

Printed in the United States of America

Library of Congress Control Number: 2016935375

For all general information, please contact Arcadia Publishing:
Telephone 843-853-2070
Fax 843-853-0044
E-mail sales@arcadiapublishing.com
For customer service and orders:
Toll-Free 1-888-313-2665

Visit us on the Internet at www.arcadiapublishing.com

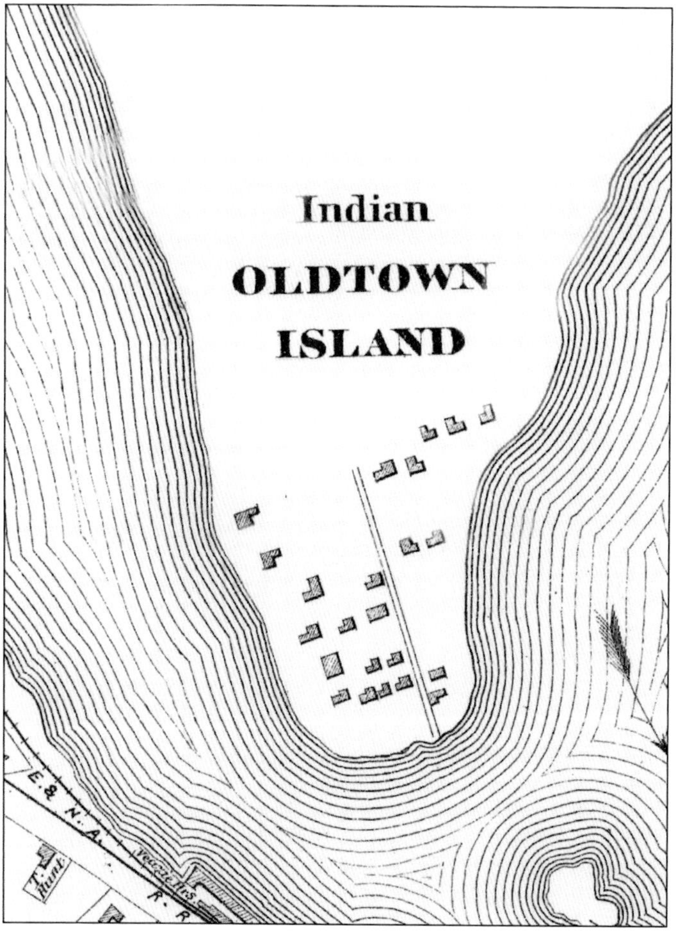

Indian Island in the Penobscot River is depicted here from a map by W.A. Sherman in his 1875 *Atlas of Penobscot County, Maine*. The Island is about one mile long and a half mile wide. During the 19th-century heyday of lumbering in Old Town, the Penobscot Nation rented shore lots to the river drivers to store their supplies and erect their living quarters. (Author's collection.)

Contents

ACKNOWLEDGMENTS

I would like to acknowledge the support of the staff of the Old Town Museum for access to its images and for their review of this book. The Old Town Public Library too has shown a level of friendship and support that made this book better than it would otherwise have been. Thanks go to Steve Thompson of Hallowell for his atlas images and for special photographic services and to Donald Angevine for his genealogical research. A special thank-you goes to Bernie and Diana Rojo Poulin for their enthusiasm, friendship, and support. I am grateful to all who lent their help.

Images from the author's collection are marked (PRS). Additional images were submitted by the Old Town Museum (OTM), the Old Town Public Library (OTPL), the City of Old Town, the Maine Historic Preservation Commission (MHPC), Diana Rojo Poulin (DRP), Bernie LaBree (BLB), Betsy H. Paradis (BHP), John and Susan Cyr (JSC), Gary and Alex Thorne (GAT), Carol L. May (CLM), Benson W. Gray (BWG), Eisso J. Atzema (EJA), Charles and Linda Weeks (CLW), James W. Kauppila (JWK), Peter W. Taylor (PWT), Larry Mishou, Clark and Ann Young (CAY), Theresa C. Hart (TCH), William A. Osborne (WAO), Charles Norman Shay (CNS), Philip A. Dunn Jr. (PAD), the Library of Congress (LOC), and Rick J. Vaillancourt (RJV).

Introduction

One of the wonderful things about being associated with the Old Town Museum is having the opportunity to explore the collections hiding in the back room of our old church. Because we cannot possibly display all of the photographs in the collection in the museum, we decided to create a photo book, so you all could enjoy them as well. We were surprised ourselves by the scores of images hiding inside our wall, but were even more overjoyed to uncover so many photographs not previously seen in the collections of the Maine Historic Preservation Commission, the Old Town Public Library, and in private collections. Our engrossing local history is now more complete than ever.

The parcel of land we call Old Town has a rich history. From the earliest settlement by the ancestors of the Penobscot Nation, through the building of a church by the French Jesuit missionaries in the early 1600s, the arrival of John Marsh in 1774, and the building of early sawmills by men named Winslow, Davis, Veazie and Wadleigh, Old Town was established and its future as a viable community was guaranteed.

For thousands of years, the Penobscot Nation lived on this land, developing an extraordinary culture and later contributing to all the important struggles for the United States to become a country, beginning even before the Revolutionary War. As we have shared the land and water, we have all delighted in knowing important Penobscots such as Joseph Nicolar, Lucy Nicolar, Molly Molasses, Louis Sockalexis, Molly Spotted Elk, Florence Shay, and Charles Norman Shay.

Hardworking men spent winters in the woods, cutting and moving trees, so they could be floated downriver in the spring, supplying these sawmills with logs from the northern reaches of the Penobscot River. One of America's first railroads was built here to carry the sawed boards and other wood products to the port in Bangor, and river steamers began carrying passengers and freight to points north on the Penobscot. Hotels, boardinghouses, and restaurants were built to accommodate lumbermen, businessmen, and travelers alike. Shoe shops to supply the woodsmen and grocery stores to feed their families were created to ease the burden of getting by, and churches were erected to serve the spirit.

And fellow Mainers too came here from all over the state to help build our town: the Folsoms from Newburgh to develop the downtown area, the Herseys from Buckfield to develop Stillwater, the Masons from Ellsworth to provide dental services, the Poors from Andover, Maine, to witness the development of our first railroad—only the second one in the United States—in 1836. Henry Varnum Poor went on to eventually found Standard & Poor's and his brother John Alfred devised a grand plan called the European and North American Railroad. When it was completed in 1871, even Pres. Ulysses S. Grant came to Maine to attend its inauguration.

A local government was created by the first communities around here, but a neighborhood was soon growing that called for its own voice to be heard. Separation was at hand finally in 1840, when we parted from neighboring Orono and became incorporated as a new town.

In the last quarter of the 19th century, the logging trade brought people with names like Pelletier, Thibodeau, Beaulieu ,and Michaud from northern Maine, Québec, and eastern Canada to our town. Thus began a robust industrial period when lumber, woolen goods, shoes, paper and paper products, canoes, caskets, and ointments were all produced in Old Town, and prosperity prevailed. Our French-speaking neighbors from the north helped to develop all of them and were welcomed warmly to our communities.

Farms too existed here—many of them, at one time. Most are gone now, no longer economically viable, but their memories surround us still. Grandstands were once filled with harness-racing fans, not only in Old Town proper, but in Pea Cove and neighboring Orono as well. They are all gone now, but once reflected the sounds of the merry-go-round, horses' hooves, and music and dancing from the dance halls.

Men named Gray, Jordan, Chapman, and Carleton were among those who built mills and factories that provided jobs and encouraged investment in the city. They brought fame to us from way beyond our country's borders. To supply these workers and their families with food, clothing, tools, and services, shops of all kinds were opened, bringing more new people to town; some were named Cutler, Goldsmith, Sklar, and Shiro. Schools were built, and clergy and teachers were put in place to minister to the citizenry and educate the youth.

Floods and fires disrupted the sense of security we worked so hard to create for ourselves. They were never welcomed, but they always were an opportunity for coming together to ponder, to hope, to plan, and to rebuild. That is what communities are for, and that is what living in Old Town has long felt like to those of us who reside here. Remarkably, we have been spared the ignominy of loud headlines proclaiming dastardly scandals, but every now and then, one pops up to remind us of just how well we can do without them.

Like in most municipalities, prosperity in Old Town has waxed and waned through the years, largely dependent on the industries mentioned before. Indeed, we are now in the midst of economic uncertainty, as our industrial base has all but evaporated and our small shops and stores have been claimed by giant retail outlets miles away. It is this flexibility of the community that makes us hopeful for the future of our city. We are confident.

Local history is no longer taught in the public schools, yet young people are hungry to know what this town is all about, how it has developed, and what will happen to it in the future. We at the Old Town Museum are grateful for this opportunity to bring together this important glimpse into our past. Indeed, we have been asked to become part of the educational community and conduct tours for high school students, perhaps starting a tradition to impart our past to the gatekeepers of our future.

This book cannot possibly be a vessel for all of our rich history. Just a few friends and neighbors sitting around a living room could no doubt spin out history more than enough for a dozen such books. The thing is, however, that this one is real—jammed chockablock full with images and stories and memories and new knowledge too—the perfect vehicle to knit more community.

We are pleased to have been approached by Arcadia Publishing for this book, and we are sure that you will enjoy it. We will always have more history for you as well at the Old Town Museum. Visit us online at www.oldtownmueum.com or on Facebook too. Better yet, drop in sometime and see us in person. We will be here for you.

—Betsy Paradis
President, Old Town Museum

One

Around Town

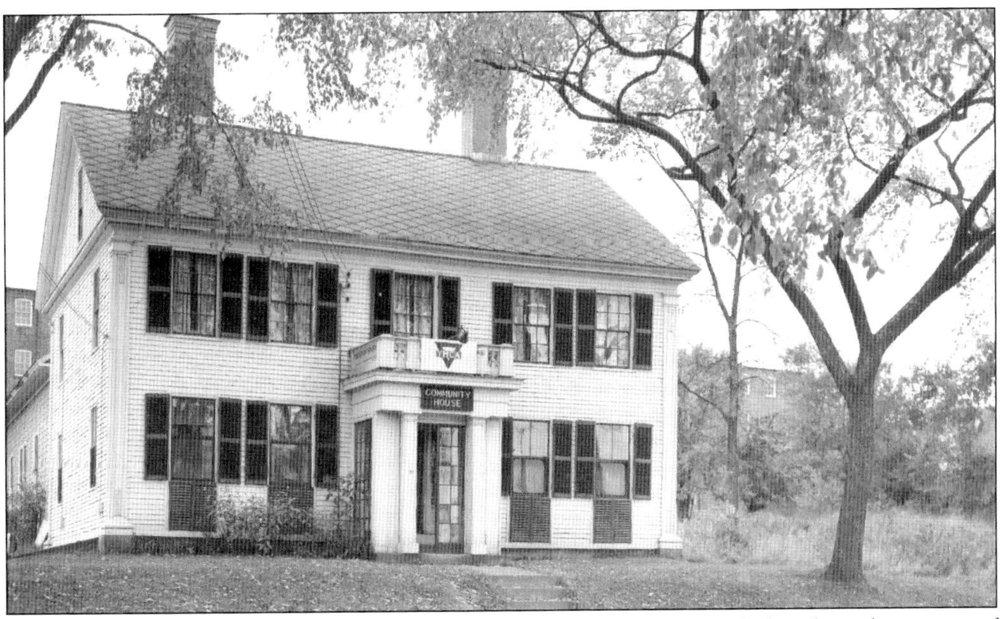

The YMCA was originally housed in the vestry of the Congregational church at the corner of Brunswick and Center Streets. In 1918, Jesse Godfrey willed her North Main Street home to the Y, with programs first offered in 1925. A professional director was hired in the late 1940s, with a gymnasium added in the mid-1950s by local contractor Herbert Sargent. In 1979, a new facility was acquired on Stillwater Avenue. (MHPC.)

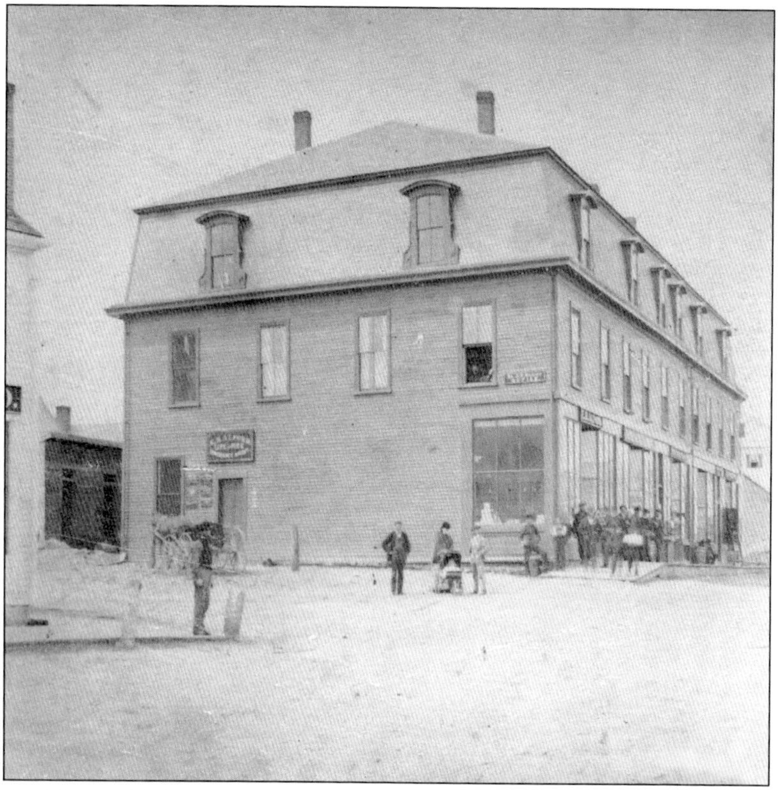

Folsom Square offered spartan comfort following completion of the Folsom Block in 1869 at the intersection of Main and Center Streets. Pedestrians were often forced to negotiate muddy roads between raised wooden walkways. E.R. Alford's Life and Fire Insurance Association sign hangs above Center Street. (MHPC.)

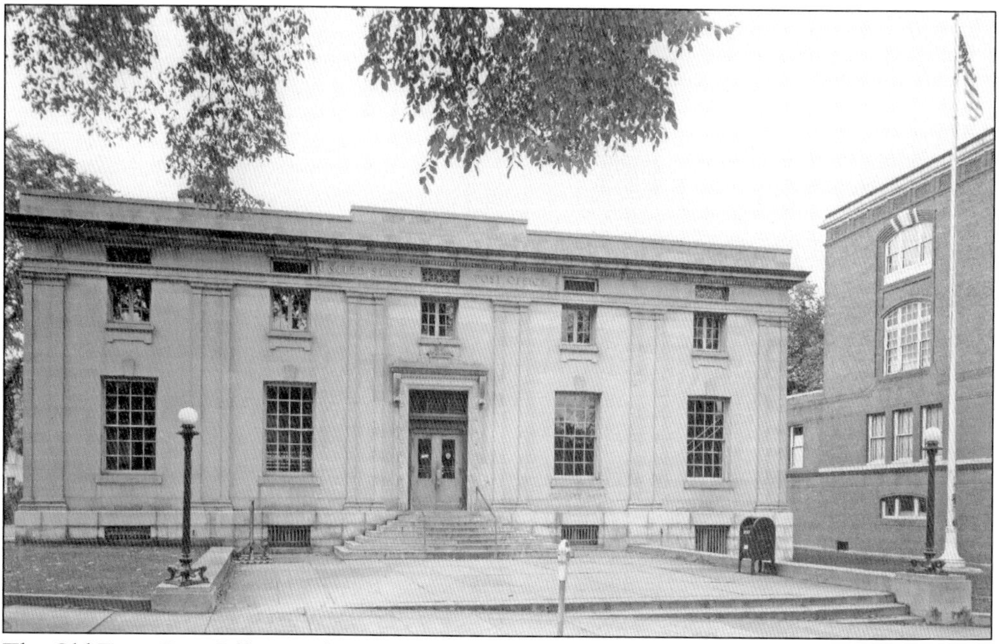

The Old Town Post Office was built on Center Street in 1914. Previously, the postal service was housed in the Folsom Block and other places over time. The design was one of six created by Oscar Wenderoth at the time. The others are in Port Jervis, New York; Medford and Pendleton, Oregon; Bowling Green, Ohio; Blue Island, Illinois; and Miles City, Montana. (MHPC.)

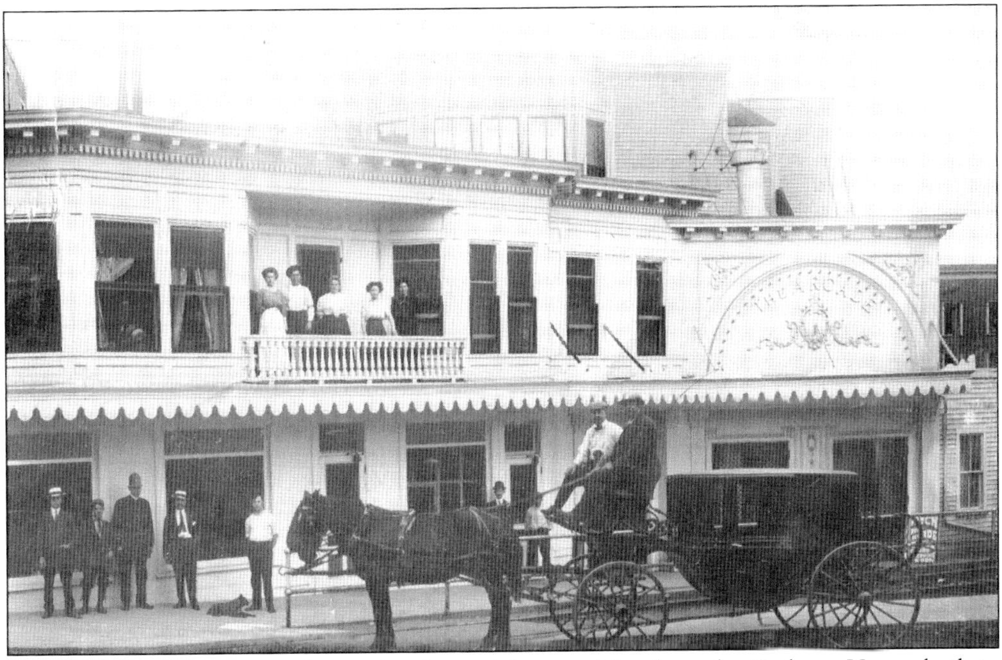

Old Town has always enjoyed a supply of overnight amenities, from the Codman House, built in 1830 by Col. William H. Smith and later operated by Ephraim Cousins, to the Oldtown Exchange. Pictured here in the early 1900s, the Eagle House was on South Main Street near the Bradbury Block. Augustus G. Perro then operated this establishment and increased his business to the point of expansion. (MHPC.)

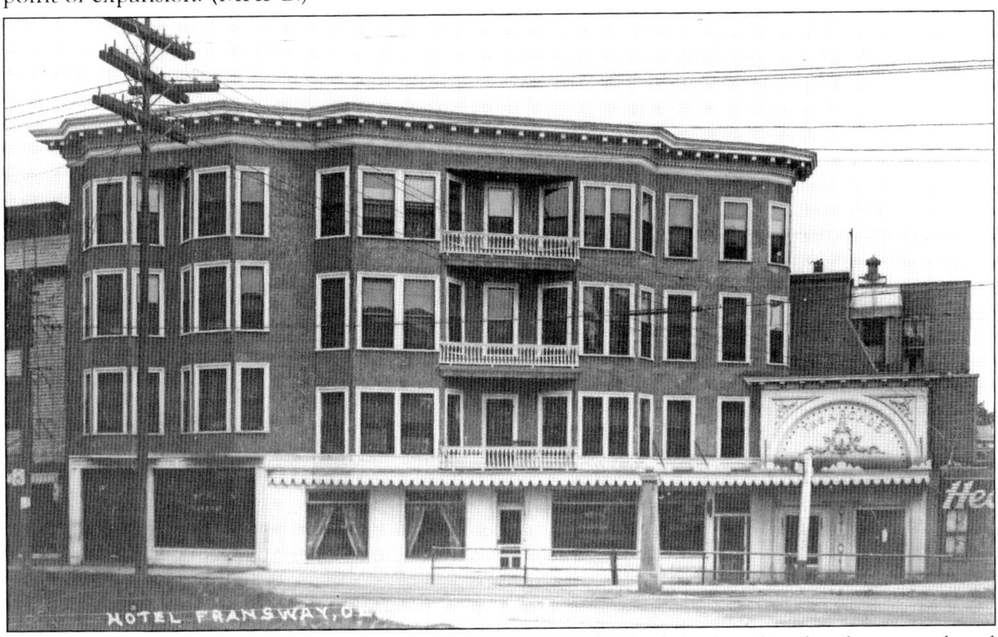

In 1912, Augustus G. Perro, operator of the Eagle House, backed the hotel with a four-story hotel facing Main Street hotel called the Fransway. Featuring a stucco exterior, the Fransway offered private baths and both the American and European plans. Automobile tours were encouraged to stop by, as were traveling salesmen. There was a deskman on duty all night long. (PRS.)

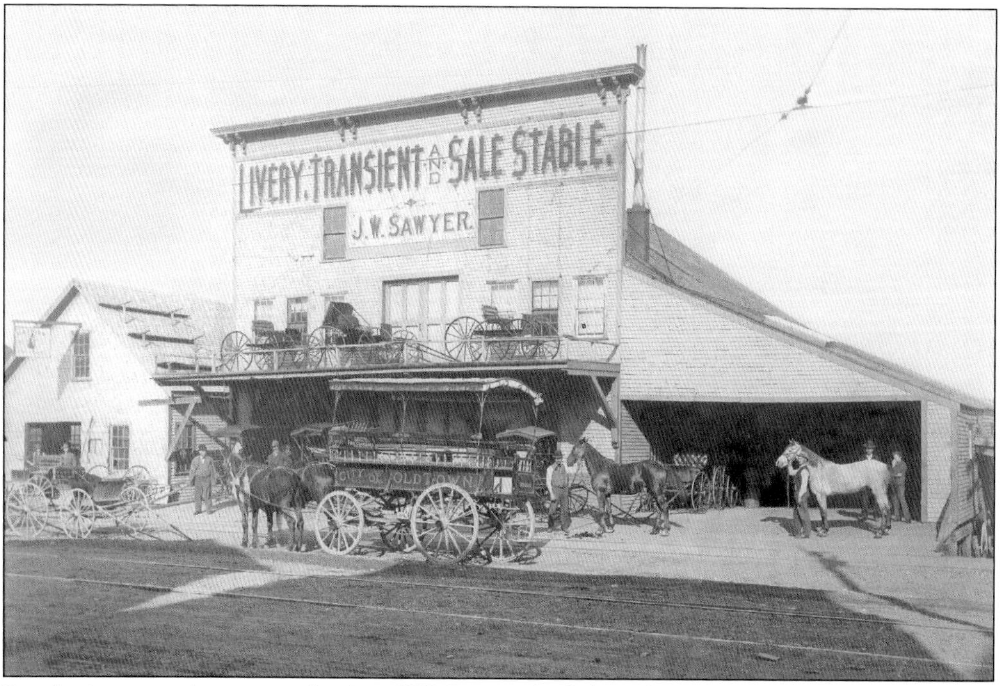

Surely, it was with great pride that J.W. Sawyer had this photograph taken of his carriage offerings, including the City of Old Town livery at the center. An 1894 trade publication notes that Sawyer is building "a large carriage repository back of his residence on Main Street to accommodate his increasing trade. Mr. Sawyer probably sells more carriages that any other man in Maine." (MHPC.)

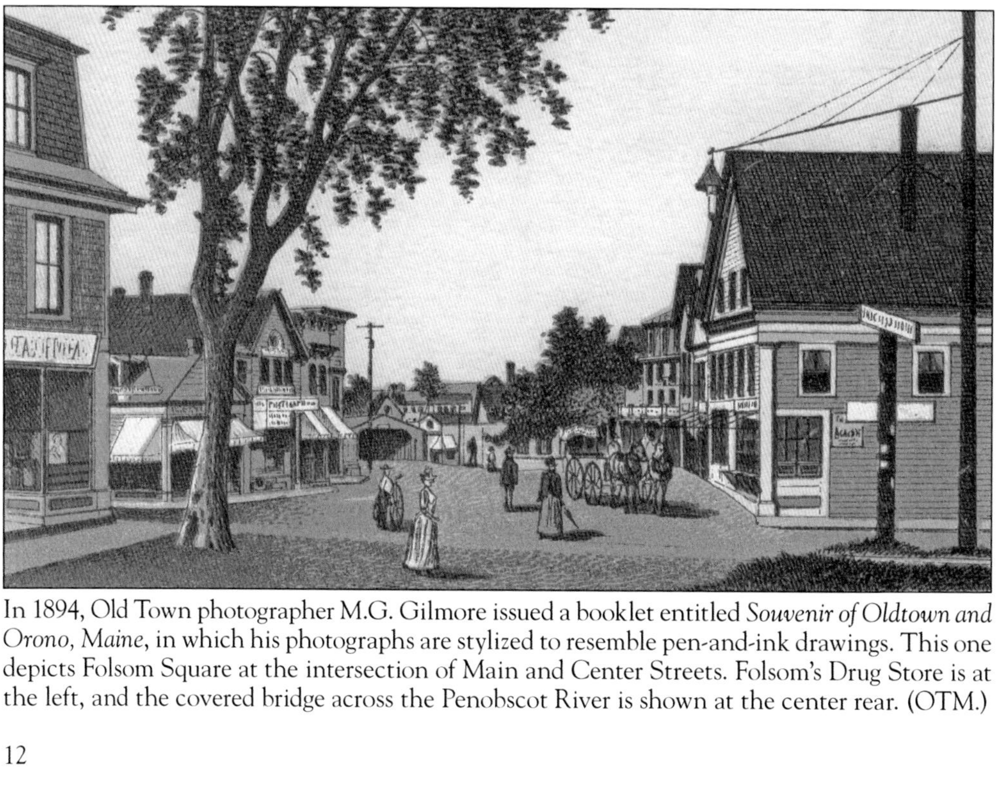

In 1894, Old Town photographer M.G. Gilmore issued a booklet entitled *Souvenir of Oldtown and Orono, Maine*, in which his photographs are stylized to resemble pen-and-ink drawings. This one depicts Folsom Square at the intersection of Main and Center Streets. Folsom's Drug Store is at the left, and the covered bridge across the Penobscot River is shown at the center rear. (OTM.)

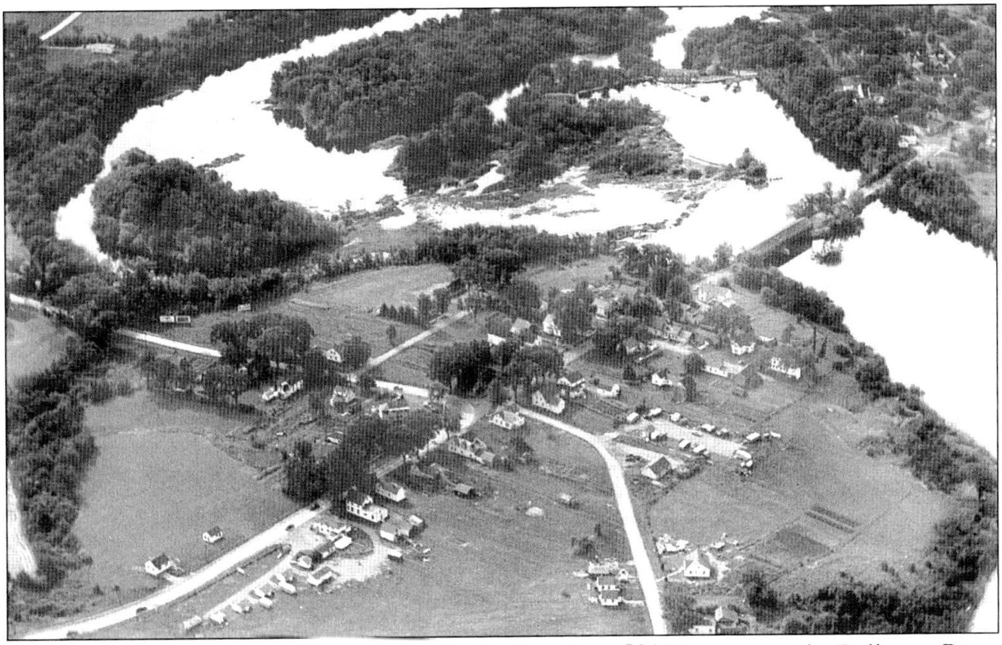

This 1940s view shows the old covered bridge leading from Old Town across the Stillwater River to the village of Stillwater. Gardens, lawns, and fields highlight the bucolic nature of this section of Old Town. The hydroelectric dam and power plant are shown at the upper right. (OTM.)

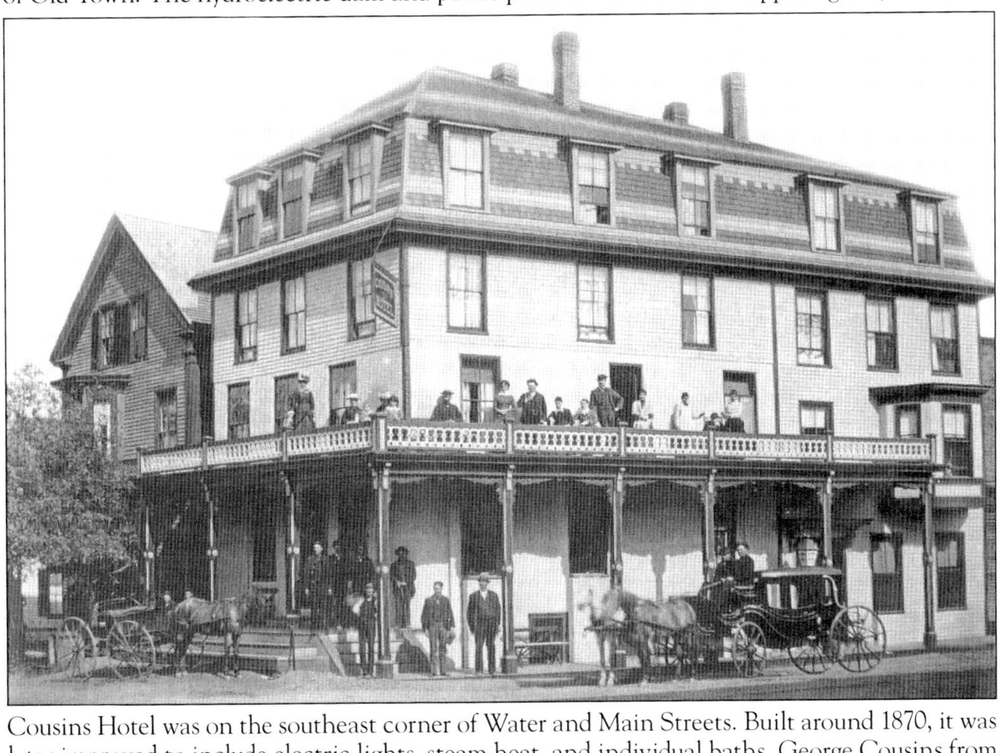

Cousins Hotel was on the southeast corner of Water and Main Streets. Built around 1870, it was later improved to include electric lights, steam heat, and individual baths. George Cousins from Ellsworth, Maine, purchased the hotel in 1899. The Cousins family had been in the hotel business in the city area for generations. The wooden hotel was replaced by the Jordan Building. (CLM.)

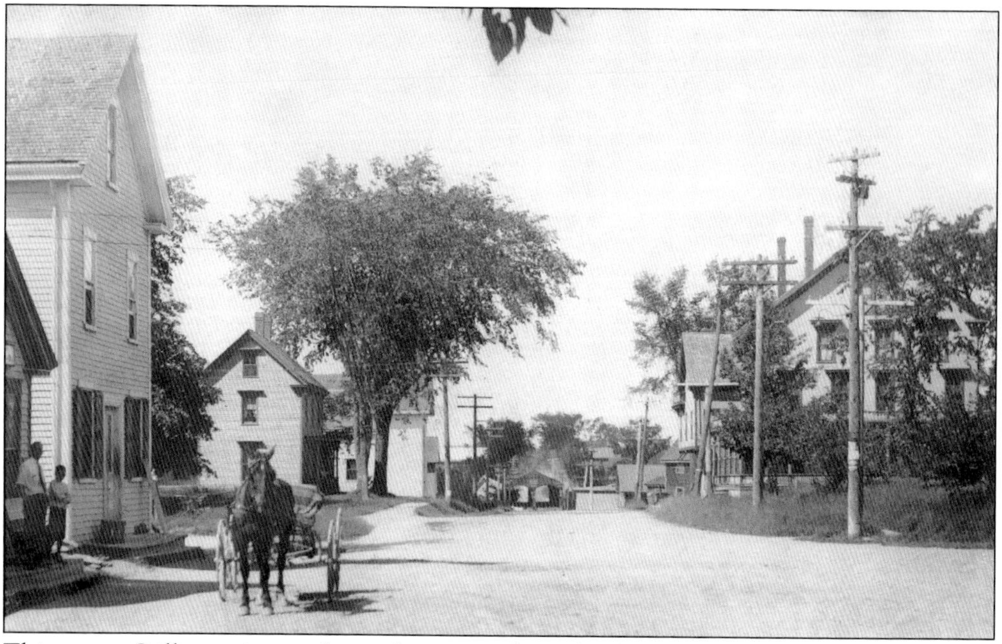

This serene Stillwater image shows the approach to the double-lane covered bridge over the Stillwater River in a view looking towards Old Town. It was once called Upper Stillwater to distinguish it from the lower village in neighboring Orono, and the name endured until the Stillwater postmaster arbitrarily dropped the "Upper." (EJA.)

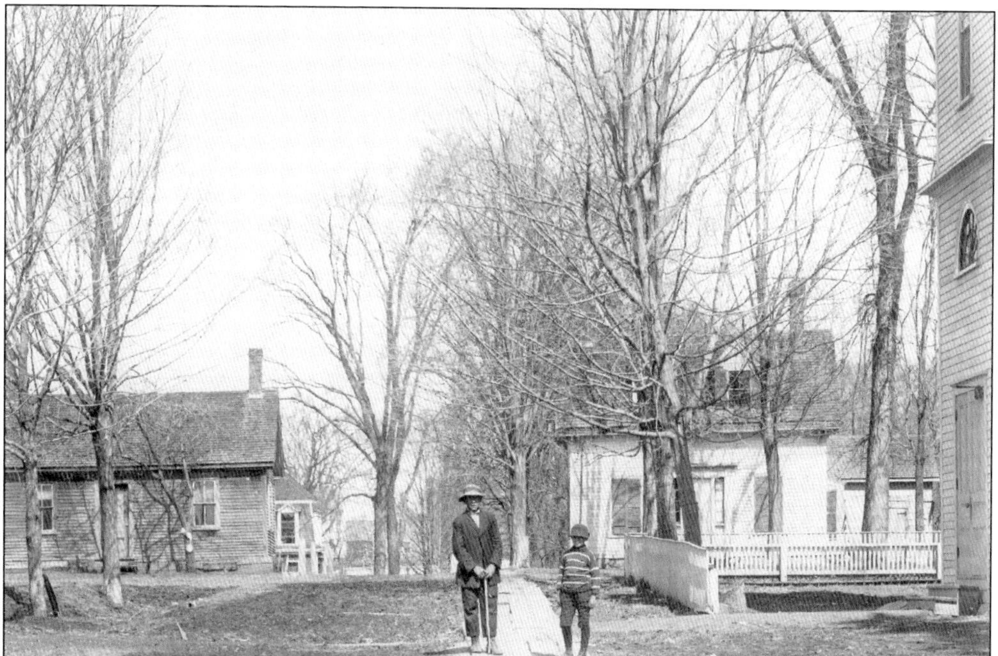

An early-20th-century view of Main Street on Indian Island is shown here. The Penobscot Nation has lived on the land and river in the Old Town area for at least 6,000 years, perhaps as many as 10,000. Old Town takes its name from the early English name for the island, Indian Oldtown. Until a bridge was built in the 1950s, the mainland was reached only by boat or over ice. (PRS.)

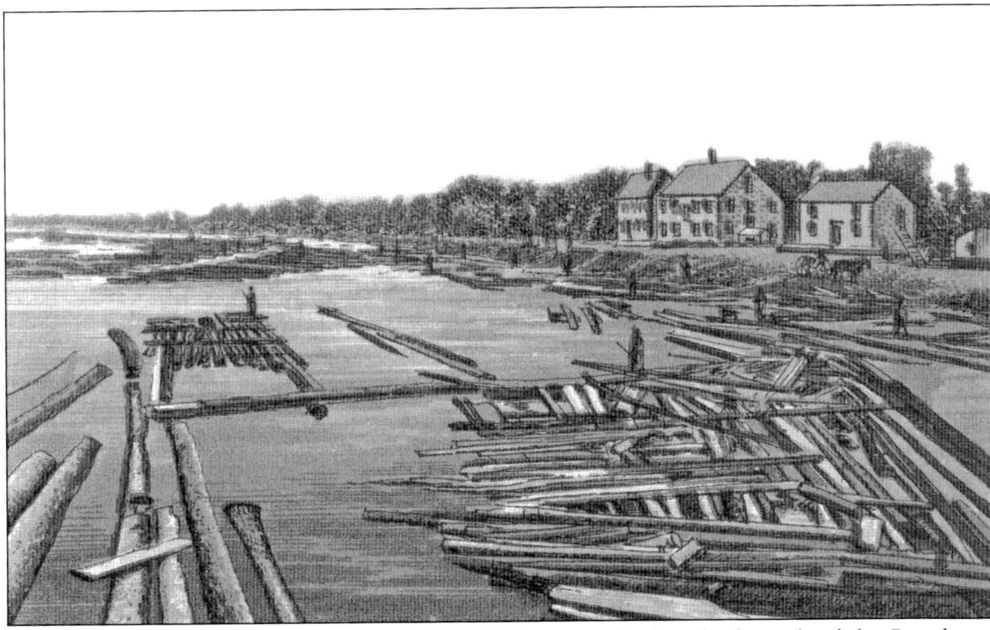

The Pea Cove section of Old Town drains both a watershed and a branch of the Penobscot River. It was ideally situated to steer logs south to mills in Old Town and Orono through the use of the sorting pens shown in this depiction by photographer M.G. Gilmore around 1900. Its commercial importance diminished greatly once river drives were eliminated in Maine in the mid-1970s. (OTM.)

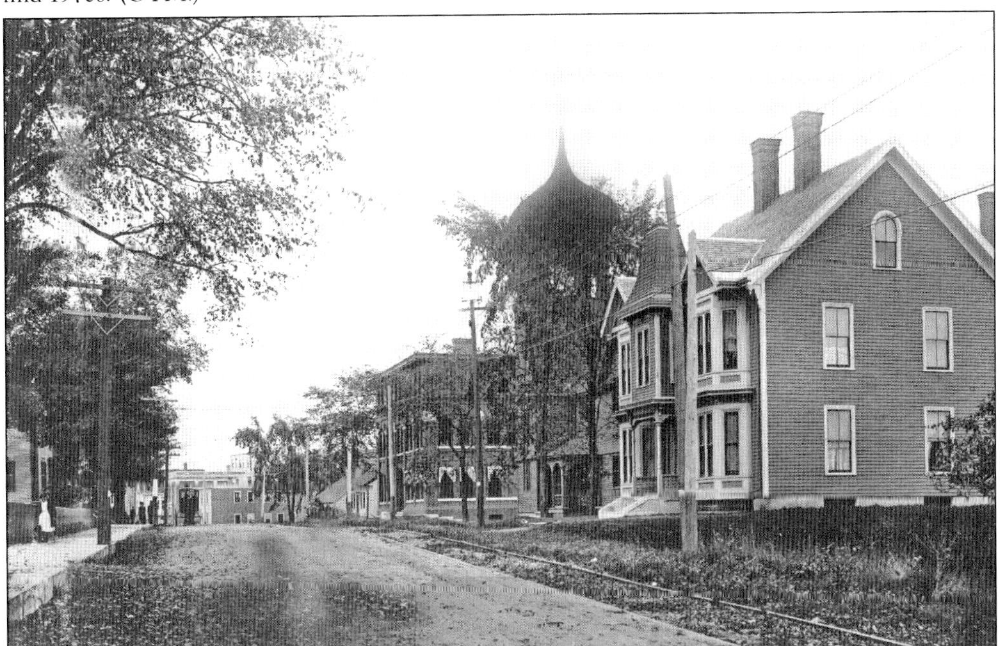

This view of Old Town looks into the center of town from South Main Street around 1910. Seen on the right are the familiar curved turret of the Universalist church and, just beyond it, the brick structure of the Bickmore Gall Company. The house on the right was once owned by the Gould family. (PRS.)

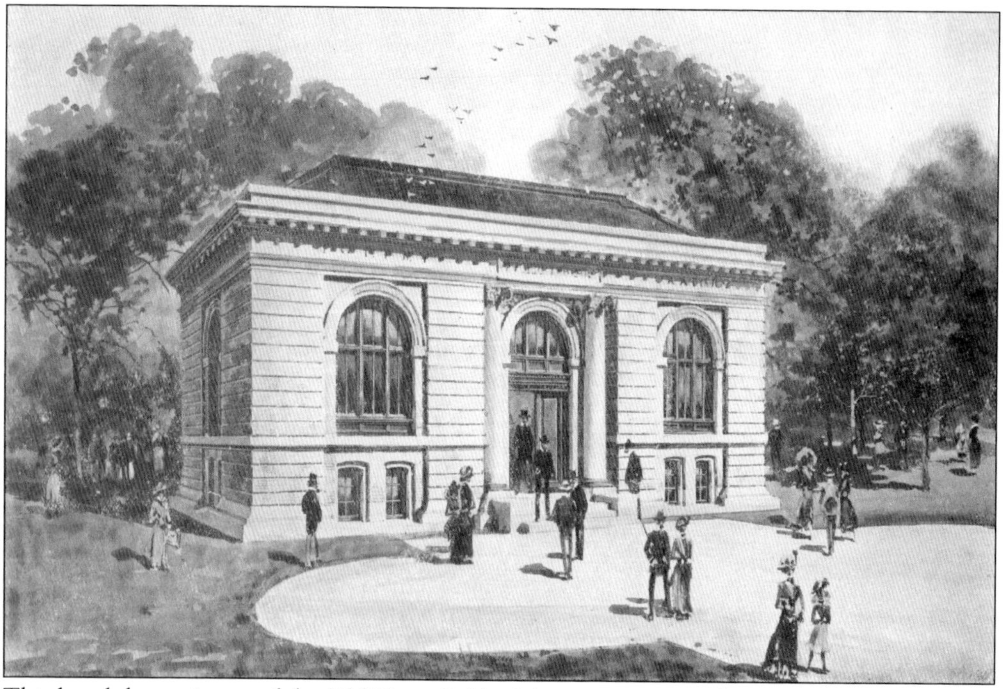

This hand-drawn image of the Old Town Public Library appears in the January 1904 *American Architect and Building News*, many months before the library was built. Financially assisted by Andrew Carnegie, the library was designed by Westfield, Massachusetts, resident Albert Randolph Ross, who also designed libraries in Pittsfield and Hinckley, Maine. (PRS.)

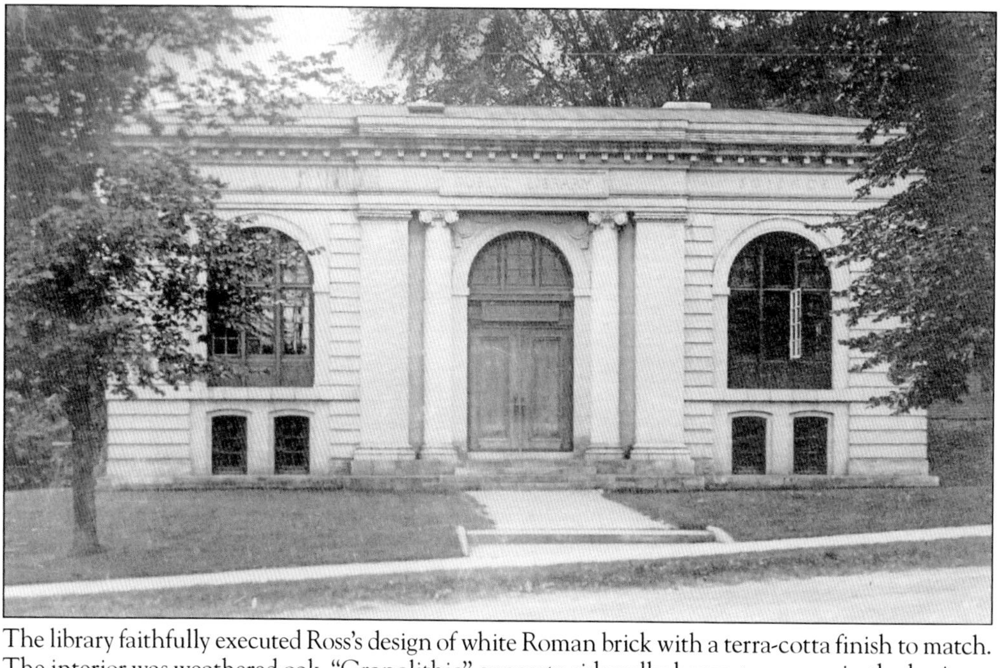

The library faithfully executed Ross's design of white Roman brick with a terra-cotta finish to match. The interior was weathered oak. "Granolithic" concrete sidewalks began to appear in the business district, particularly along North Main, Center, and Middle Streets, running up to the library. Other Carnegie libraries were being built at the University of Maine and Bangor. (PRS.)

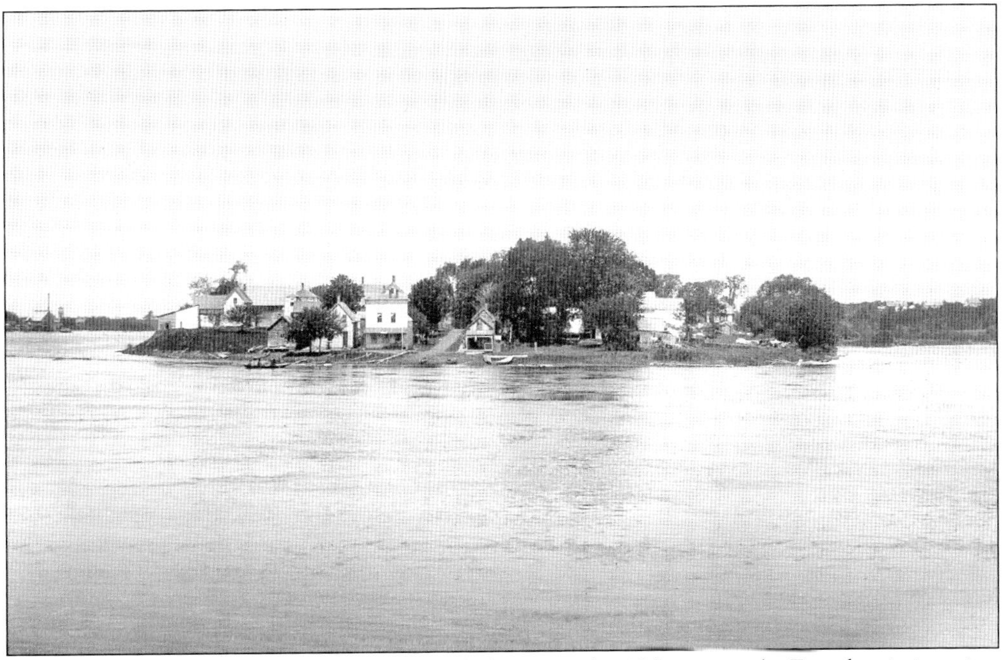

The Penobscot Nation was converted to Catholicism in the 16th century by French missionaries. The earliest church on Indian Island was built in 1688. Treaties negotiated with the United States, Massachusetts, and Maine have not always aligned with each other, causing tensions from time to time between the Penobscot Nation and the State of Maine. (OTPL.)

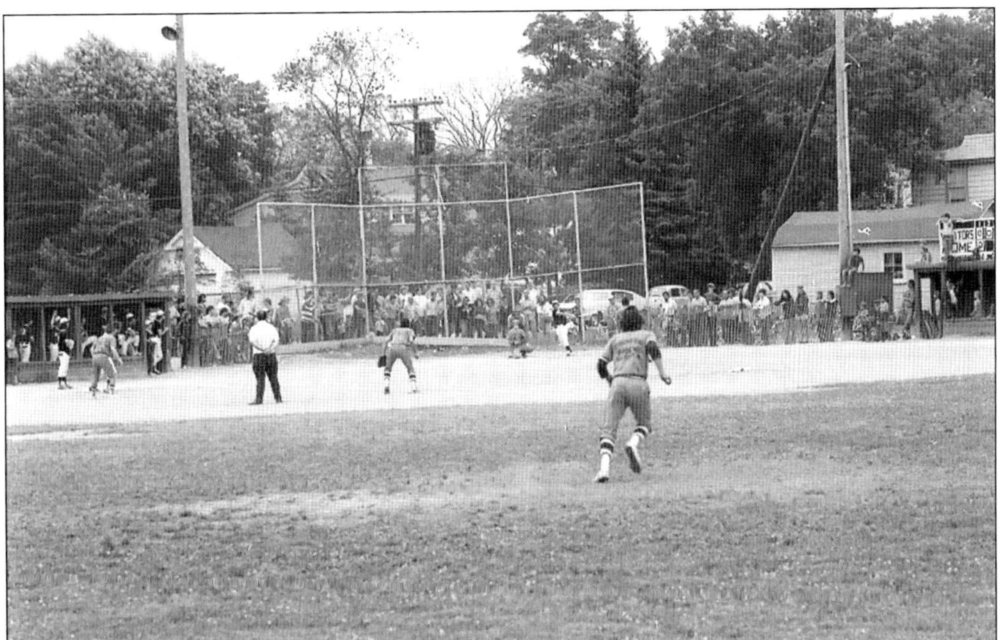

Treat and Webster Island became known as French Island in recognition of the hundreds of Québécois families who came here to live while working in the lumber, woolen, and pulp and paper mills that provided Old Town with a robust industrial base from the 1880s to the 1970s. Softball was enjoyed by generations of French Island residents as shown in this 1960s image. (PWT.)

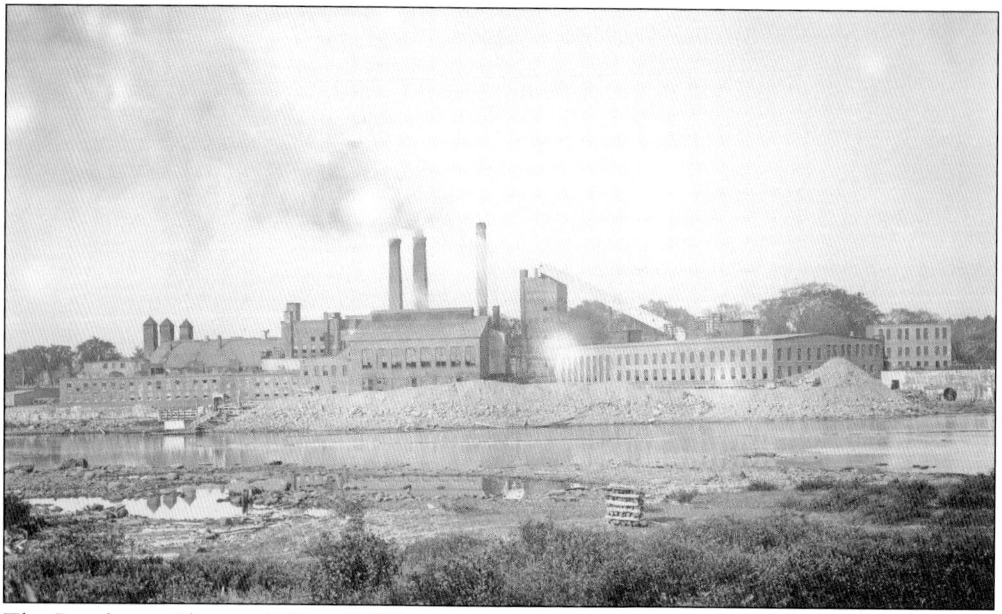

The Penobscot Chemical Fibre (PCF) Paper Mill in the Great Works section of Old Town is shown here in this 1911 image. Established in 1882, PCF was a mainstay in Old Town for more than a century before the world economy developed and undercut it on price. Like many such mills in Maine, it soldiered on for many years before recently closing. (OTPL.)

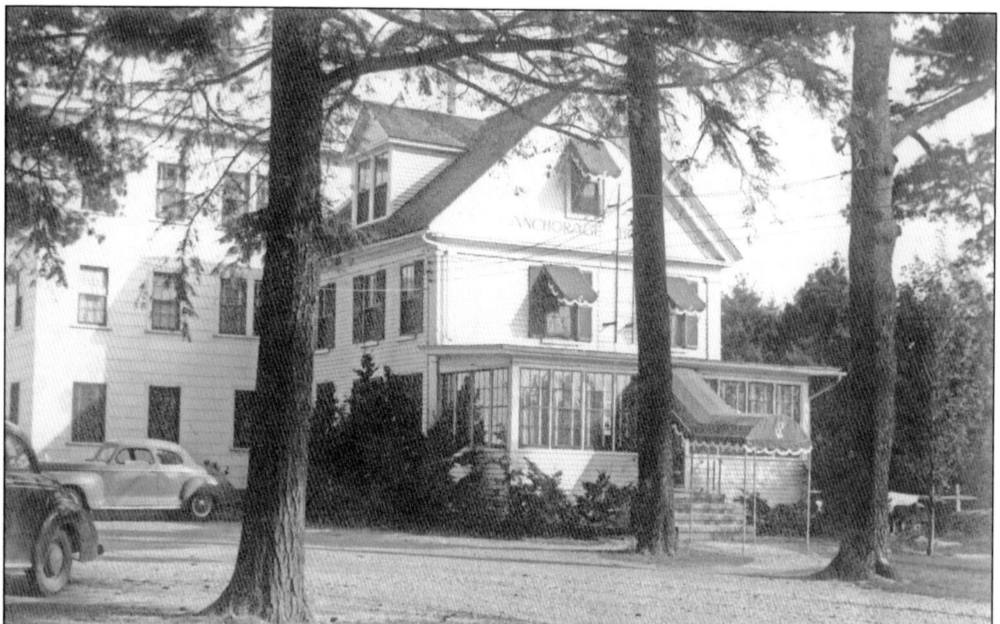

The Anchorage Hotel stood at the crest of Academy Hill on Stillwater Avenue. Long an attraction for the weary traveler or for those who craved lively music, the hotel also catered to the hunter and fisherman. Civic clubs, such as Rotary International, met here for years. Razed in 2005, the Anchorage was replaced by condominiums. (BHP.)

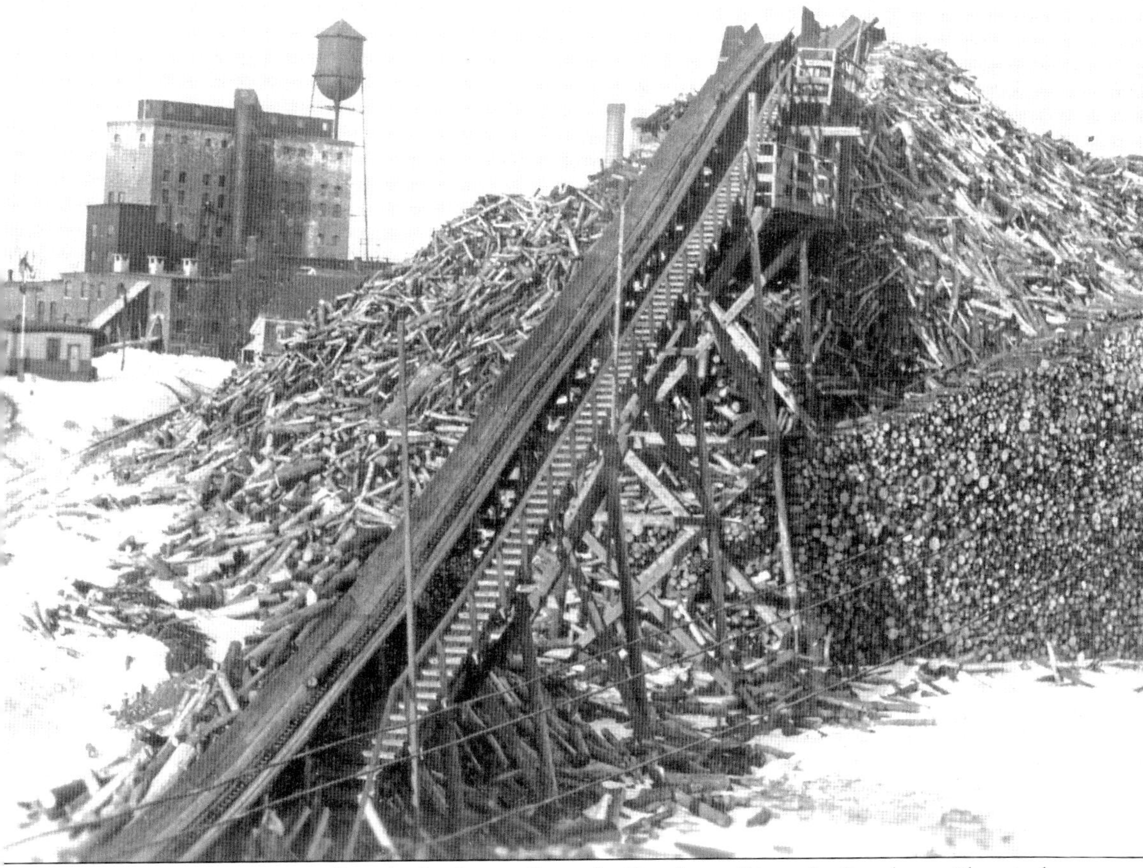

Erected on the site of one of hundreds of sawmills on the Penobscot River, the Penobscot Chemical Fibre Company changed hands several times over the years, becoming known as the Penobscot Company, the Penobscot Division of Diamond International, the James River Corporation, the Georgia-Pacific Corporation mill, and, finally, as Expera Specialty Solutions. It ceased operation at the end of 2015 after more than 130 years in business. (CLM.)

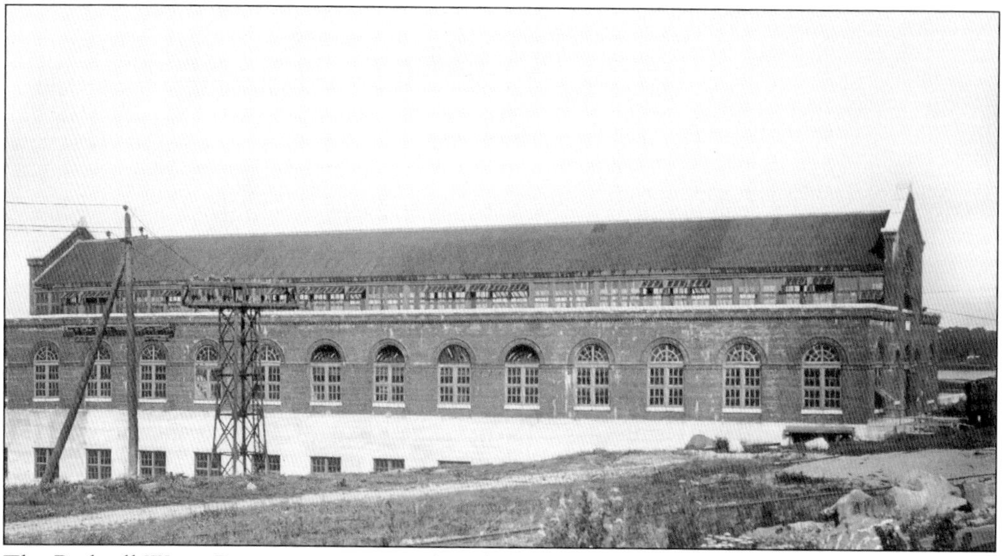

The Bodwell Water Power company was founded in the 1880s in Milford, across the Penobscot River from Old Town. At the time, it was among the largest producers of electricity in the country. Joseph R. Bodwell, late governor of Maine, died in office less than a year after his inauguration; nonetheless, he enhanced the child welfare system and improved labor conditions. (MHPC.)

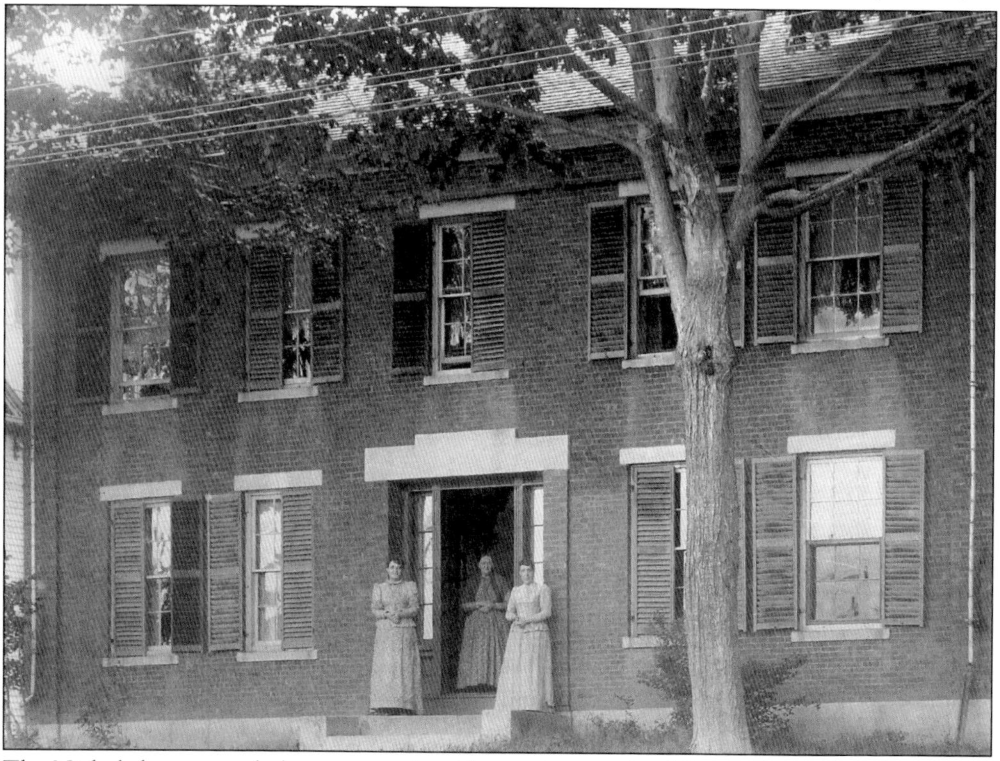

The Nichols home stood along a row of residences just south of Center Street on South Main Street. It is shown in this mid-1880s image with Belinda Fuller Braley (center) and her two youngest children, Ever (left) and Sarah. Ever married Fred Nichols. This home was demolished in the late 1970s to make room for the Marsh Island Apartments for the elderly. (BWG.)

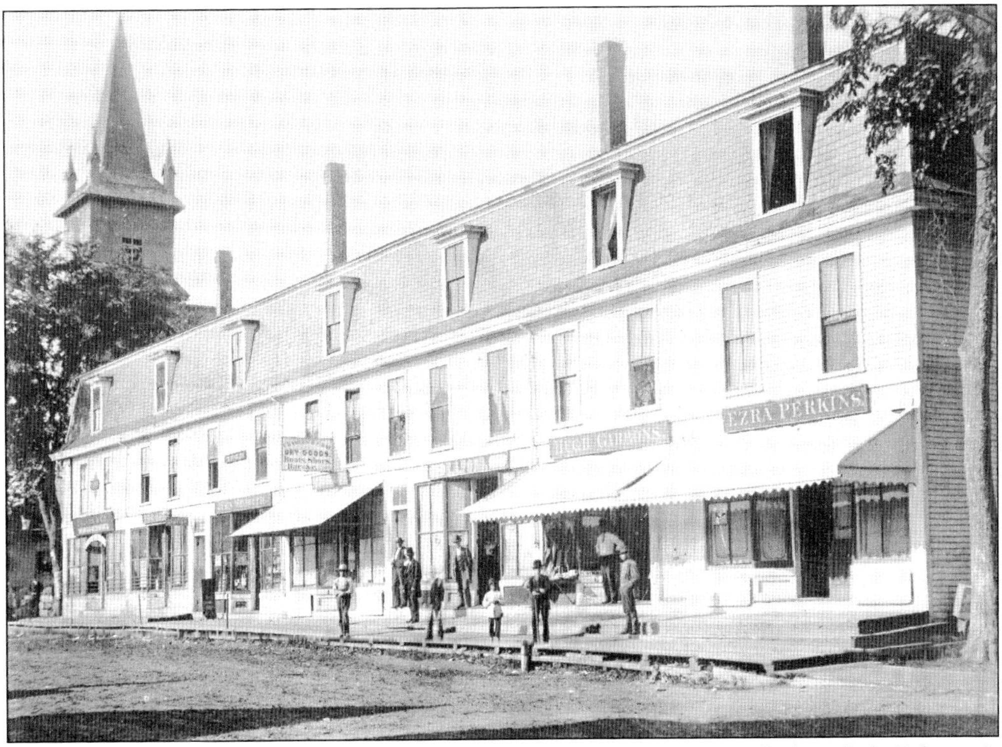

The businesses in the Folsom Block, shown before electricity was installed, include Folsom & Co., drugs and medicines; the US post office; James Weymouth; and Charles H. Gray, dry goods. E.A. Pond, Hugh Gibbons, and Ezra Perkins all sold boots and shoes. Weymouth, Gibbons, and Perkins would later help found the Old Town Electric Company. (MHPC.)

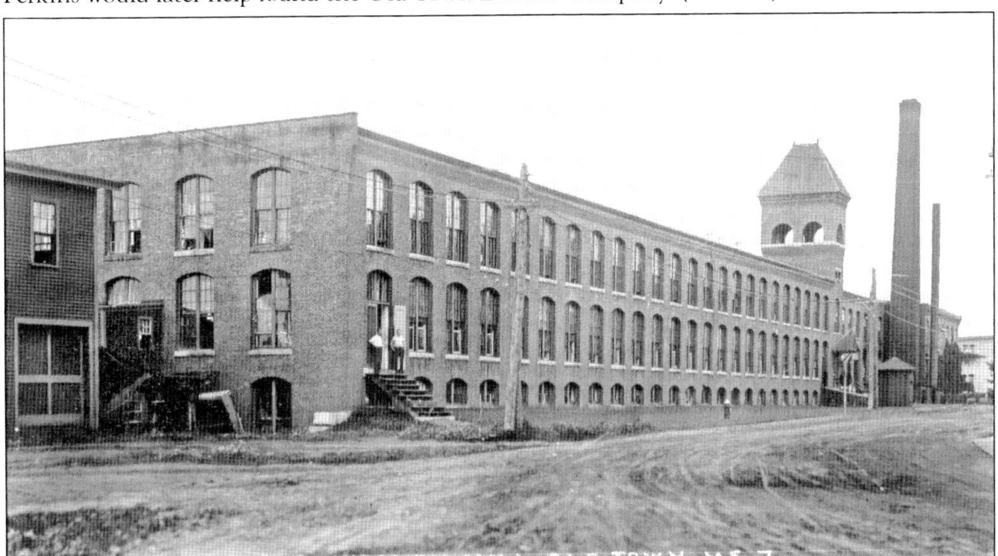

The Old Town Woolen Company on North Main Street was managed by Herbert Gray and Fred Phelps. The plant operated on a 24-hour schedule to keep up with demand. Over 500 employees worked at its plants in Old Town, Sangerville, and Guilford in Maine. In 1917, Gray's son Maurice, five years out of college, would manage the Guilford plant. (MHPC.)

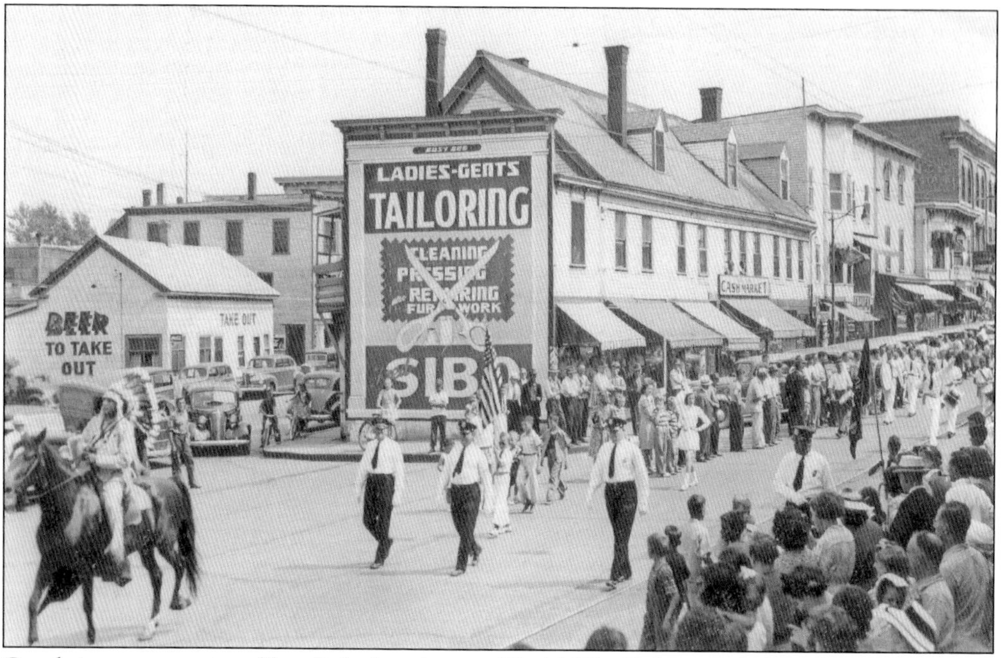

Good times were enjoyed by all during the pre–World War II days, including this parade at the intersection of Water and North Main Streets. Fred P. Sibo's tailoring and dry-cleaning business is shown here, while over the Old Town Cash Market, two young ladies enjoy an unobstructed view. Chief Poolaw from Indian Island leads the procession north through town. (OTM.)

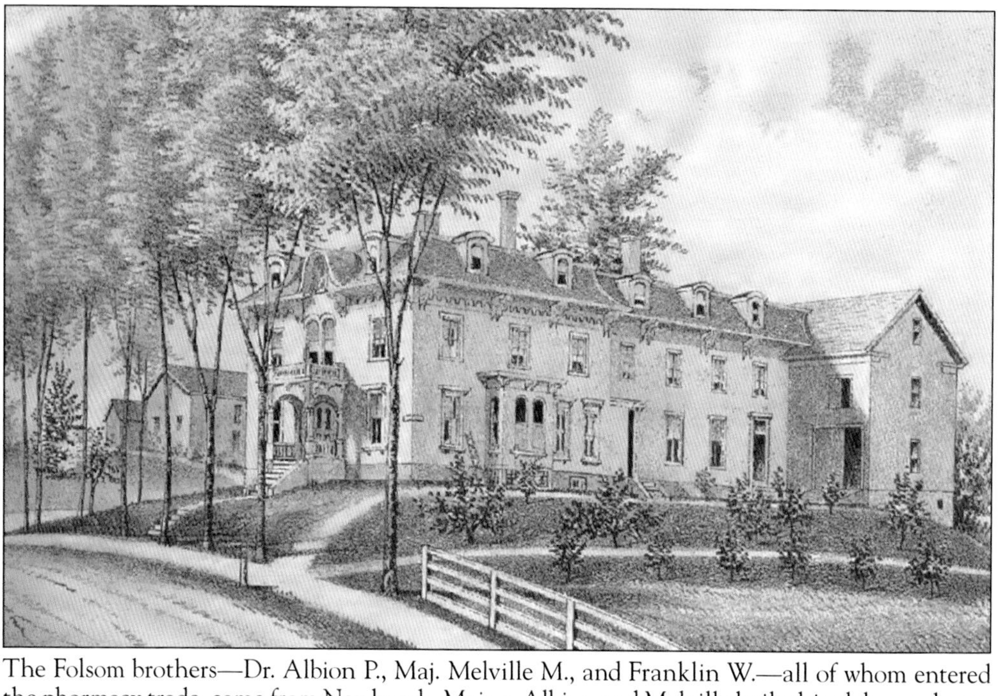

The Folsom brothers—Dr. Albion P., Maj. Melville M., and Franklin W.—all of whom entered the pharmacy trade, came from Newburgh, Maine. Albion and Melville built this elaborate home at the corner of Center and Brunswick Streets, which still stands. They also erected the Folsom Block in 1869, and Melville was once mayor of Old Town. (PRS.)

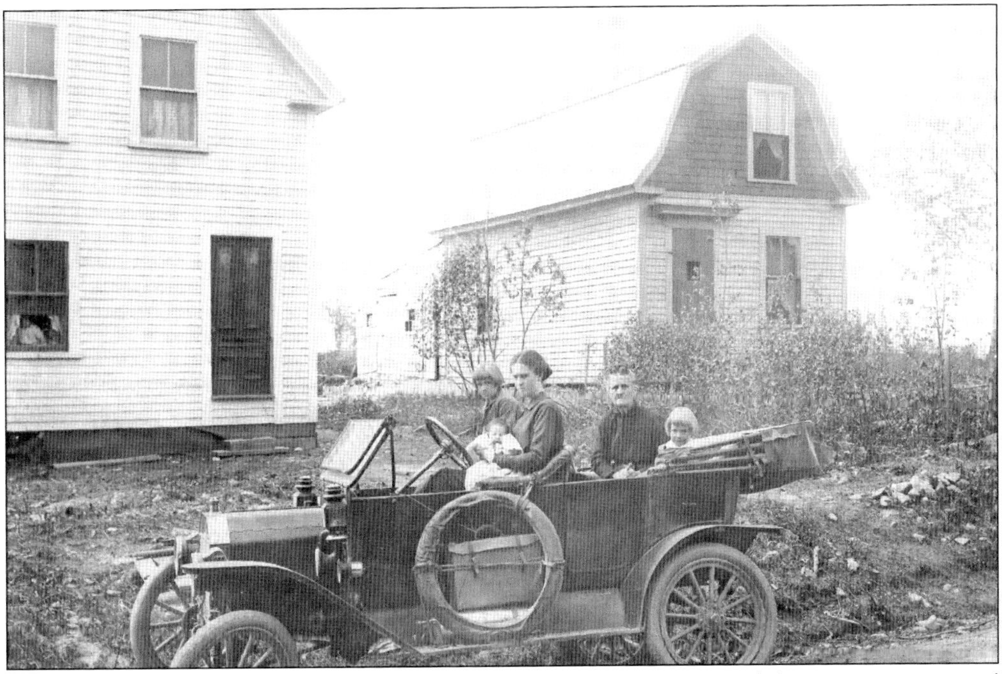

Across the river in Milford, Edith L. Sleeper, at the wheel of her automobile, appears concerned as she holds little Greg, with his brother George Jr. beside them. In the backseat, her mother, Julia Longley, tends to little Kenneth. Pictured is the Sleeper home on the County Road. (OTM.)

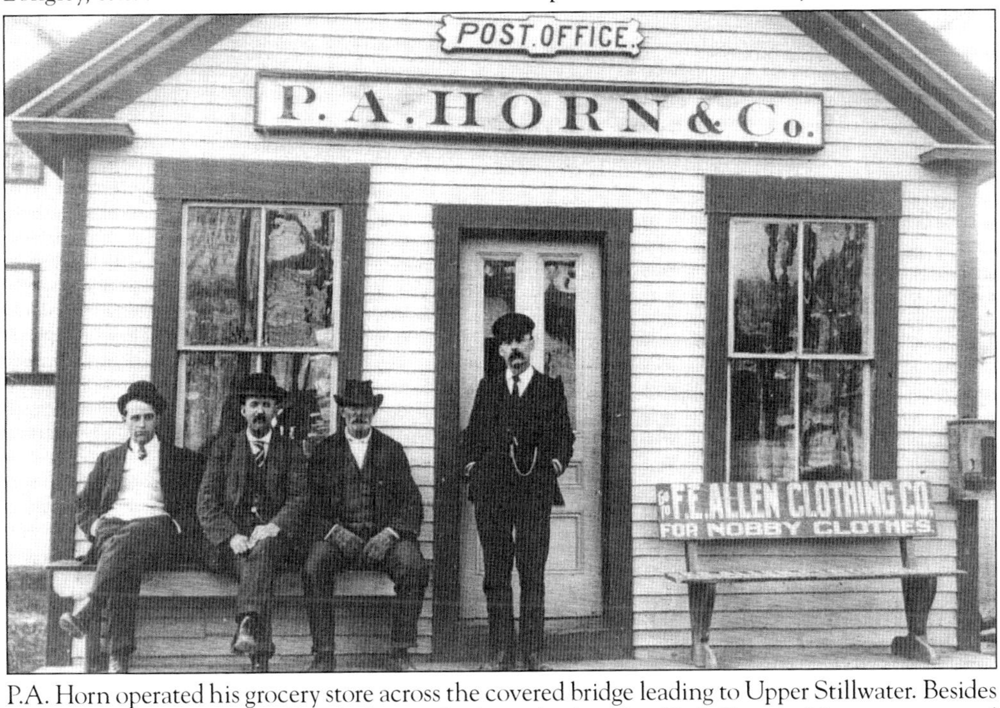

P.A. Horn operated his grocery store across the covered bridge leading to Upper Stillwater. Besides groceries, he advertised Nobby clothing, which was both a New York City clothing company and a term meaning "spiffy" or "swell." In Horatio Alger's 1867 novel *Ragged Dick*, Frank asks Dick, "What's a swell?" Dick replies, "O, a fellow that wears nobby clothes like you." (EJA.)

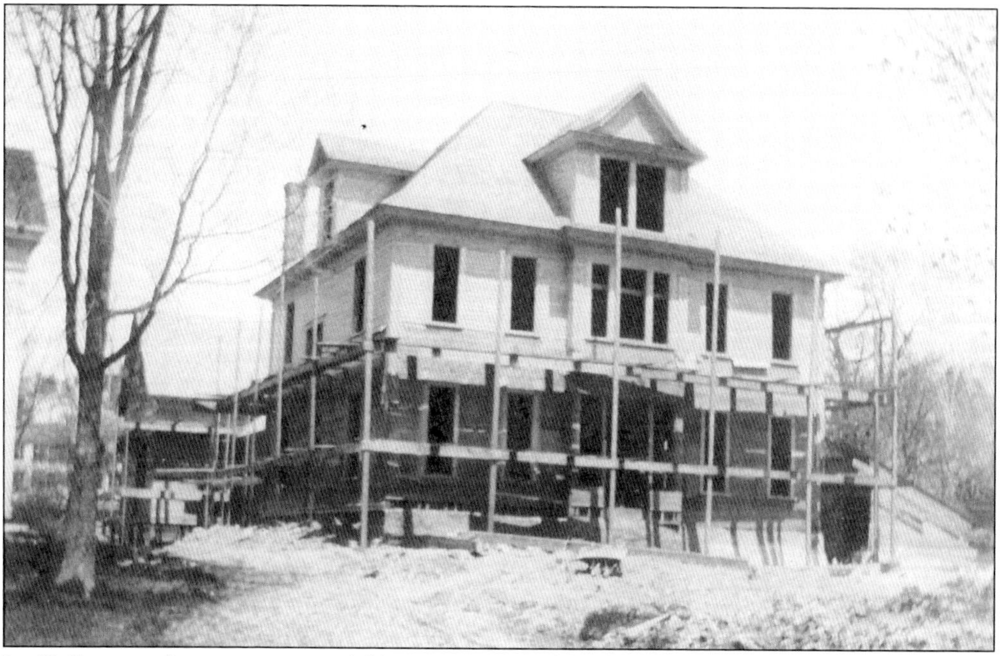

Ira D. Eastman became a successful businessman and lumber dealer in Old Town in the 1890s. He also surveyed wildlands for the James W. Sewall Company and the State of Maine. In 1906, he began construction of his residence on Center Street, which came to be called Three Gates because of its three entrances through a wrought iron fence. (DRP.)

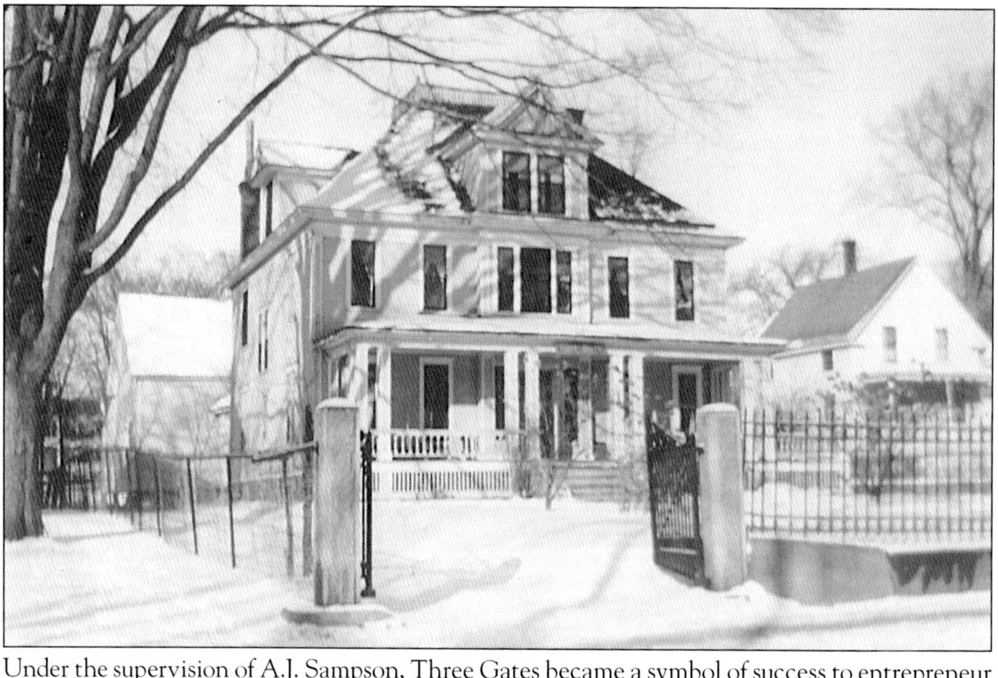

Under the supervision of A.J. Sampson, Three Gates became a symbol of success to entrepreneur Ira D. Eastman. In 1906, he erected this home, about which the *Enterprise* declared that when completed, "it will add one more to the handsome residences and grounds of this city." The same year, Eastman offered a house on Fourth Street and his camp at Pushaw for sale. (DRP.)

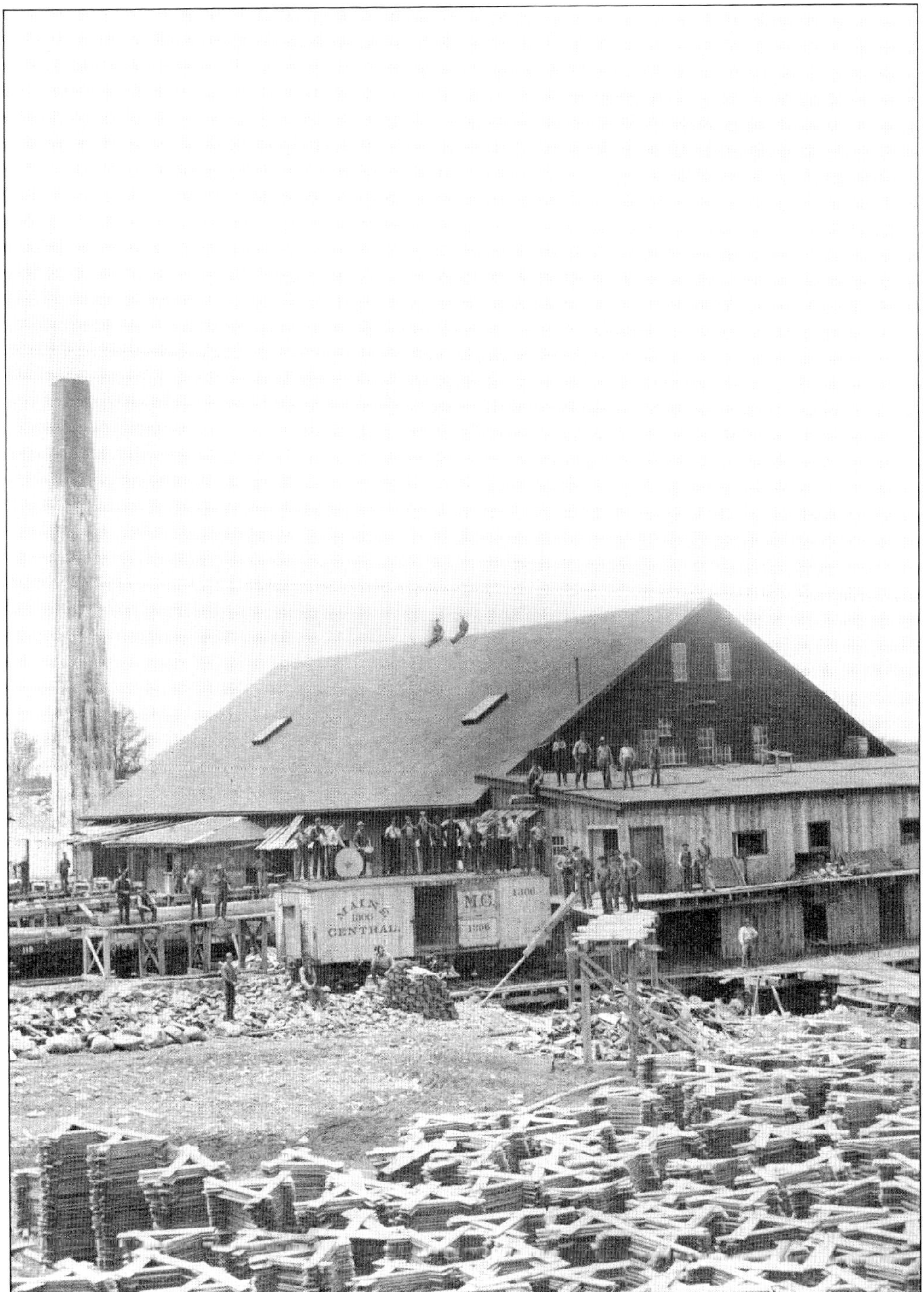

Workers at the Cassidy steam mill in Stillwater take time out from their jobs to pose for a group picture. Lumber from their hard work is air-drying in the yard in front of them. The Maine Central Railroad car is waiting to be filled with products destined for market. During its existence, the mill was often idled from a lack of orders. (MHPC.)

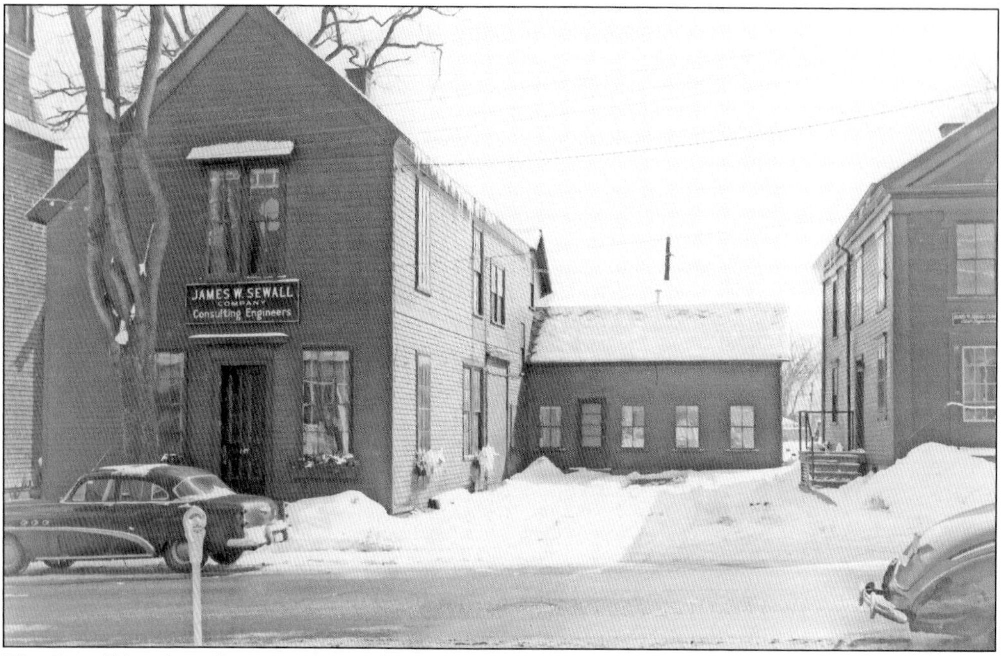

The Sewall brothers, James and Joseph, founded the James W. Sewall Company in 1880 to provide forestry management, surveying, and other services. The firm's office is shown here in the 1970s as its 100th birthday was approaching. Today, the company is known all around the world and has done work for NASA and NOAA. (OTM.)

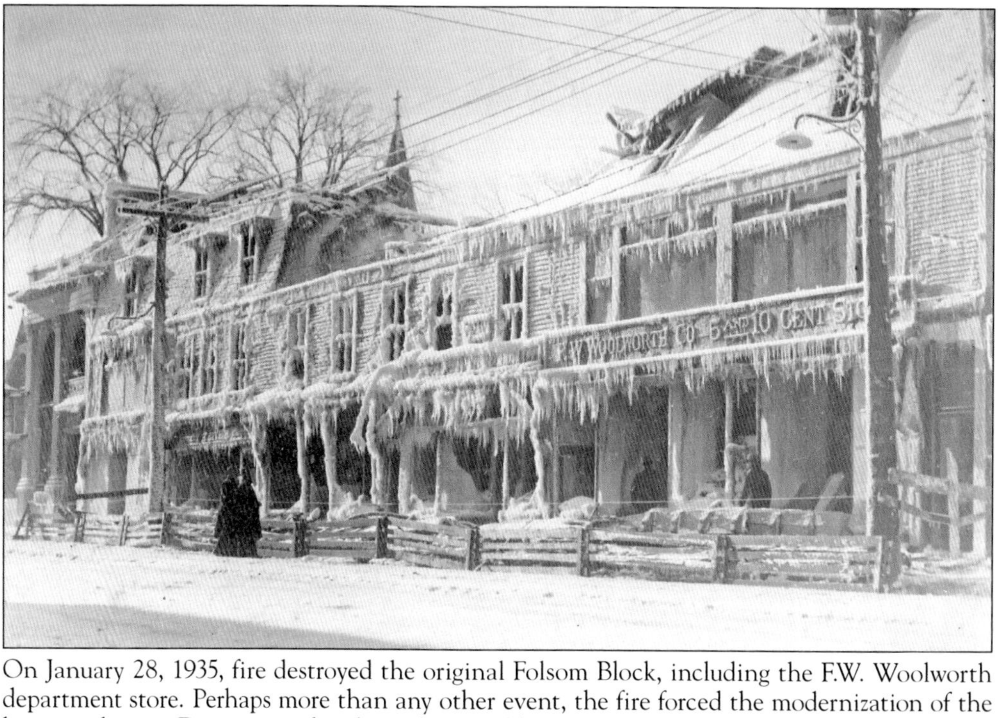

On January 28, 1935, fire destroyed the original Folsom Block, including the F.W. Woolworth department store. Perhaps more than any other event, the fire forced the modernization of the business district. Devastating fires have driven Old Town's fate, beginning with the Lincoln Fire of April 19, 1865, the day of the town's tribute to the recently slain president. (OTM.)

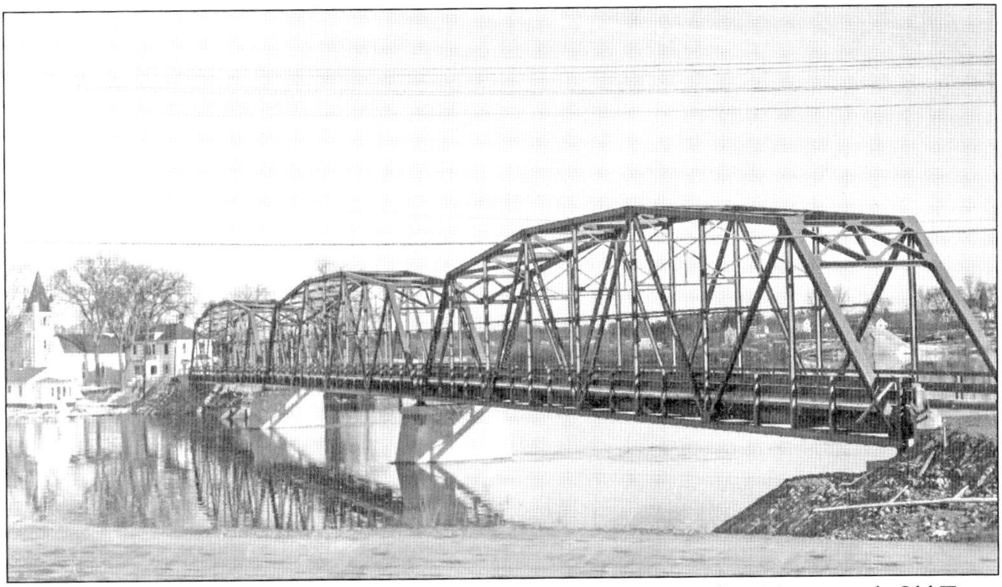

In 1951, the Indian Island bridge finally connected the Penobscot Indian Nation with Old Town proper and the world at large. Individual members of the nation had previously achieved worldwide fame, but the bridge improved everyday life for all its members. By the 1940s, tribal members were increasingly enrolled in regular Old Town public schools. (MHPC.)

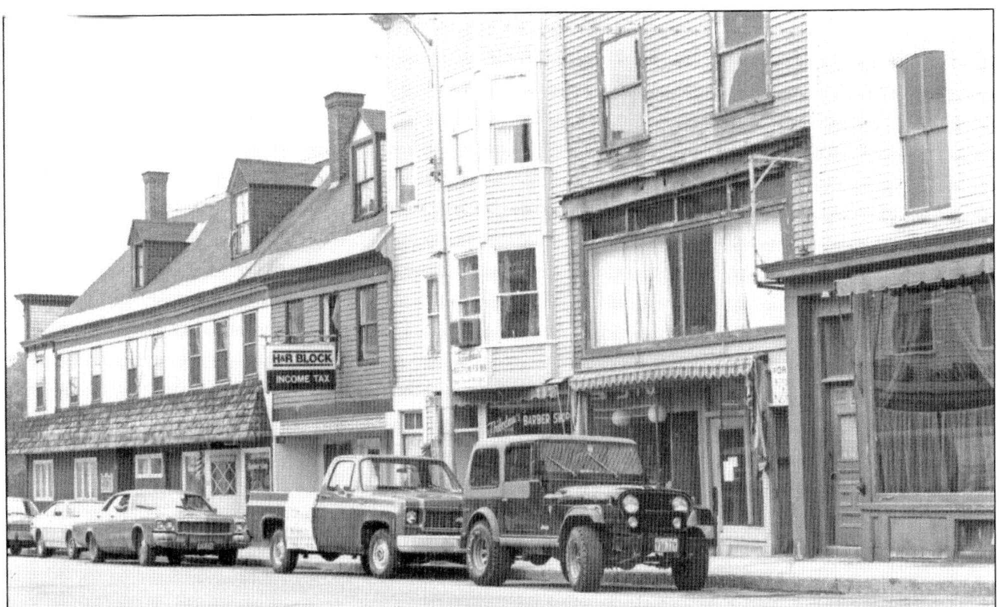

Over the years, the area of North Main Street undergoing the least amount of dramatic change has been the section shown here abutting Center Street and backed by Water Street. Gray's Hardware and Gray's Market were originally located here in the early 1860s. (CLM.)

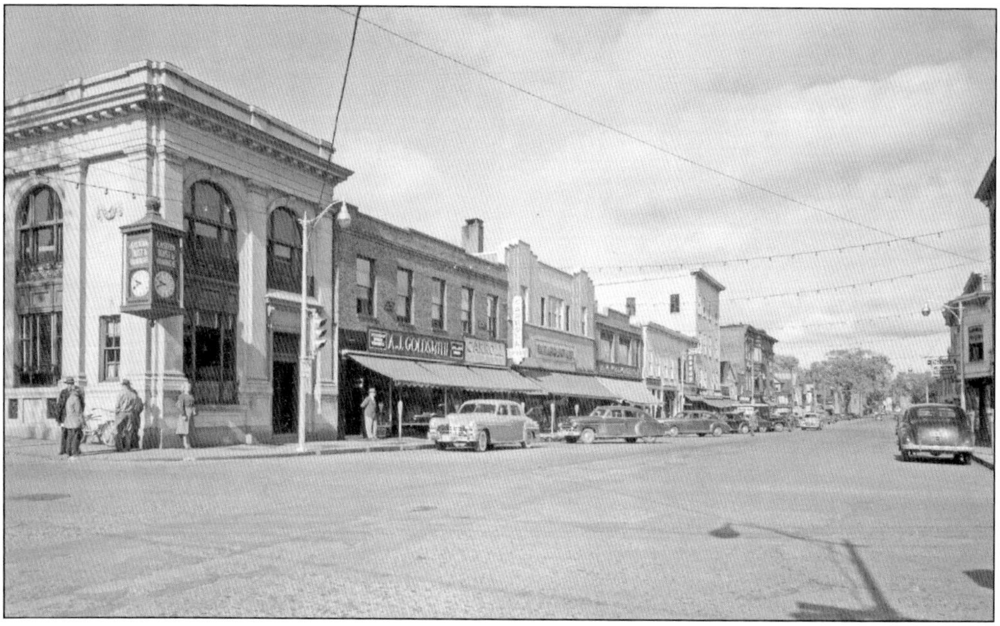

In this early 1950s view, the site of the Folsom Block has been completely transformed. The block burned in 1935, and its reformation brought in national chain stores, including the Carroll Cut Rate store, and the W.T. Grant and F.W. Woolworth department stores. Nationalization of local shopping habits would continue unabated. (MHPC.)

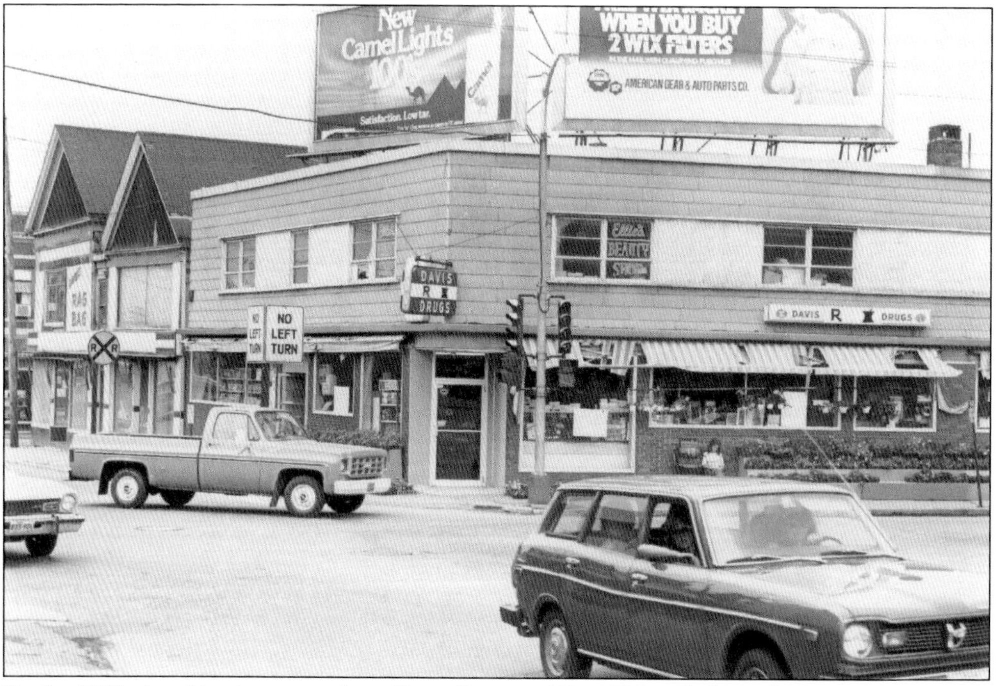

By the 1970s, local businesses such as Davis Drug and Ben Sklar clothing, longtime community institutions, would feel the twin pinches of modernization and out-of-state competition. With the cards stacked against them, these and other businesses withered and died. Today, this block of stores has been completely razed and replaced by grass and benches. (CLM.)

Two

Canoes and Cures

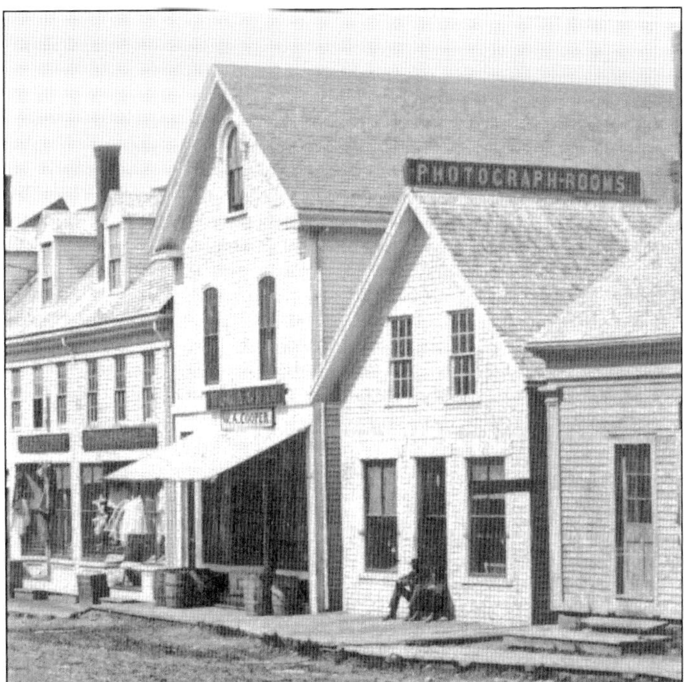

A reasonable guess is that photographer M.L. Averill took this image of his shop from the west side of North Main Street in the 1870s. Importantly, he also captured an image of the shop of Alexander Gray's sons Wilbur and George. Next door, their cousin William Cooper, from Jefferson, Maine, ran a meat shop. The Grays were on their way to becoming a shaping force in Old Town's history. They would later founded the Old Town Canoe Company, for which the city is best known. Businesses all over town benefitted from their acumen, including the Bickmore Gall Cure Company. (BWG.)

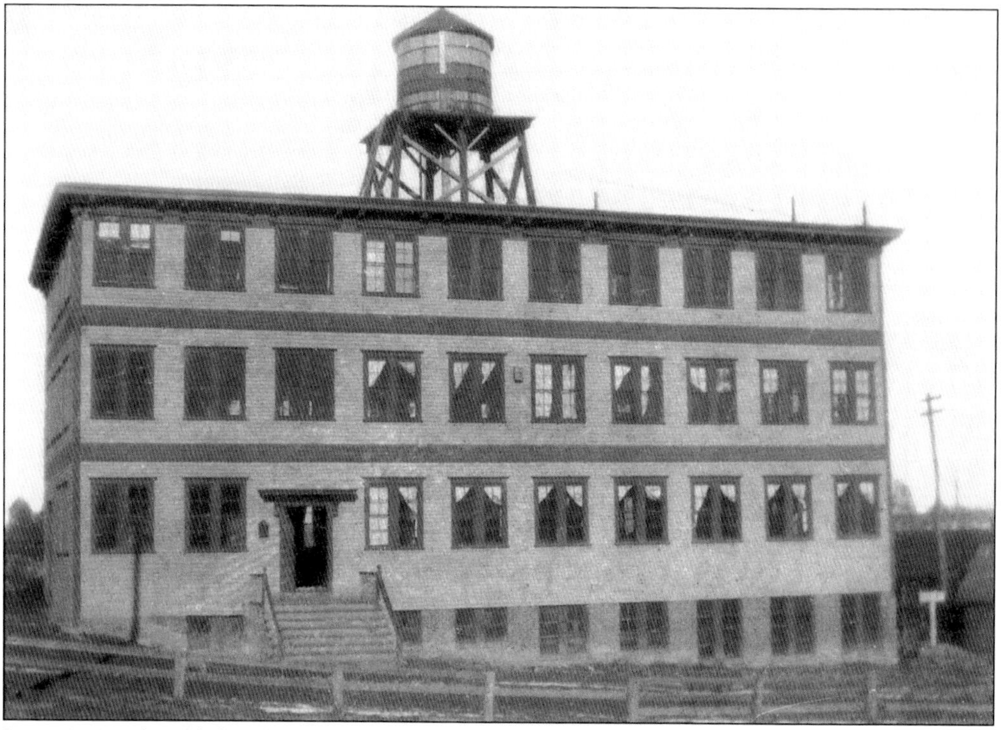

Justin L. Keith sold the shoes made in his Middle Street factory (shown here) in his Old Town Shoe Store in the Folsom Block in the late 1800s. Hundreds of lumberjacks and sawmill workers had swarmed the Old Town area since the early 1800s, propelling the rise of many such stores, often side-by-side, to cater to their footwear needs. (BWG.)

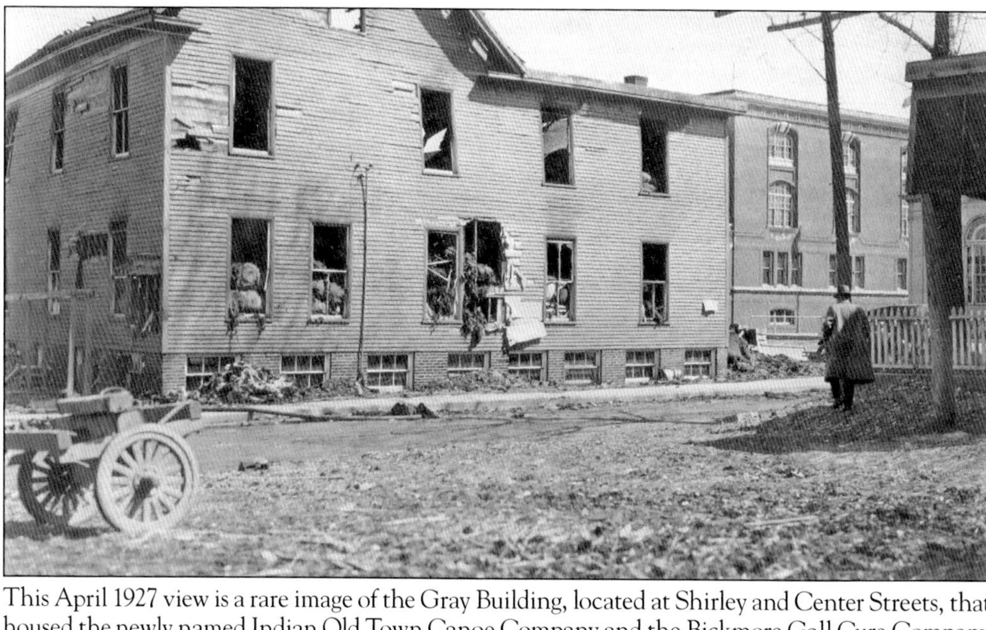

This April 1927 view is a rare image of the Gray Building, located at Shirley and Center Streets, that housed the newly named Indian Old Town Canoe Company and the Bickmore Gall Cure Company in the 1890s. Before the fire, Philip Barron's waste products, including bales of shoddy produced by the woolen mills, were stored here. The Masonic Hall is shown to the right. (OTPL.)

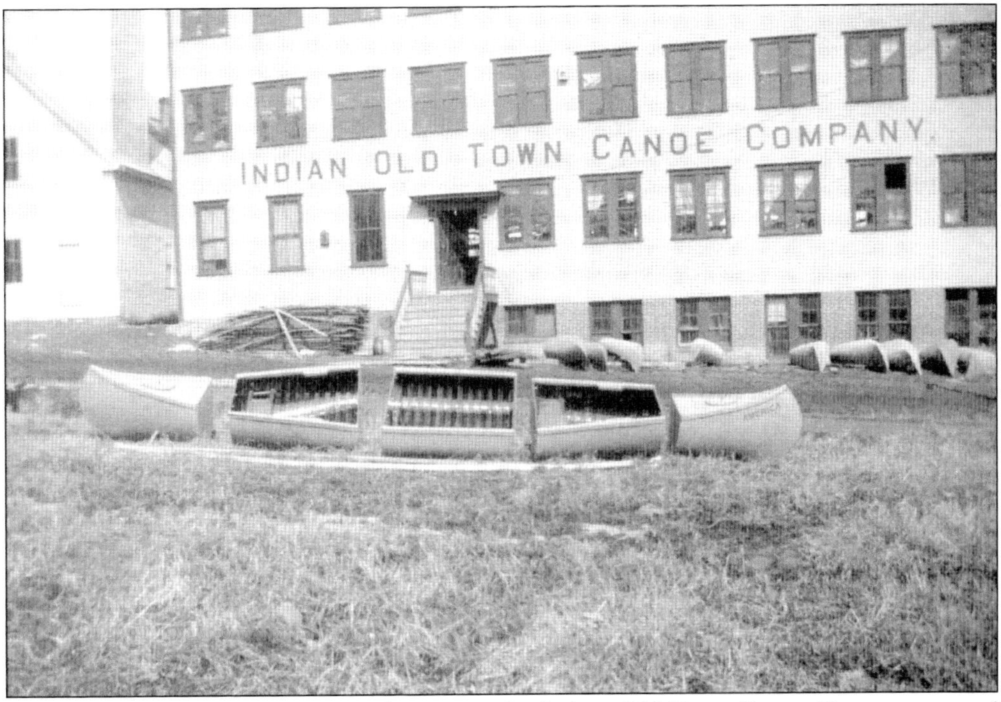

As sales expanded with strategic advertising, the Indian Old Town Canoe Company moved into the bottom floors of the Keith Shoe Company building on Middle Street around 1900. The Bickmore people moved with them, occupying the top floor. The segmented canoe shown here was made for a North Pole explorer whose mission was ultimately unsuccessful. (PRS.)

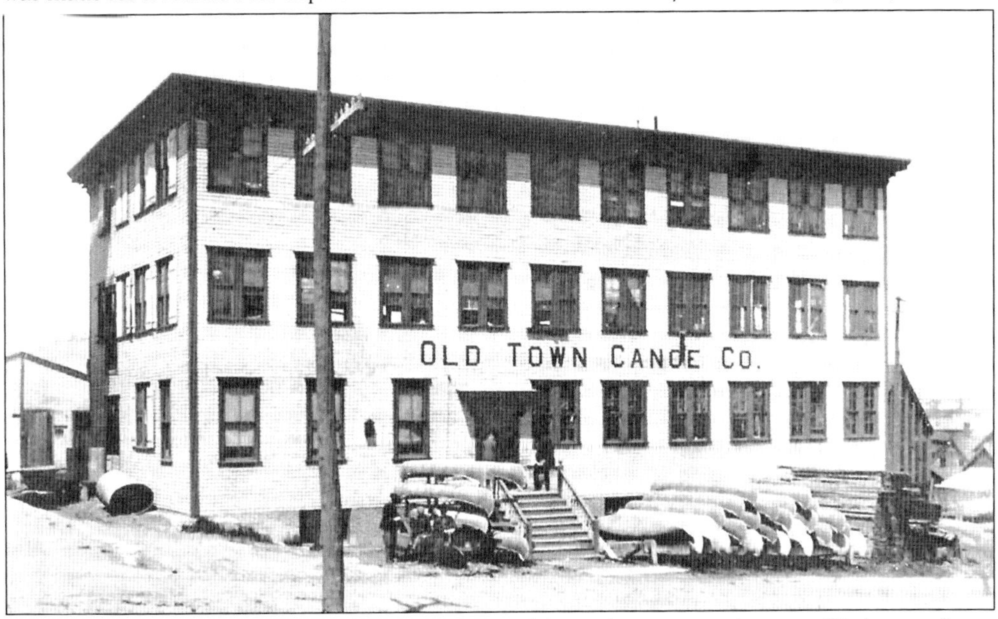

Soon after its incorporation, "Indian" was dropped from the company's name. "Robertson" was added briefly before John R. Robertson, who had come from Massachusetts to help organize the business, returned there. With his departure, the name settled into the Old Town Canoe Company, long known worldwide for its top-notch products. (BWG.)

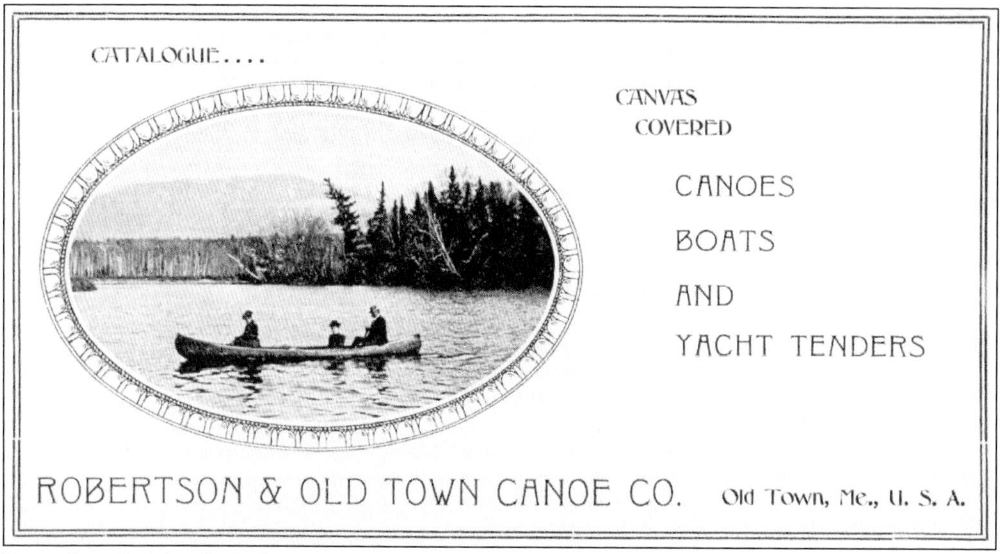

Even though John R. Robertson was with the company only a short time, advertising with the word "Robertson" in the company name was produced. The reasons he left Maine and returned to Massachusetts remain unclear. At the company's incorporation, Herbert Gray was chairman and George H. Richardson was secretary, with stockholders George A. Gray and Robertson later becoming directors. (BWG.)

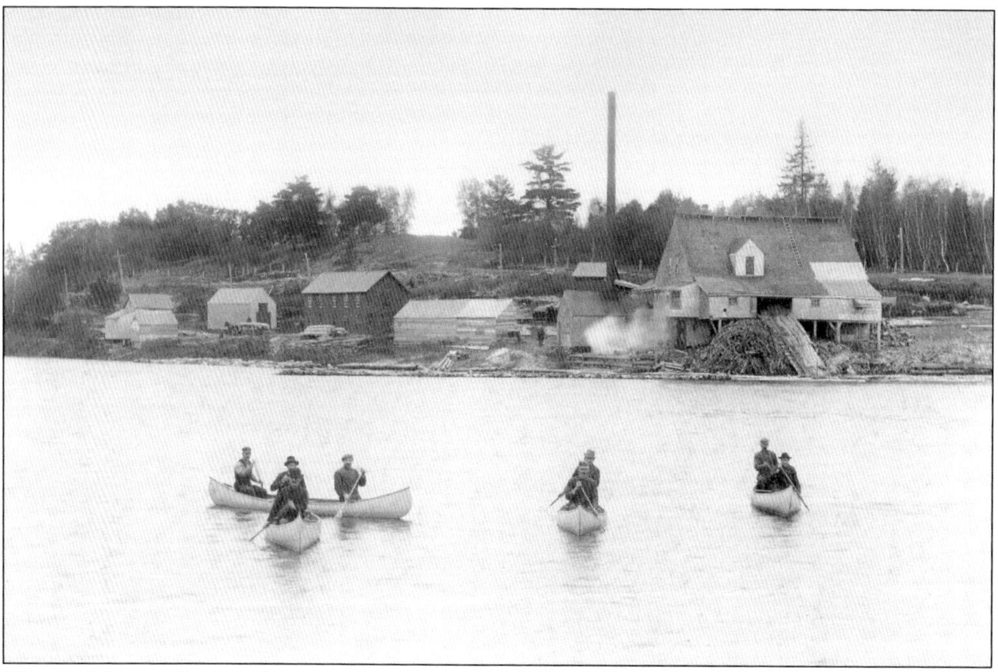

The Old Town Canoe Company was not the first in the area. The Guy Carleton Company had been making bateaux since the 1870s on the banks on the Penobscot near the present-day Knights of Columbus building. Canoes were added to its product line about 1888; some of them are pictured here in this late 1890s image showing the Carleton sawmill and factory in the background. (BWG.)

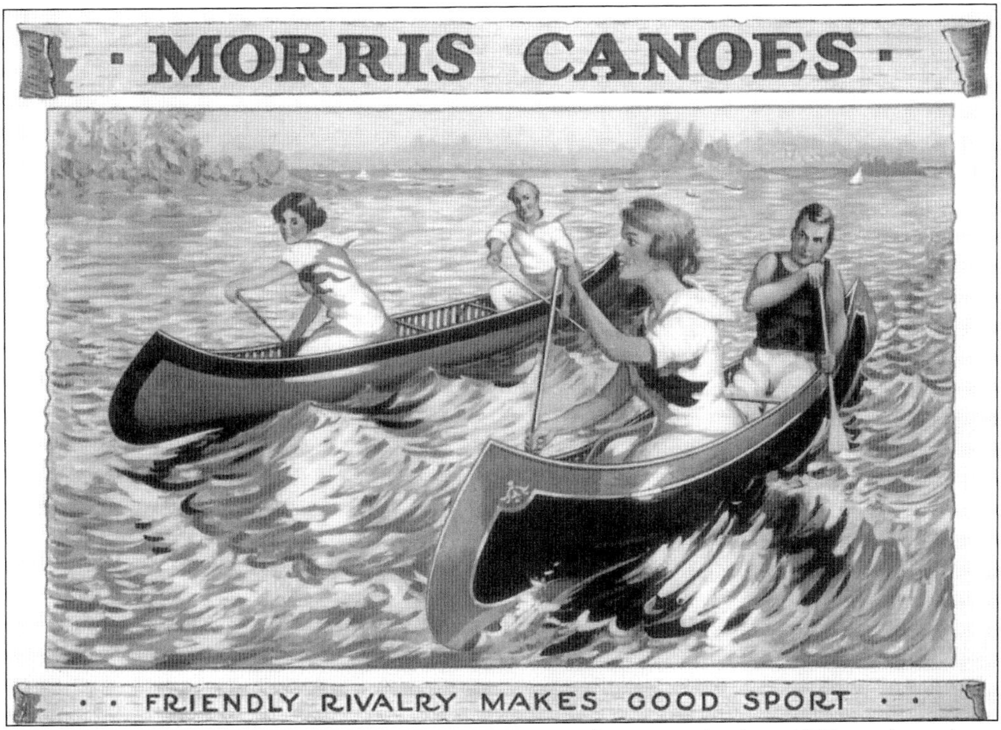

The Bert N. Morris canoe business in Veazie, Maine, began in the late 1880s and was later known as simply Morris Canoe. A fire ended the Morris production line in 1910, with many of its workers gravitating to the Old Town Canoe Company. Today, the Stucco Lodge occupies this space along US Route 2. (OTM.)

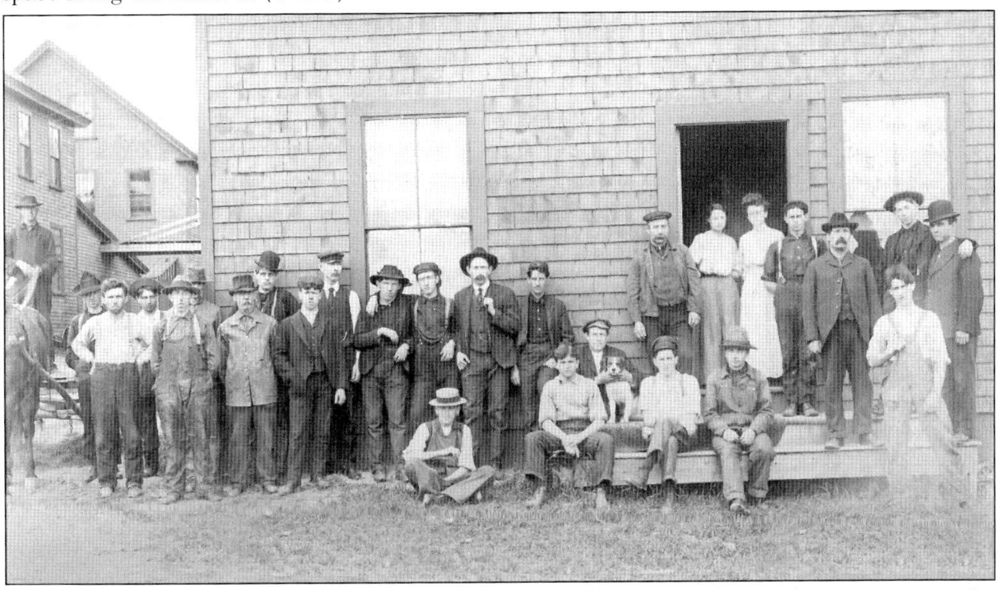

This is a rare image of Morris Canoe's workforce. There was a lot of mutual respect among the canoe manufacturers of the area. They kept up with each other's products and lent a hand when needed. To help Old Town Canoe grow its business, several workers from Morris Canoe taught the craft of canoe making to its workers. (BWG.)

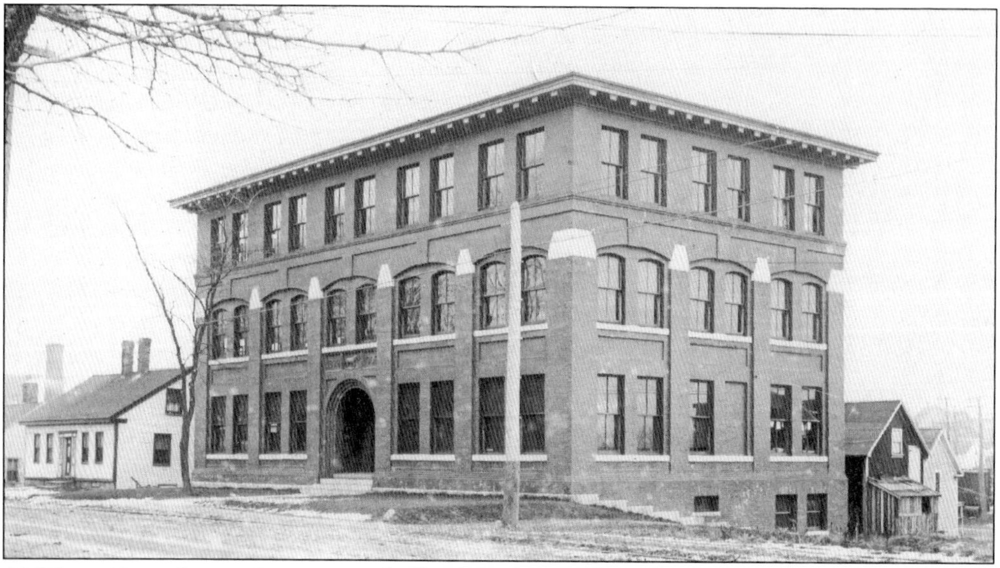

Old Town Canoe's growth was exceeded by that of the Bickmore Gall Cure Company; in 1906, it built new headquarters on South Main Street on the former Lucy Bachelder property. It was the third move in 10 years. Word of mouth advertising worked for its gall cure, leading Bickmore to market across the United States at first and then to Canada, Europe, and Australia. (OTM.)

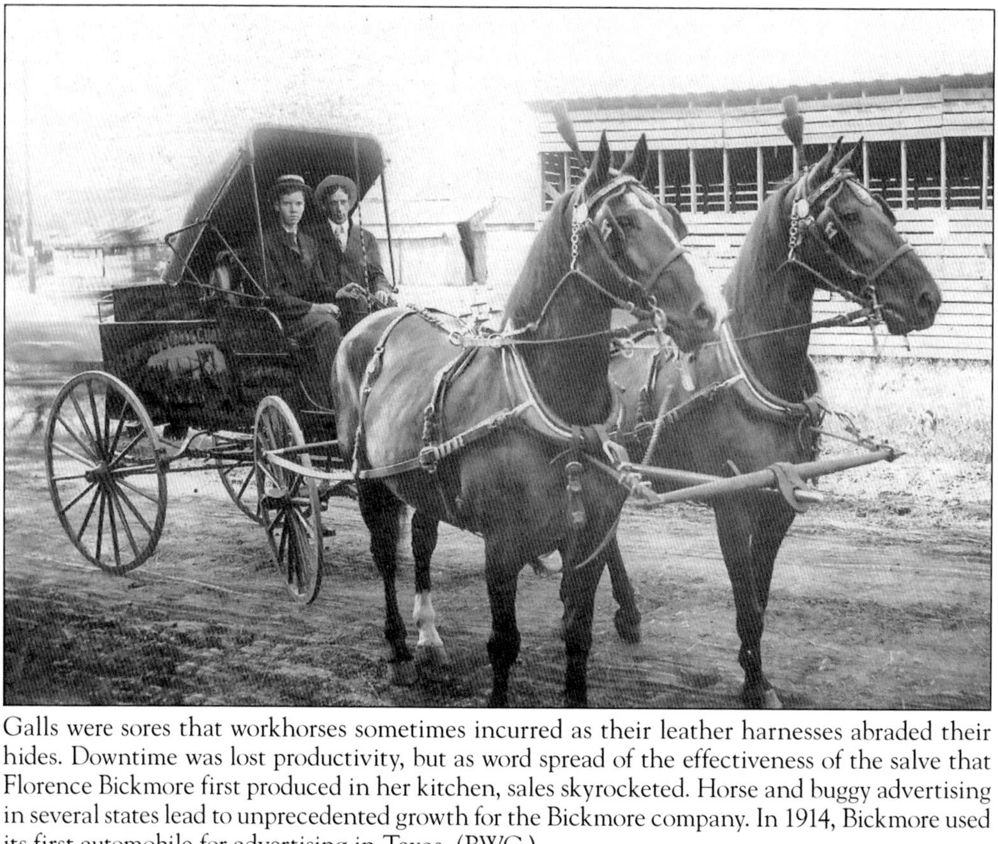

Galls were sores that workhorses sometimes incurred as their leather harnesses abraded their hides. Downtime was lost productivity, but as word spread of the effectiveness of the salve that Florence Bickmore first produced in her kitchen, sales skyrocketed. Horse and buggy advertising in several states lead to unprecedented growth for the Bickmore company. In 1914, Bickmore used its first automobile for advertising in Texas. (BWG.)

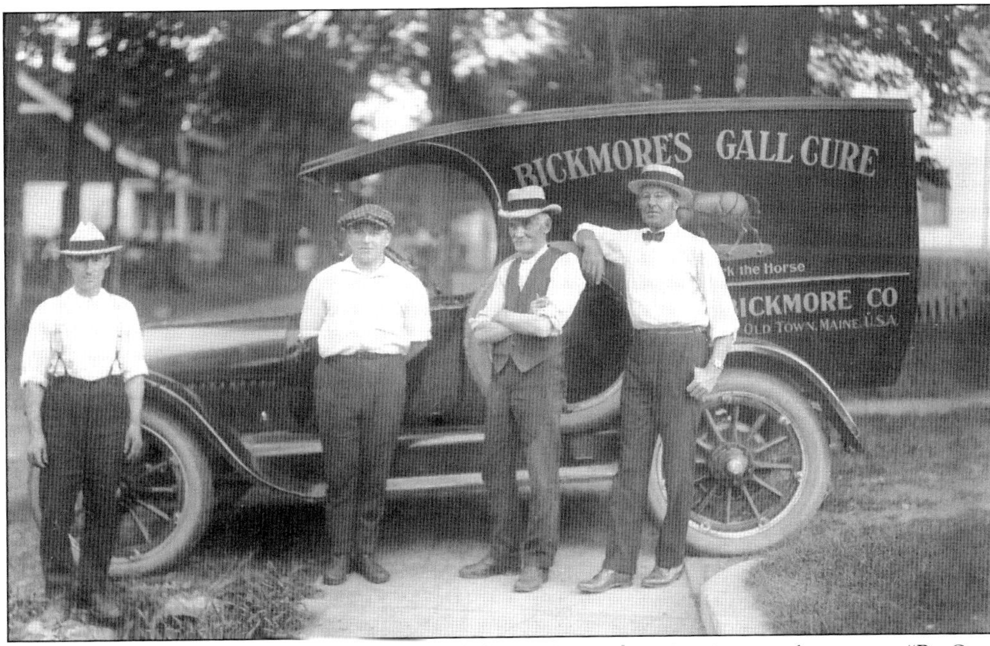

In 1915, Bickmore outfitted its first automobile in Maine, keeping its popular motto, "Be Sure and Work the Horse." Trading the horse for an engine-powered van marked an ironic milestone day in the company's development. Shown here with his glasses carefully removed for the picture, Abiel Bickmore (second from right) poses with, from left to right, Carl Merrill, Edward Keith, and Jesse Gray. (JWK.)

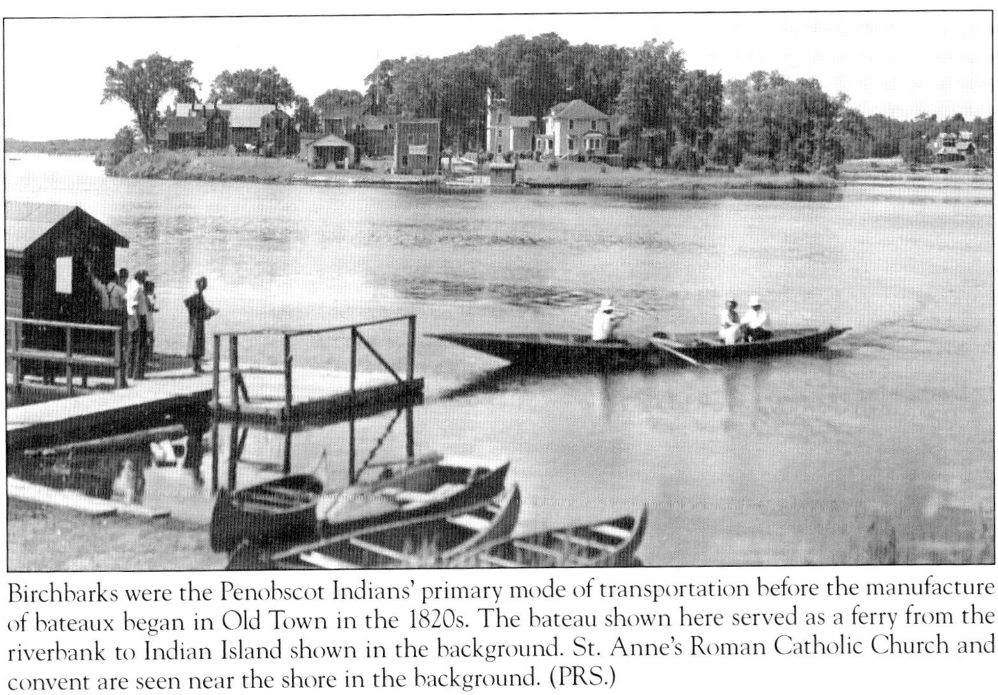

Birchbarks were the Penobscot Indians' primary mode of transportation before the manufacture of bateaux began in Old Town in the 1820s. The bateau shown here served as a ferry from the riverbank to Indian Island shown in the background. St. Anne's Roman Catholic Church and convent are seen near the shore in the background. (PRS.)

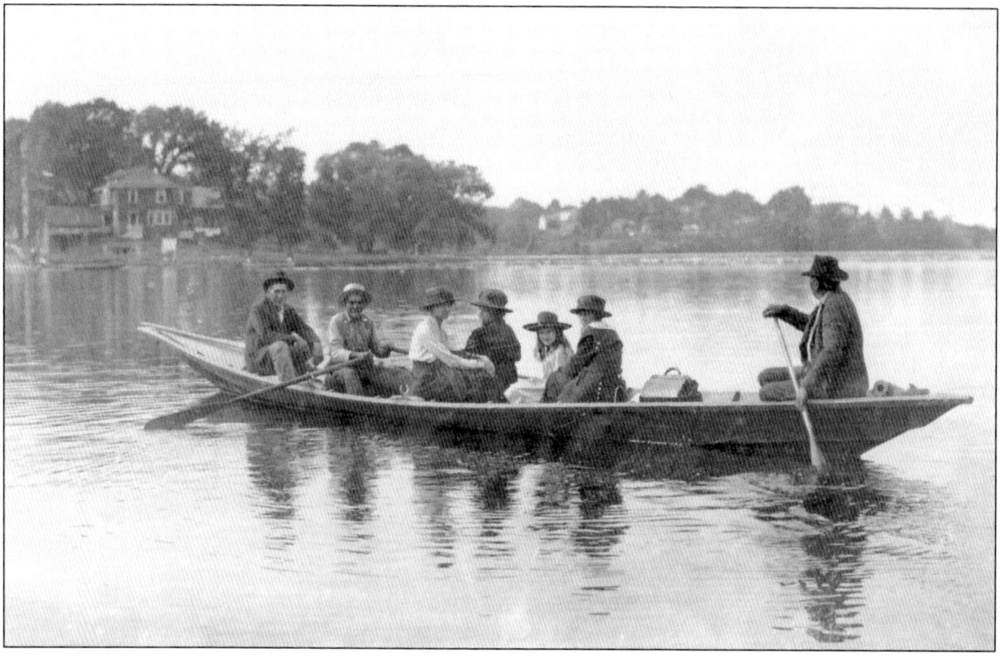

Bateaux were strictly utilitarian watercraft, flat on the bottom and elongated at either end, which made entrance and egress possible without getting one's feet and clothing wet. The bateau pictured here around 1920 is transporting several passengers to Indian Island. The difficulties of Indian children attending school in town were compounded by transportation challenges. (PRS.)

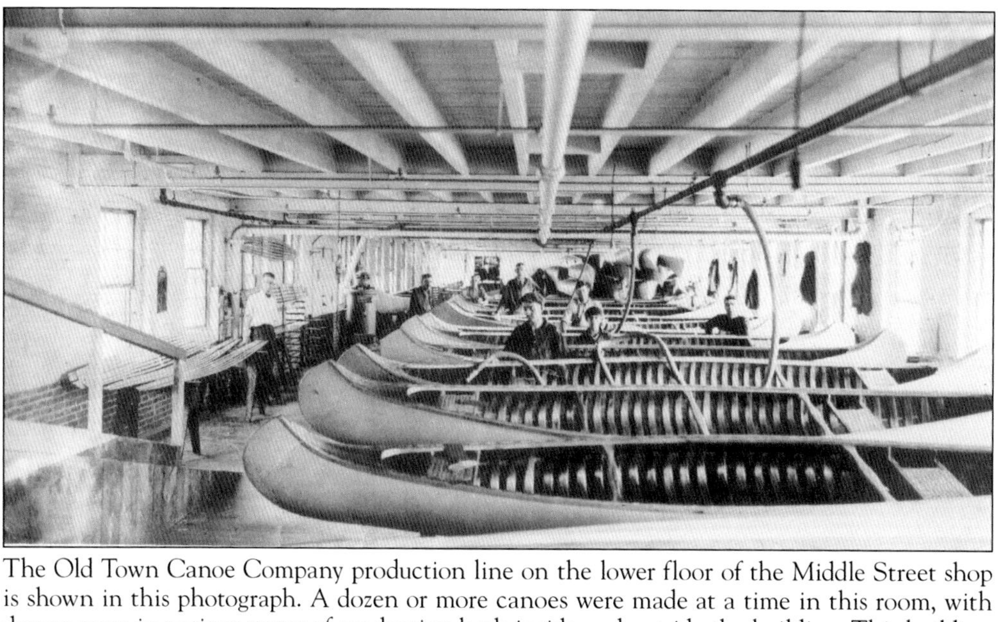

The Old Town Canoe Company production line on the lower floor of the Middle Street shop is shown in this photograph. A dozen or more canoes were made at a time in this room, with dozens more in various stages of production both inside and outside the building. This building was abandoned in 2009 as its new owner, Johnson Outdoors, relocated the canoe-building process to keep pace with technology and demand. (BWG.)

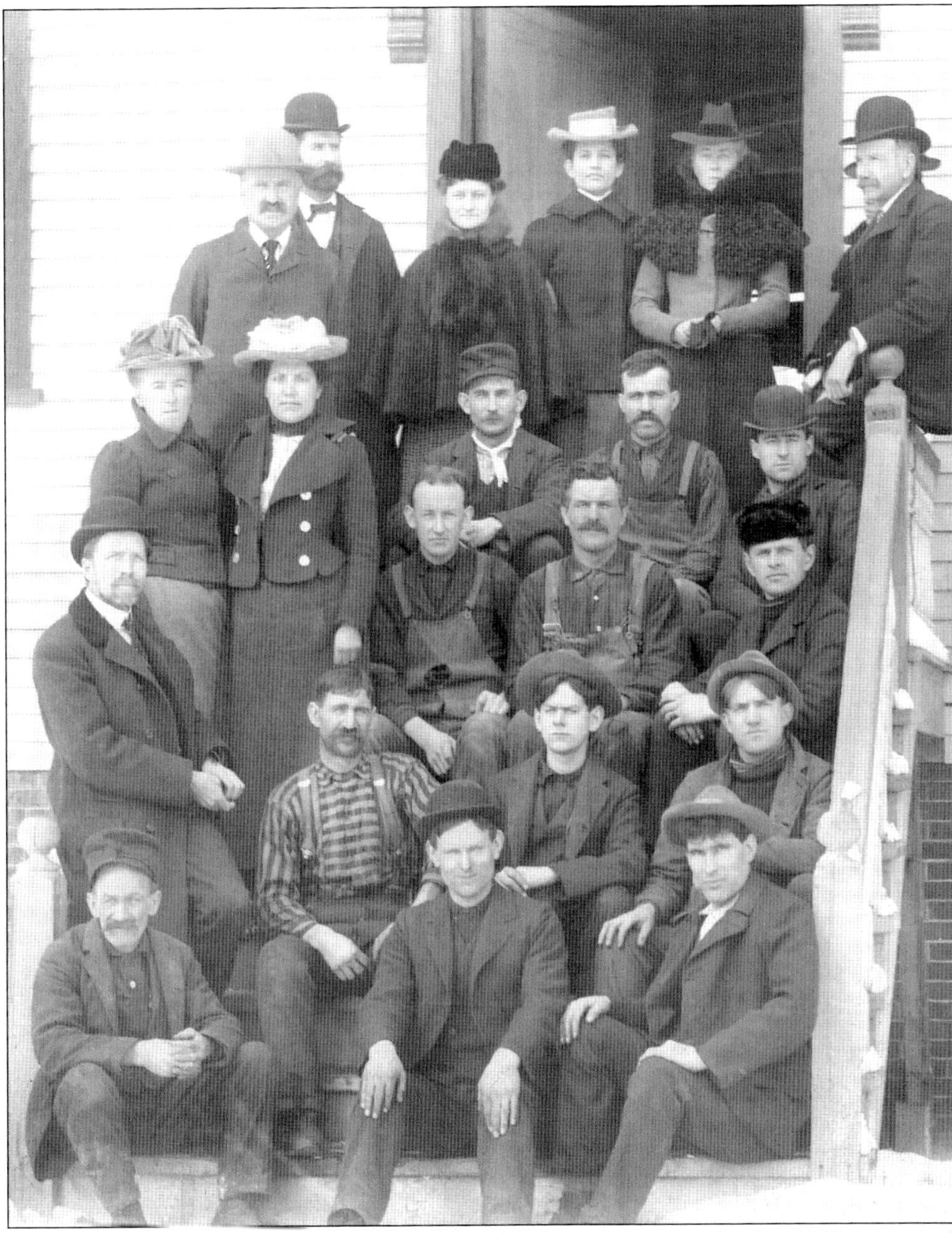

The Bickmore and Gray families supported each others' businesses. In this 1902 image, a few Old Town Canoe and Gray Hardware employees mingle with those of the Bickmore Gall Cure Company amidst freshly-fallen snow. All the female employees shown worked for Bickmore. Canoe builder John R. Robertson is at the rear left. In front of him is George A. Gray and at the top right is George's brother Herbert. Standing at the lower left in the derby is George H. Richardson, manager and treasurer of Bickmore as well as an official with the canoe company. He was also an amateur ornithologist, once building a 17-room birdhouse that he populated with wrens, sparrows, and purple martins. His effort was featured in the March 1910 issue of *Nature and Culture* magazine. (BWG.)

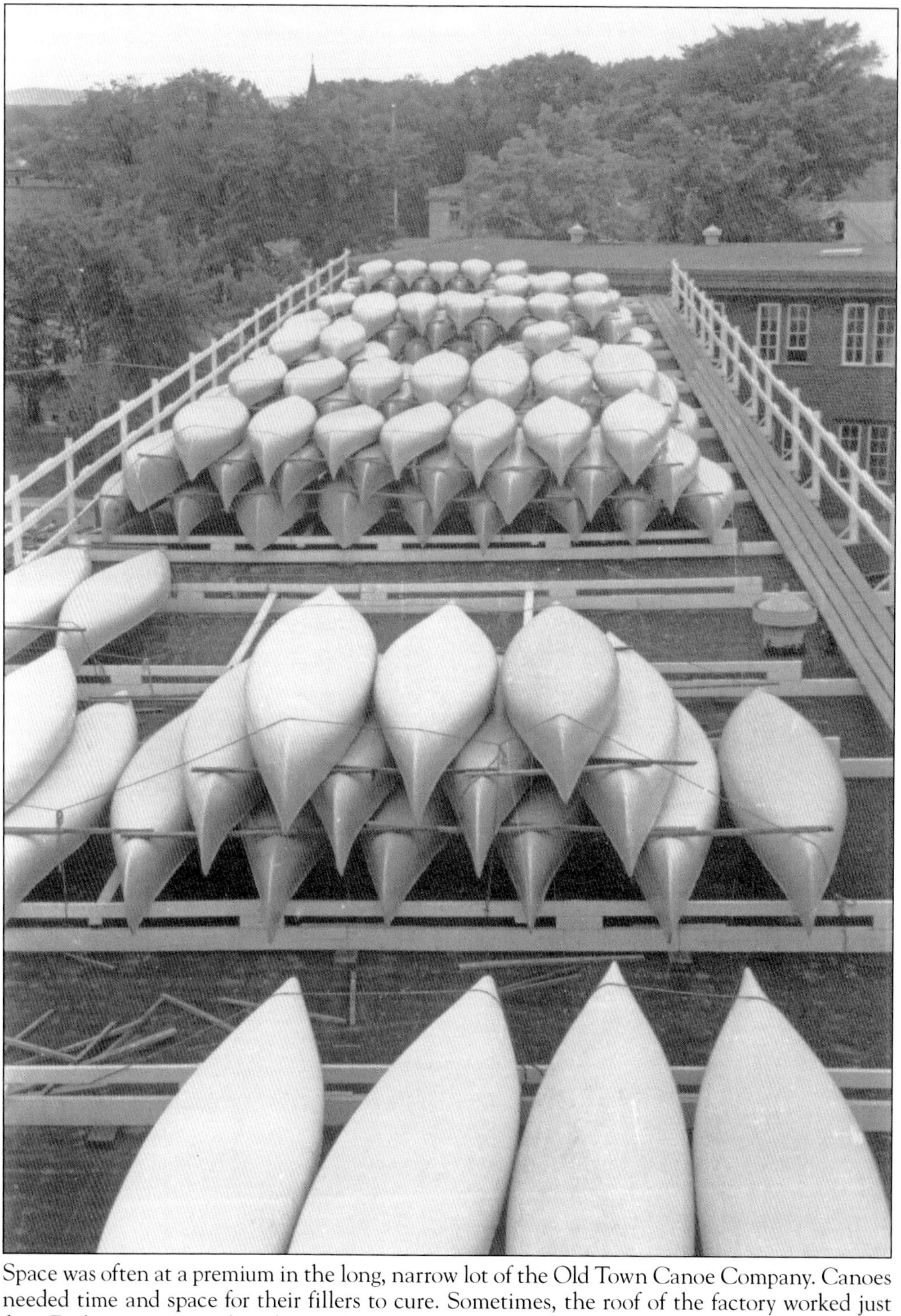

Space was often at a premium in the long, narrow lot of the Old Town Canoe Company. Canoes needed time and space for their fillers to cure. Sometimes, the roof of the factory worked just fine. Each canoe was tethered securely to guard against damage or injury from high winds. The drying process would take several weeks depending upon weather conditions, a variable that always required careful planning regarding space usage. (BWG.)

Abiel P. Bickmore developed an international company from the stovetop remedy developed by his wife, Florence, for sores and ailment affecting the working horse. Astute advertising of the Bickmore Gall Salve promoted the notion that no downtime was needed for the cure to show its healing magic. The Bickmores were long considered upstanding Old Town citizens who worked tirelessly to improve the city's fortunes. (OTM.)

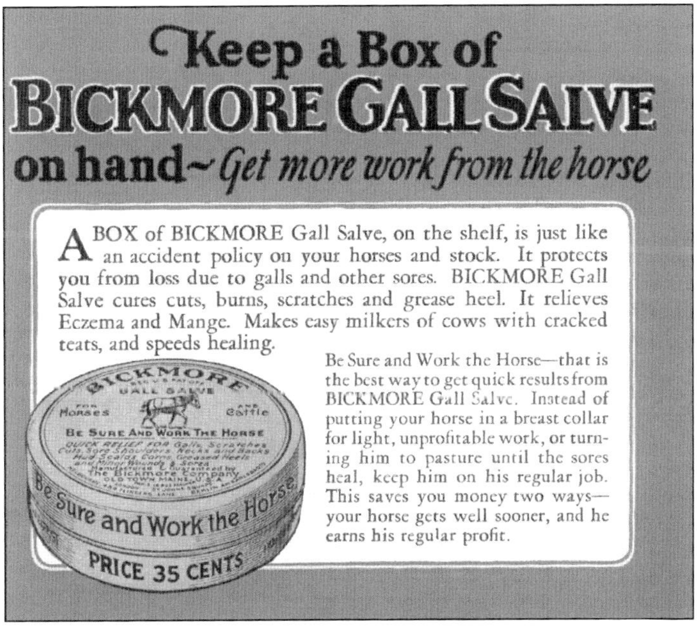

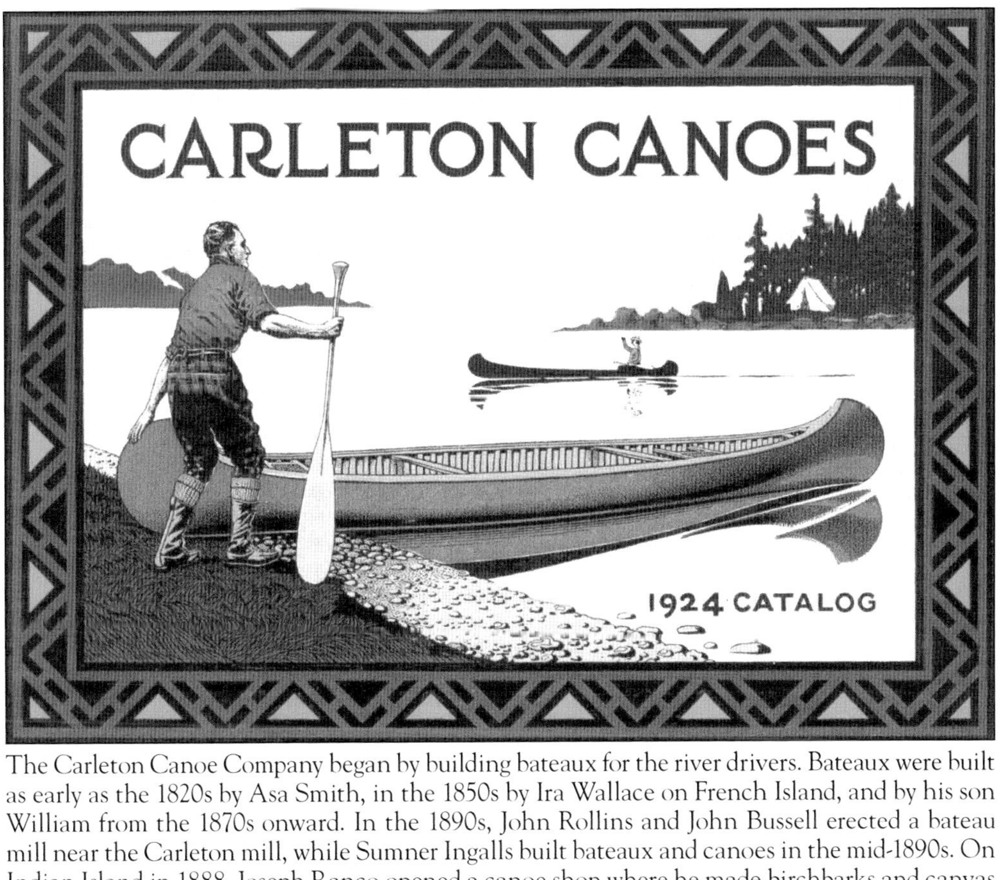

The Carleton Canoe Company began by building bateaux for the river drivers. Bateaux were built as early as the 1820s by Asa Smith, in the 1850s by Ira Wallace on French Island, and by his son William from the 1870s onward. In the 1890s, John Rollins and John Bussell erected a bateau mill near the Carleton mill, while Sumner Ingalls built bateaux and canoes in the mid-1890s. On Indian Island in 1888, Joseph Ranco opened a canoe shop where he made birchbarks and canvas canoes in the form of birchbarks. (BWG.)

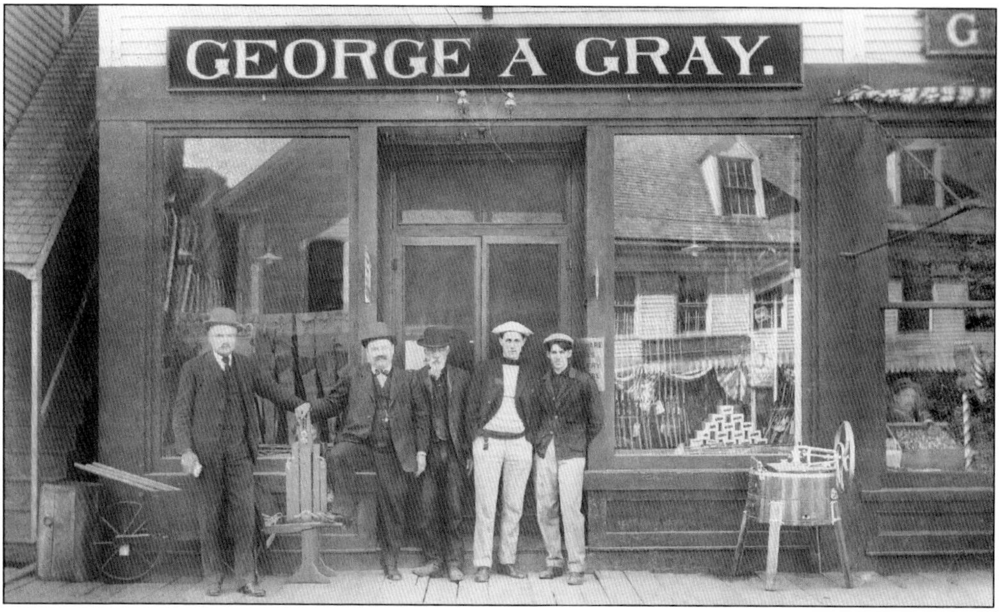

Both George A. Gray and his older brother Wilbur had moved their stores across the east side of Main Street to the left when this picture was taken of George (far left). The others are not identified, but there is some feeling that the man on the right may be Alfred Wickett, a founding craftsman of the Old Town Canoe Company. The face in the window far right may be Wilbur's. (BWG.)

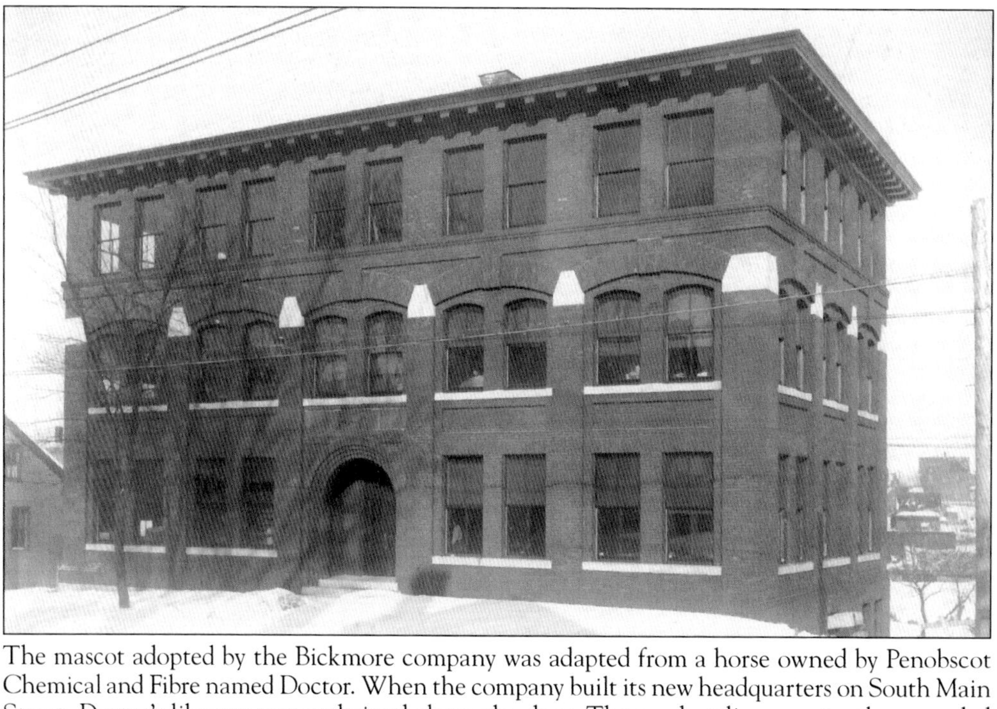

The mascot adopted by the Bickmore company was adapted from a horse owned by Penobscot Chemical and Fibre named Doctor. When the company built its new headquarters on South Main Street, Doctor's likeness was enshrined above the door. The product line constantly expanded from the Bickmore Gall Cure to mortician's powder, toothpaste, shaving cream, cold cream, disappearing cream, and XYZ skin ointment. (BWG.)

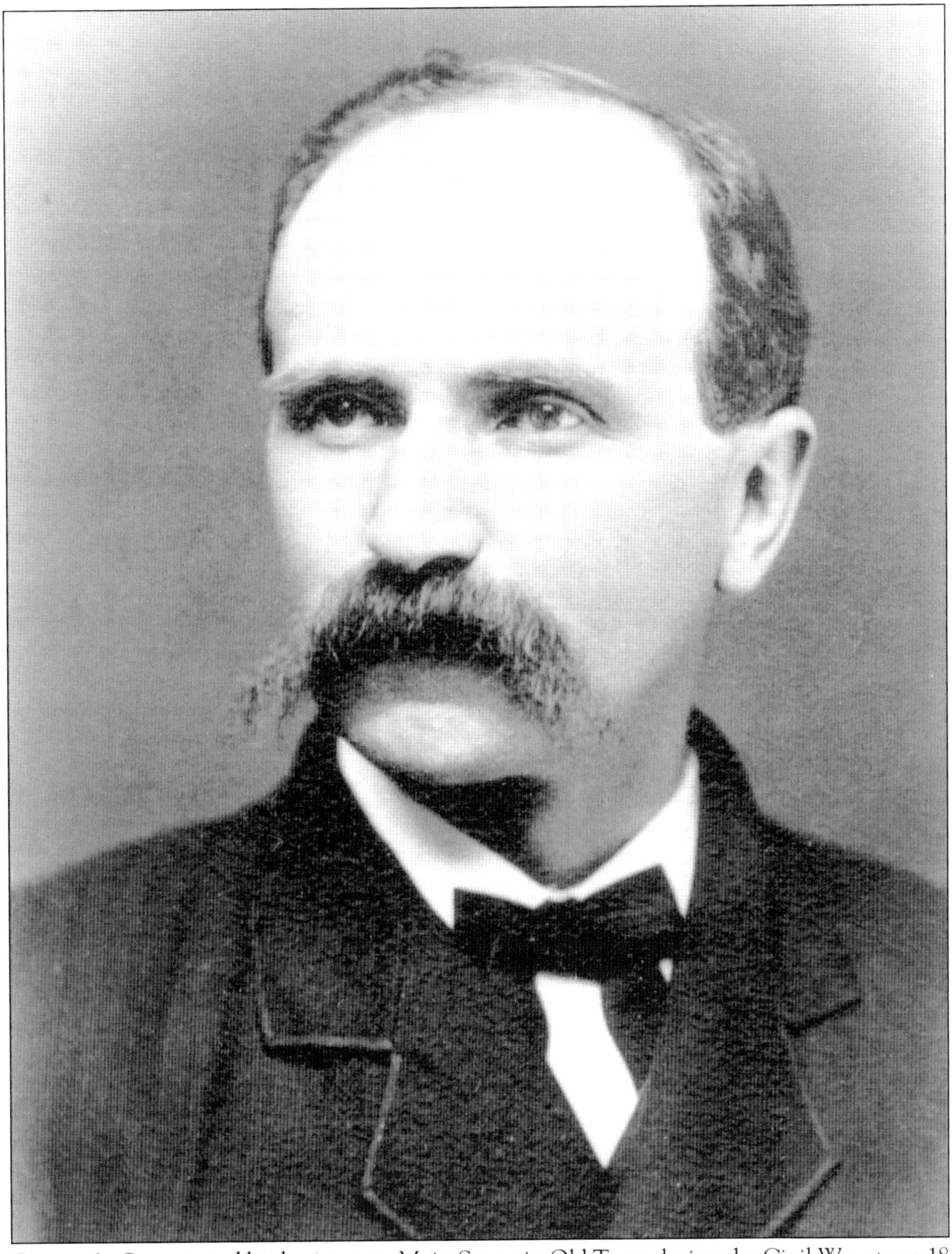

George A. Gray started his business on Main Street in Old Town during the Civil War at age 18 with his older brother Wilbur. Soon, he moved his business to the other side of the street, and Wilbur moved in next door to him. George had established himself as an astute hardware dealer, attending as well to the family lumber business. Old Town Canoe Company lore holds that he was approached by Alfred Wickett seeking work. Learning that Wickett could build canoes, Gray hired him to do just that, with the first canoes built in a shed behind the hardware store. Soon, demand grew, and Gray joined Guy E. Carleton and Edwin M. White in the canoe-making business; years later, Gray bought out both his rivals. (BWG.)

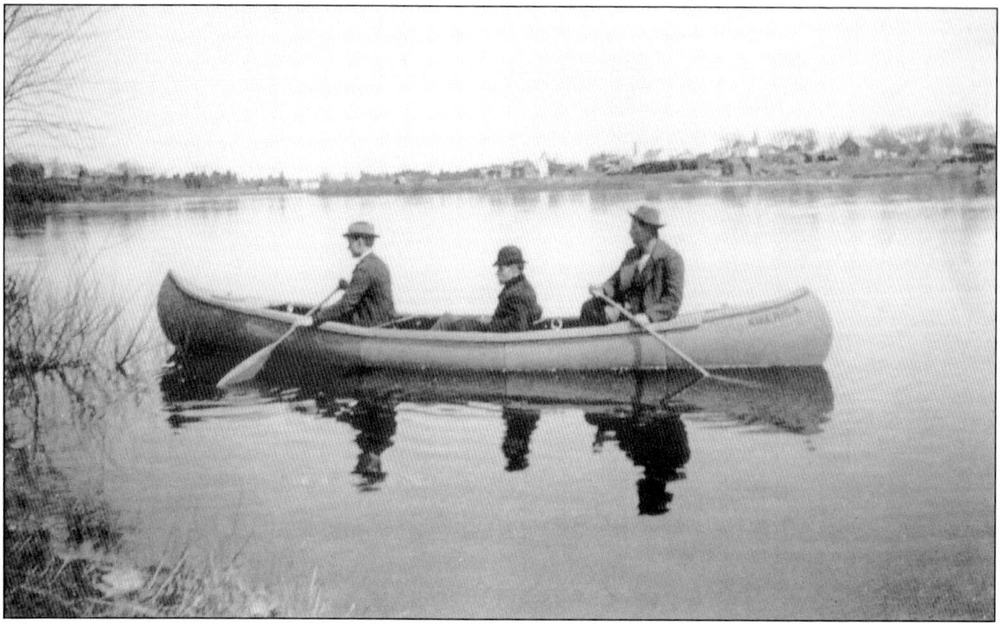

This image offers another glance at the segmented canoe built for the Baldwin-Ziegler explorers, who intended its use on their 1901 North Pole mission. However, ice prevented the delivery of the coal needed for the trek. A second mission in 1903 also failed. The men were led by explorer Robert Peary's meteorologist, Evelyn Baldwin. Samuel B. Gray is pictured, with George Richardson in the middle. The identity of the stern man is unknown. (BWG.)

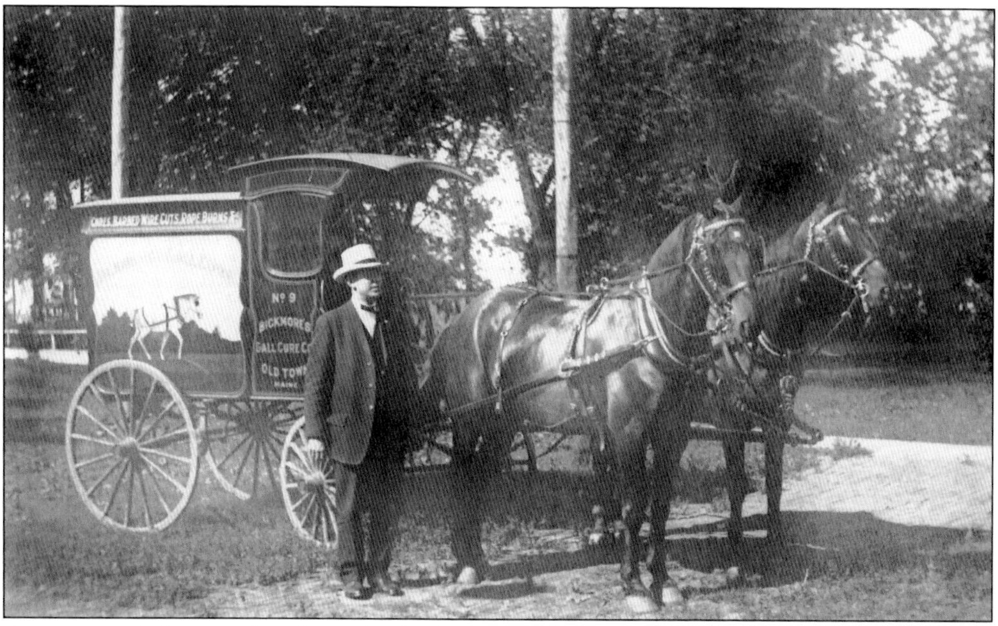

As it expanded its product line, the Bickmore Gall Cure Company also changed its name, although not before this image was captured. The new name, the Bickmore Company, reflected its growth in products for people such as fly ointment and shaving cream. Ever supportive of each other's products, the Bickmore salesmen early on pitched the Old Town Canoe product line to its growing nationwide customer base. (BWG.)

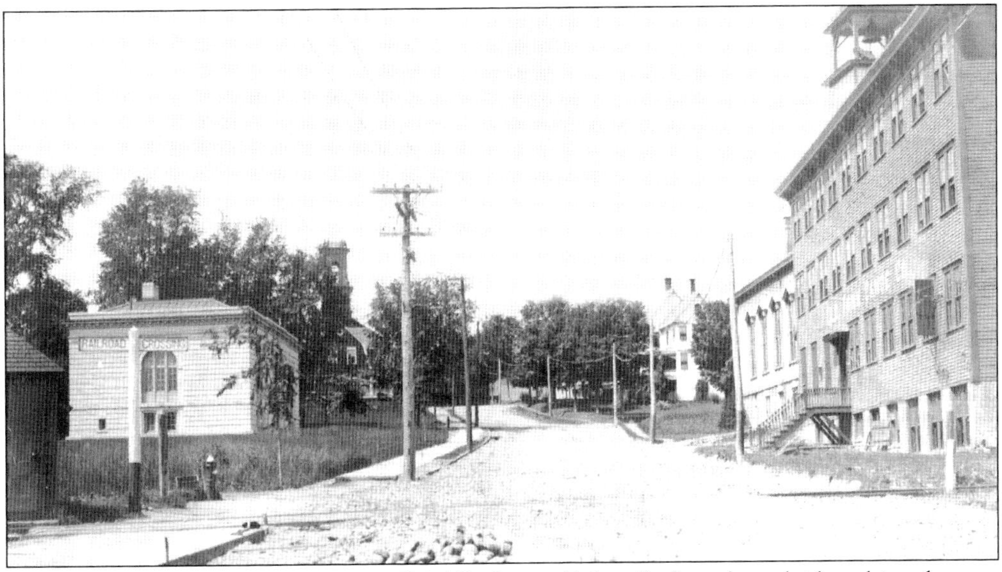

Change is afoot is this c. 1907 image of Middle Street. Sidewalks have been laid, making the new library more easily accessible. A break just before and after the Maine Central Railroad crossing indicates there is more work to be done. The bell tower of the fire station looms over the Old Town Canoe factory, while toward Brunswick Street, the city hall is shown on the right. (BWG.)

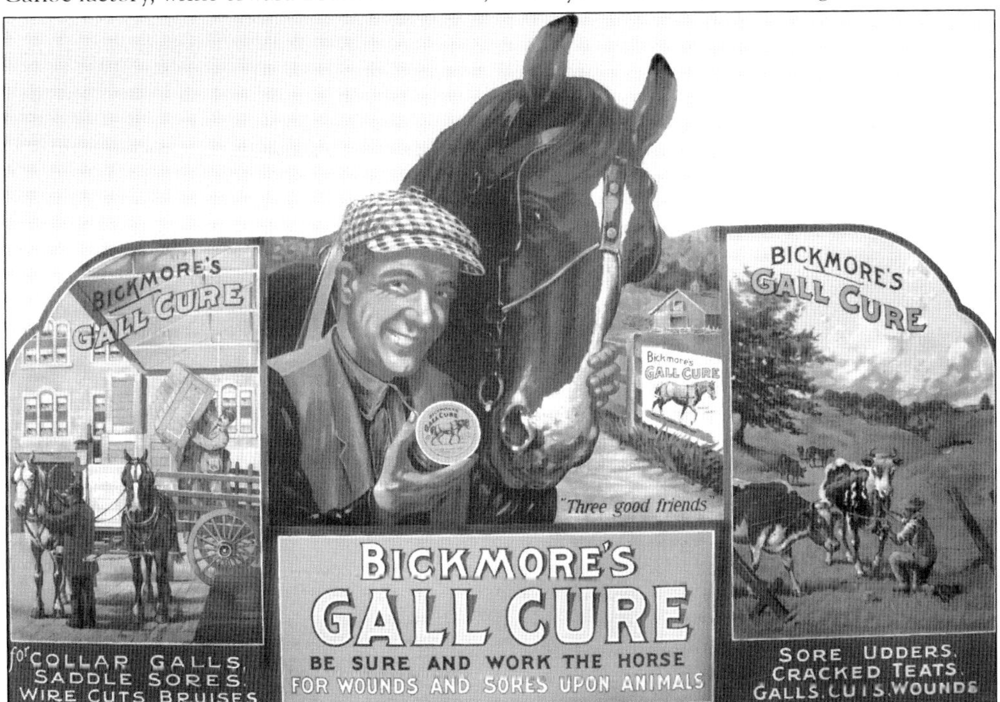

As the company grew, so did its advertising. This well-crafted cardboard counter poster measures three feet wide and incorporates the core Bickmore theme of working the horse to cure the ailment. Cleverness was a hallmark of Bickmore ads; an 1888 ad shows a run-down horse on its way for the cure. On its return, a happy animal has regained its vigor, displaying the gait of a disciplined trotting horse. (OTM.)

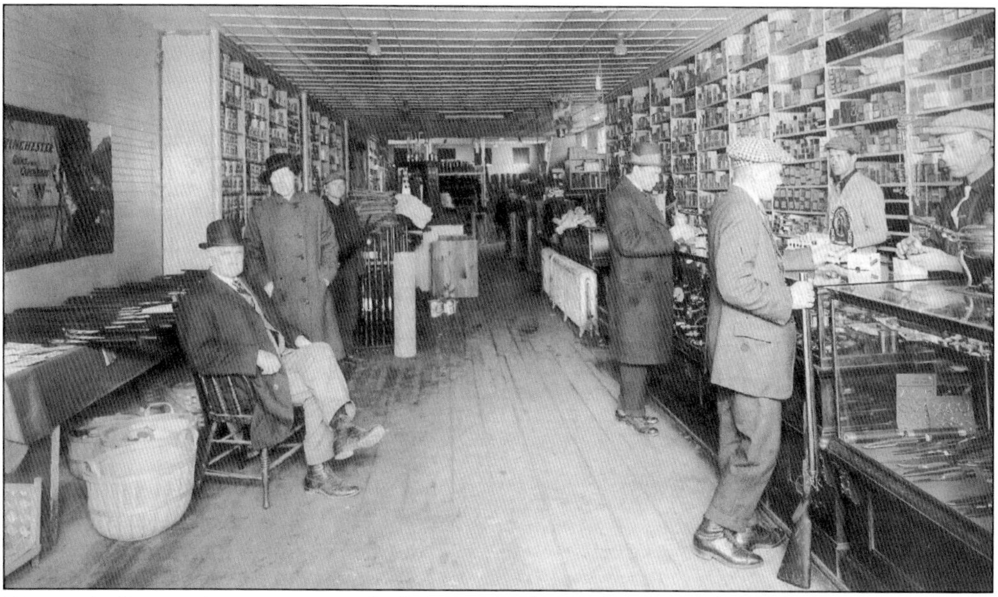

George A. Gray is shown sitting at the left wearing his traditional derby in this c. 1920 picture of Gray's Hardware Store on North Main Street. The store's emphasis on catering to the sporting trade is apparent with the plethora of guns and ammunition on display. One customer seems ready to purchase some shotgun shells to go with his new hunting weapon. (BWG.)

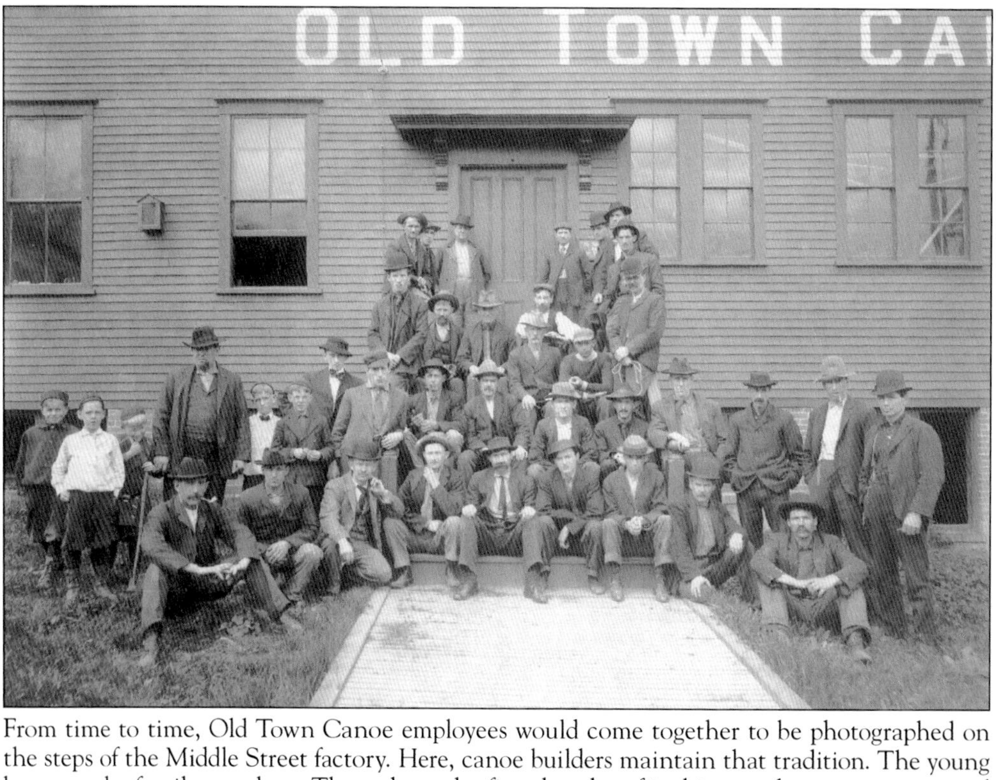

From time to time, Old Town Canoe employees would come together to be photographed on the steps of the Middle Street factory. Here, canoe builders maintain that tradition. The young boys may be family members. Throughout the first decades of its history, the company stressed its high-quality craftsmanship and dedication to excellence. (BWG.)

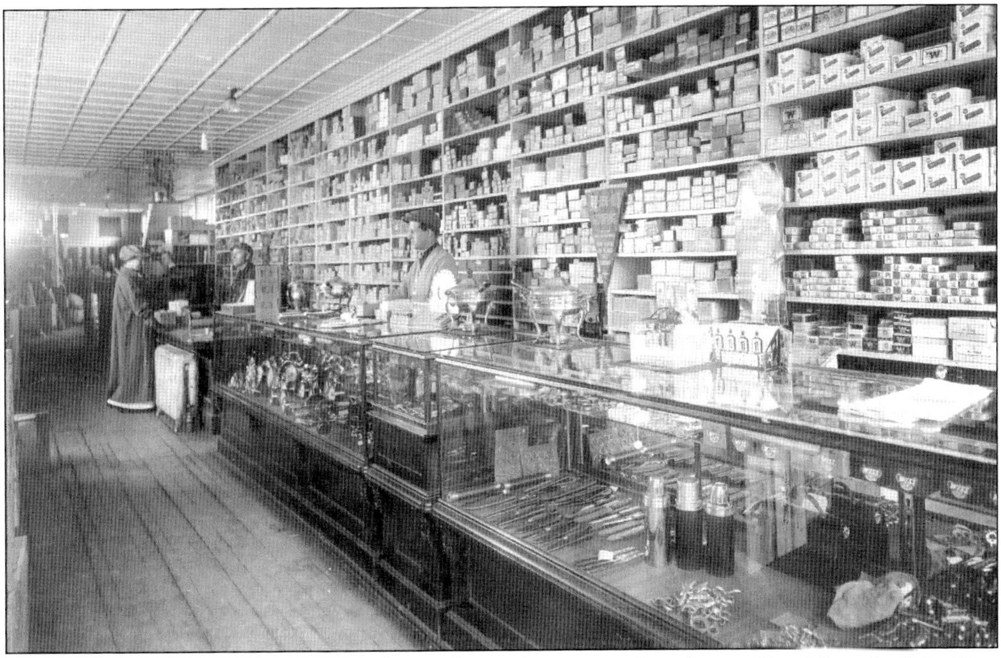

An alternate view of the Gray's Hardware shows the range of products offered for sale: 3-in-One lubricating oil, Ru-Ber-Oid roofing products, padlocks, aluminum collapsible cups, key rings, alarm clocks, thermos bottles, hunting knives, Wiss Cut Clear products, and this: "No dark corners in your home with this Eveready electric lamp." (BWG.)

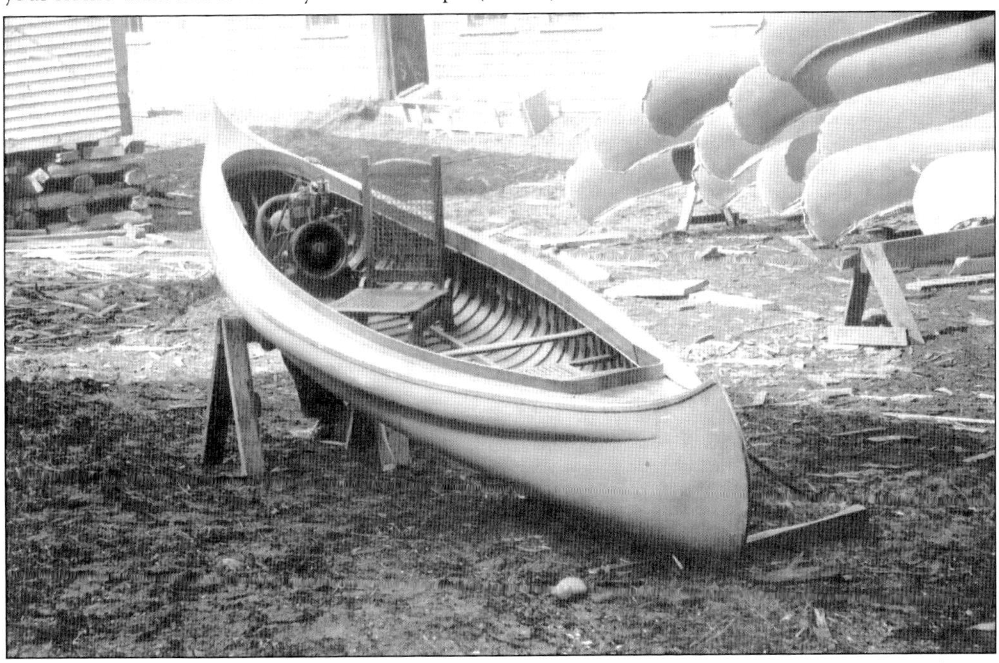

Old Town Canoe produced its first motor craft in 1905 with this model featuring a sponson design to help the craft from capsizing. Other manufacturers had produced motorized craft for several years before Old Town Canoe's customers began inquiring about them. The specially adapted chair soon gave way to more integrated designs. (BWG.)

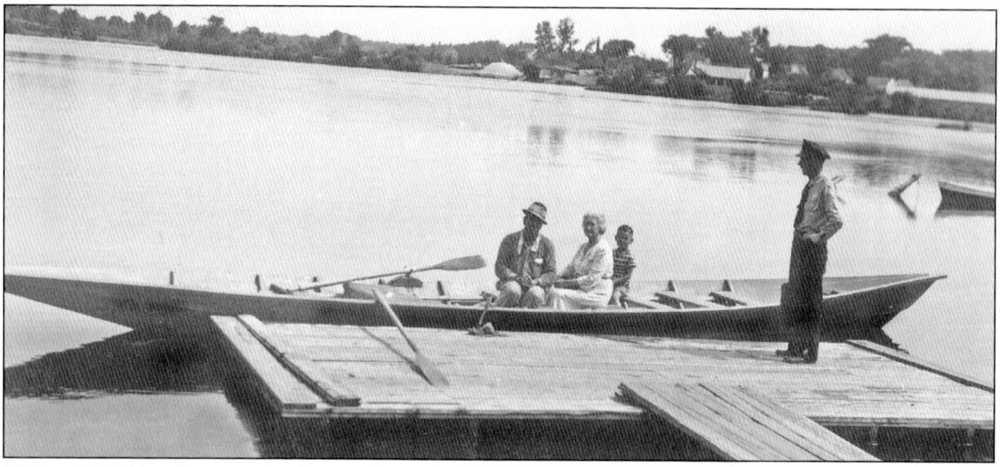

This mid-1940s photograph shows a bateau used as a ferry between Old Town and Indian Island, a mode of transportation that would continue until 1951, when a connecting bridge was built. Early Old Town bateaux makers were Guy E. Carleton, Sumner L. Ingalls, and William W. Wallace; the latter sold his boatbuilding business in 1888 to C.W. Hayes of Orono, who used it for carriage painting. (BWG.)

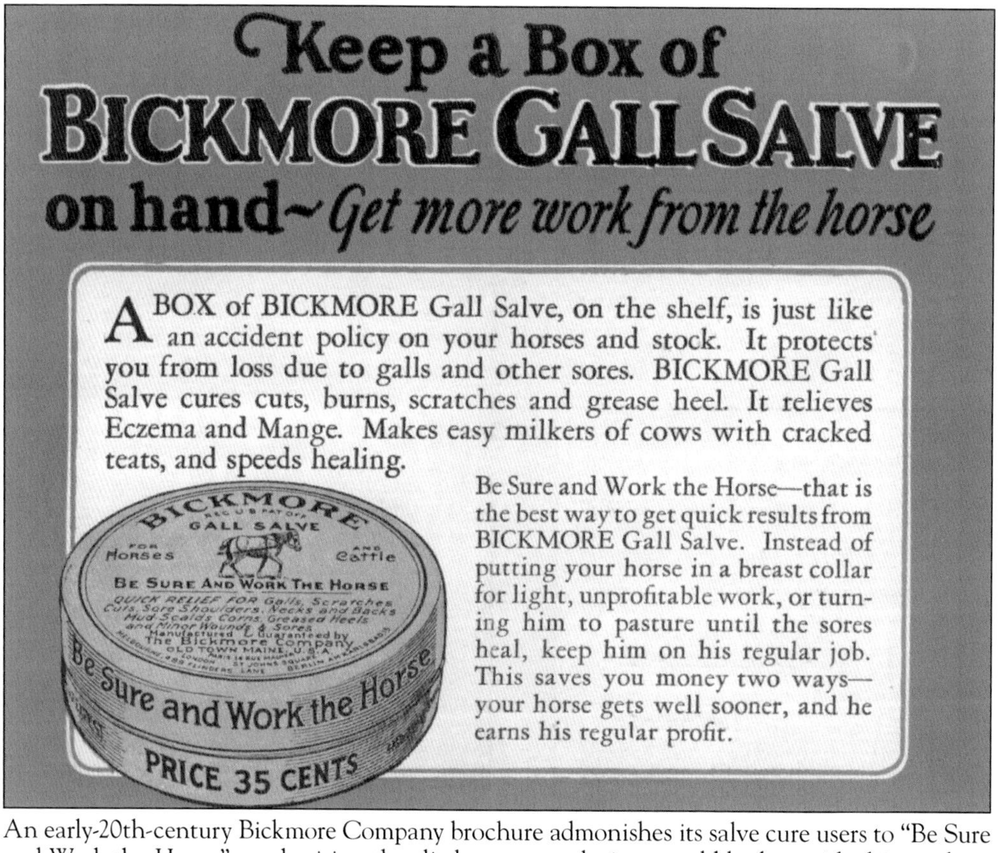

An early-20th-century Bickmore Company brochure admonishes its salve cure users to "Be Sure and Work the Horse," emphasizing that little or no work time would be lost with this product. After the company's founders died, management fell to entrepreneur Herbert Gray, who became president, and his son Maurice, who became treasurer and general manager. (OTM.)

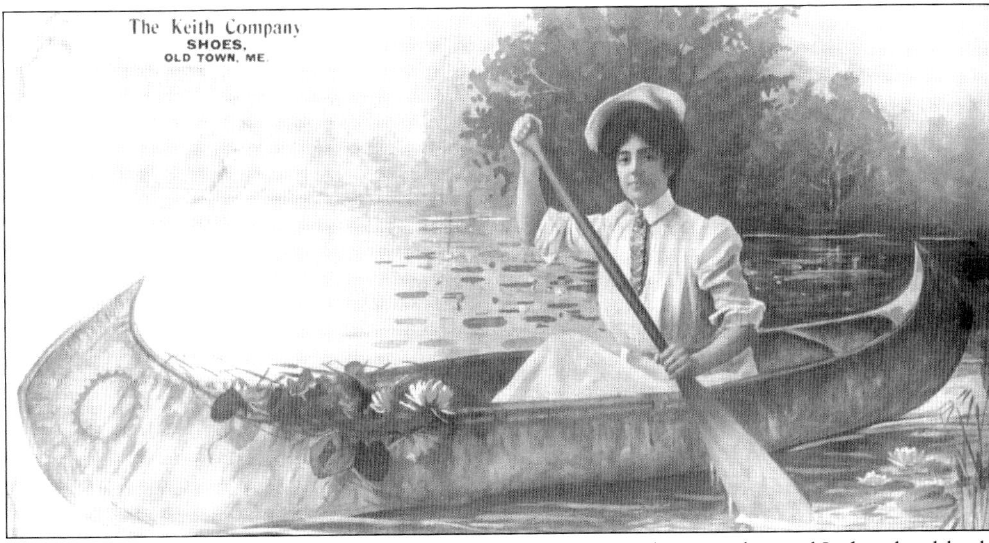

This early Keith Shoe Company advertisement features a damsel in a traditional Indian birchbark. One interpretation might be that the shoe company had yet to be colocated with the Old Town Canoe company, as both businesses were subsequently located on Shirley Street and later on Middle Street along with the Bickmore Gall Cure Company. (OTM.)

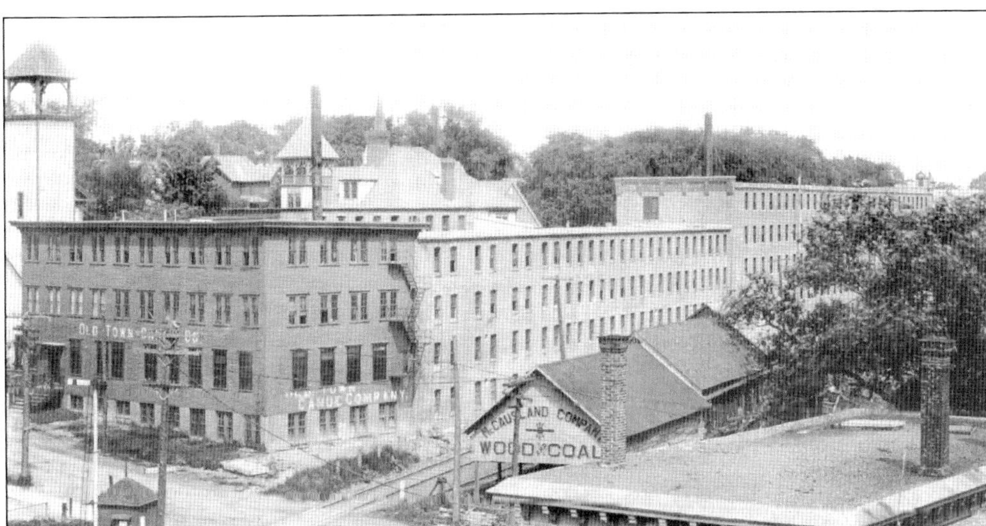

The full panoply of the Old Town Canoe's endless stretch of buildings along North Brunswick Street is shown in the early-20th-century image. At left, the bell tower of the fire department looms above the factory. To its right, the bell tower of the McKinley School, which burned in 1917, can be seen. To its right is the steeple of the Methodist church. At bottom right, the McCausland Wood and Coal business hugs the railroad tracks. (BWG.)

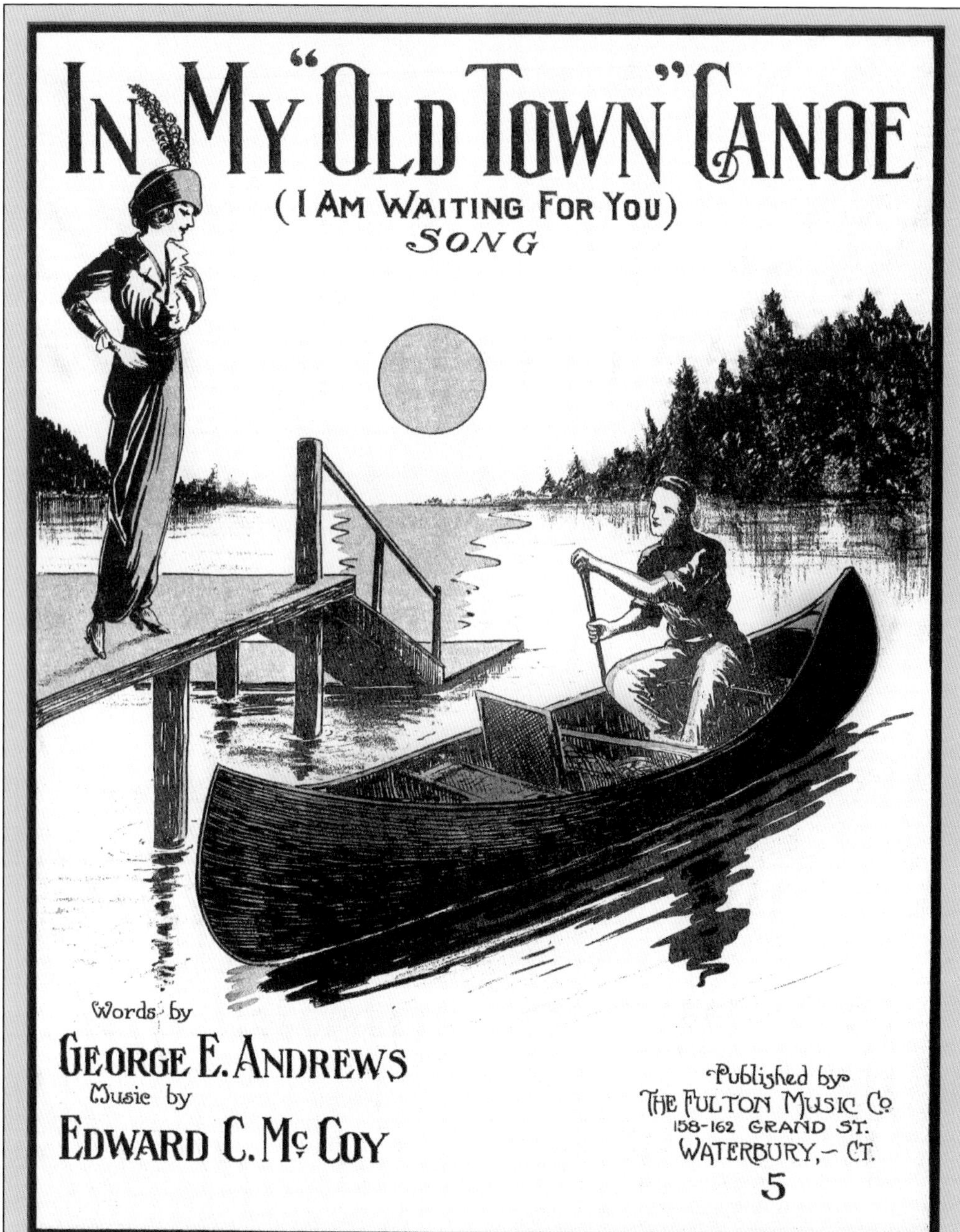

Old Town canoes became known far and wide, partly as a result of shrewd co-marketing by the Bickmore Gall Cure Company, but also through its own carefully placed print ads. By 1916, a musical produced by students at the University of Michigan featured the song "Out in My Old Town Canoe," including the lyric, "Each little ripple enchants you, whispering a hint of love." The success of the "courting canoe" was assured. (OTM.)

Three

LIVING AND WORKING

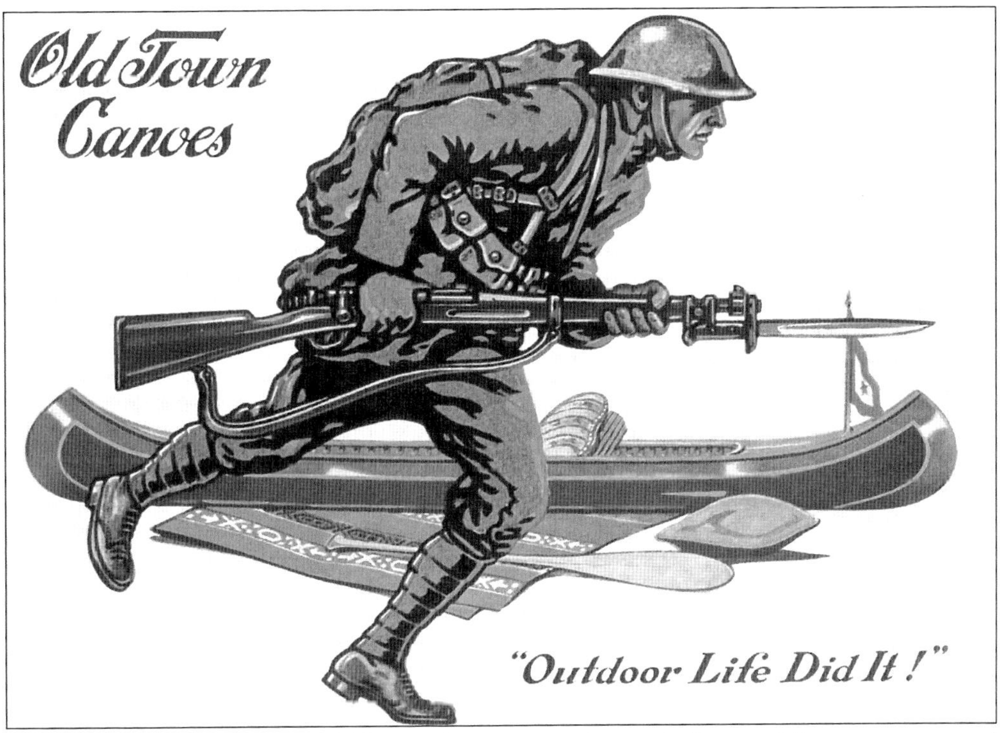

As World War I closed in 1919, Old Town Canoe teamed up with *Outdoor Life* magazine to extol their mutual effects on the fitness of the American soldier. Beginning in the 1870s, canoe making, a skill learned from the Penobscot Indians, had been a source of employment for hundreds of Old Town workers. From master craftsmen such as brothers Alfred and Richard Wickett at Old Town Canoe to the artisans at E.M. White and the Bert N. Morris Company in nearby Veazie, the canoe and bateau industry made making a living somewhat easier. Bateaux making, begun in the 1820s, survived for more than 100 years. With the advent of aluminum and plastics, canoe making faced daunting challenges, and those in the boat-manufacturing industry who were faint of heart endured years of economic uncertainty. (BWG.)

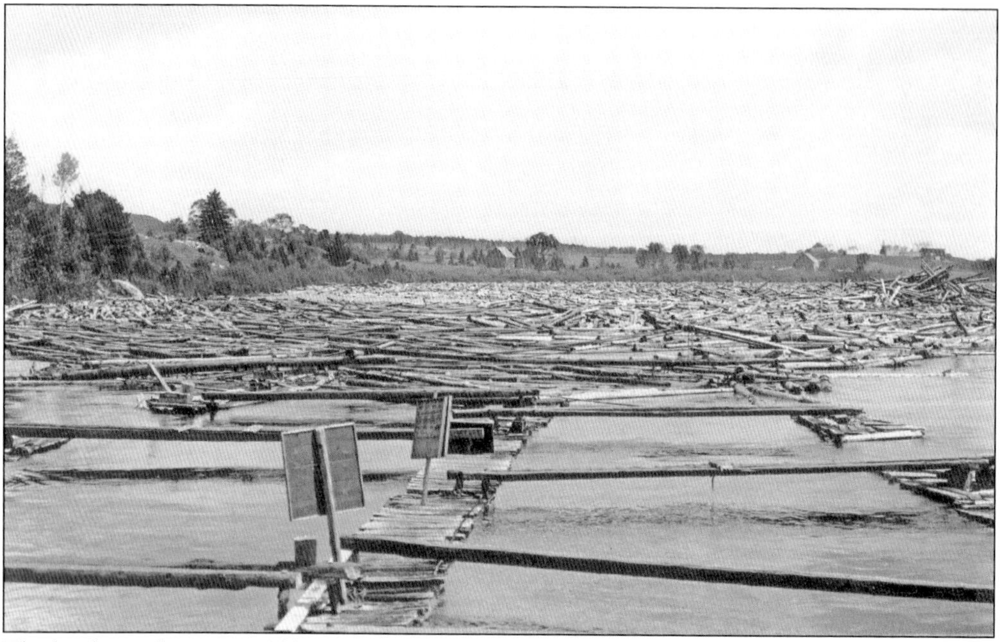

The lumber industry put Old Town on the map at the expense of the Penobscot Nation. In 1833, the State of Maine sold off 100,000 acres of tribal lands, fully 95 percent of the Penobscots' holdings, clearing the way for massive lumbering operations. Gen. Samuel Veazie's relentless pursuit of the forest's bounty focused on the falls at Old Town to power his mills and turn lumber into wealth. In this image, thousands of logs pile up against the booms, waiting to be sorted. (OTM.)

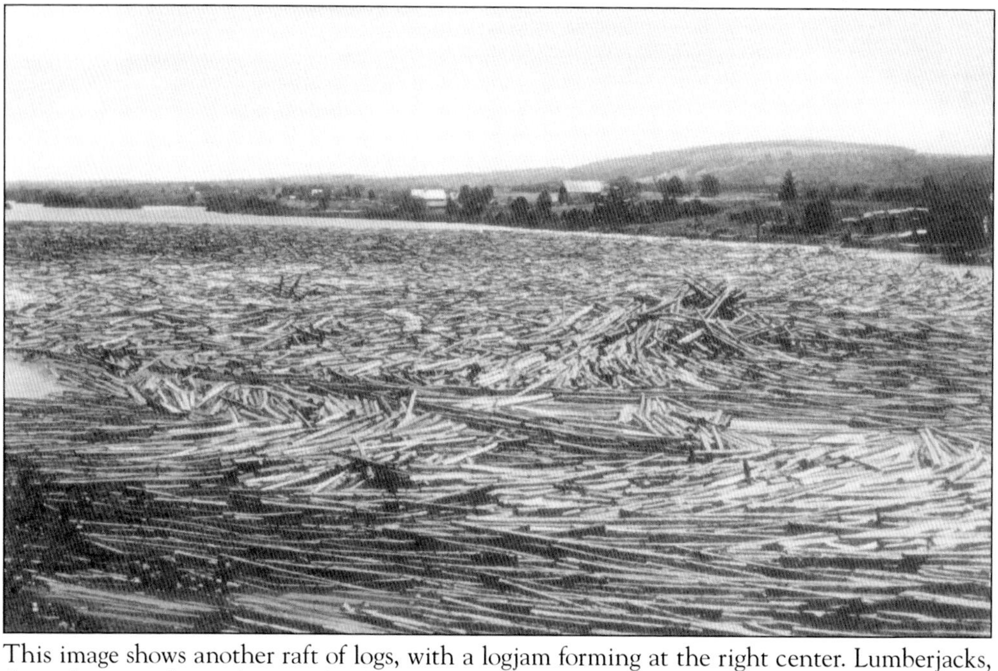

This image shows another raft of logs, with a logjam forming at the right center. Lumberjacks, dressed in river driver shirts and spiked boots, clambered into the middle to break up these rafts. Sometimes, as the jam was broken, sudden shifts in the log piles could propel men into the air or under the water, sometimes leading to loss of life. (BWG.)

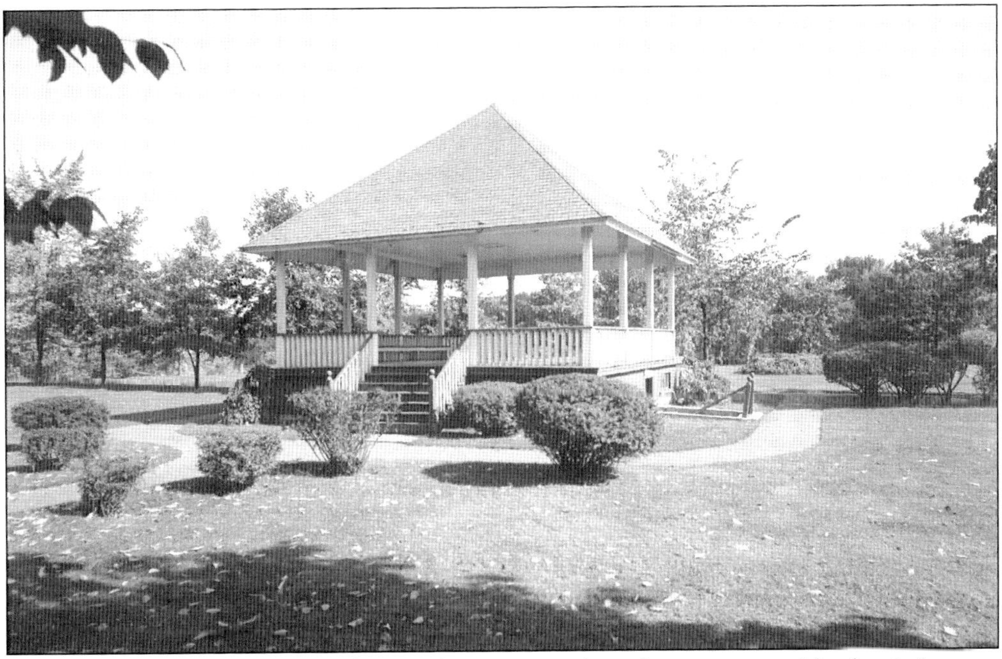

At one time, this location on North Main Street was used as a dumping ground for the city's waste, but in 1938, several women's clubs took the lead with government officials and motivated citizens to create City Park. It featured lawns, sidewalks, restrooms, shade trees, flowers, and shrubbery. Today, a new bandstand shines as one of the city's treasured symbols. (WAO.)

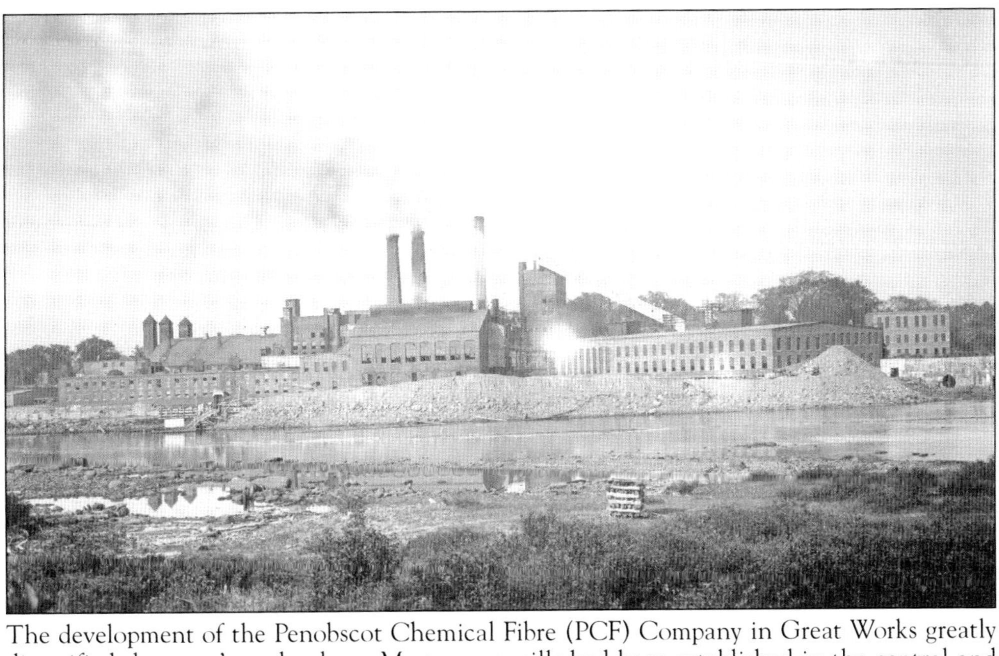

The development of the Penobscot Chemical Fibre (PCF) Company in Great Works greatly diversified the town's worker base. Most paper mills had been established in the central and western portions of the state, but PCF was one of a series of paper mills built in the northern section that eventually overtook the older areas in terms of numbers of factories and papermaking capacity. (MHPC.)

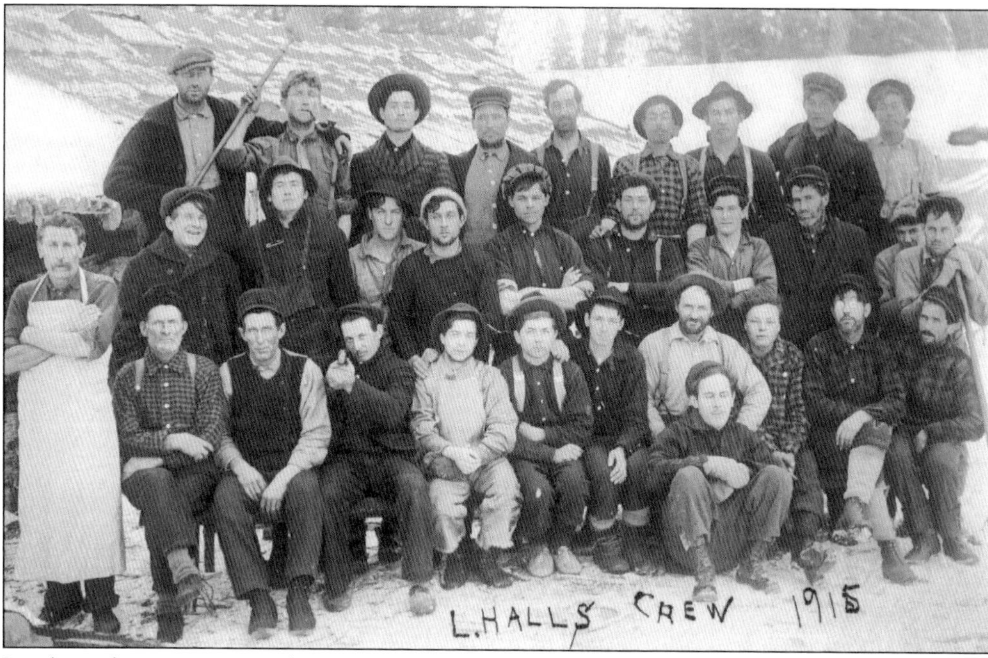

Lumberjacks were in great demand during the winter months when ice and snow facilitated the moving of heavy logs over the ground. Lumber crews delighted in having their pictures taken for their families, sometimes displaying the tools of their trade, including their hunter, who points his weapon directly at the camera. (OTM.)

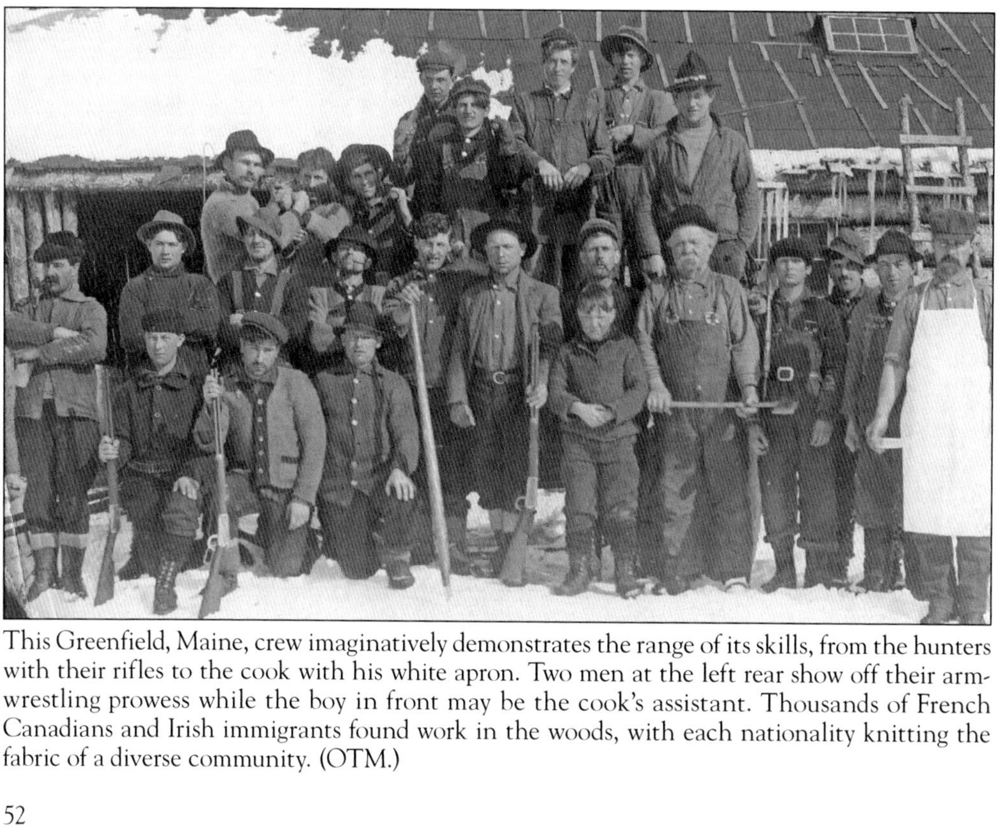

This Greenfield, Maine, crew imaginatively demonstrates the range of its skills, from the hunters with their rifles to the cook with his white apron. Two men at the left rear show off their arm-wrestling prowess while the boy in front may be the cook's assistant. Thousands of French Canadians and Irish immigrants found work in the woods, with each nationality knitting the fabric of a diverse community. (OTM.)

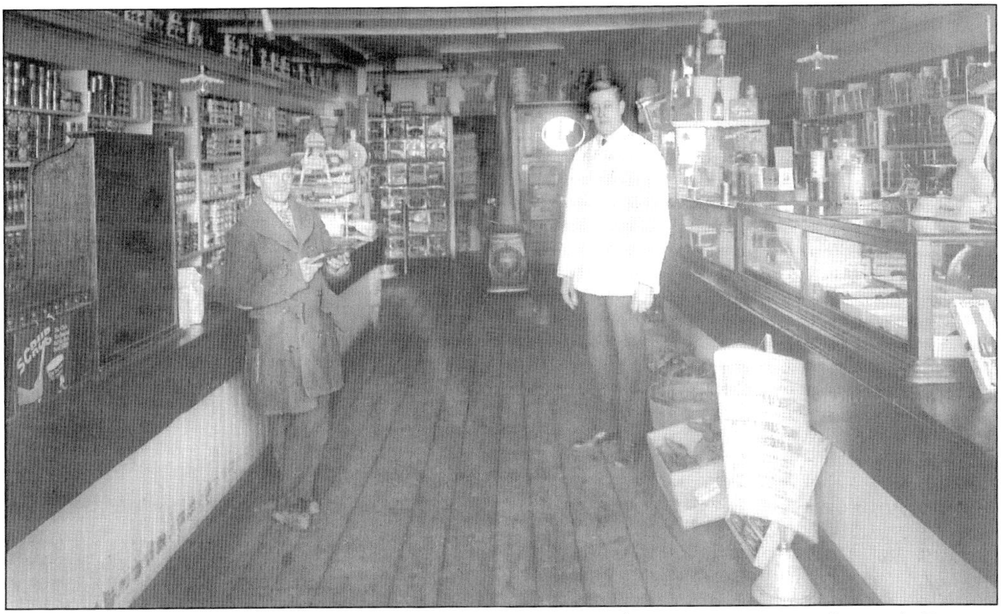

Charles O. Stevens (right) operated a grocery store on North Main Street near Boutin's Corner, where Nina's Little Big Store was later located. Customers were greeted by an advertisement with the Old Dutch Cleanser maid and her club that "Knocked Half the Rub Out of Scrub." To the right, 20 Mule Team Borax chips are available. The containers on the floor are filled with sweet potatoes and other vegetables. (DRP.)

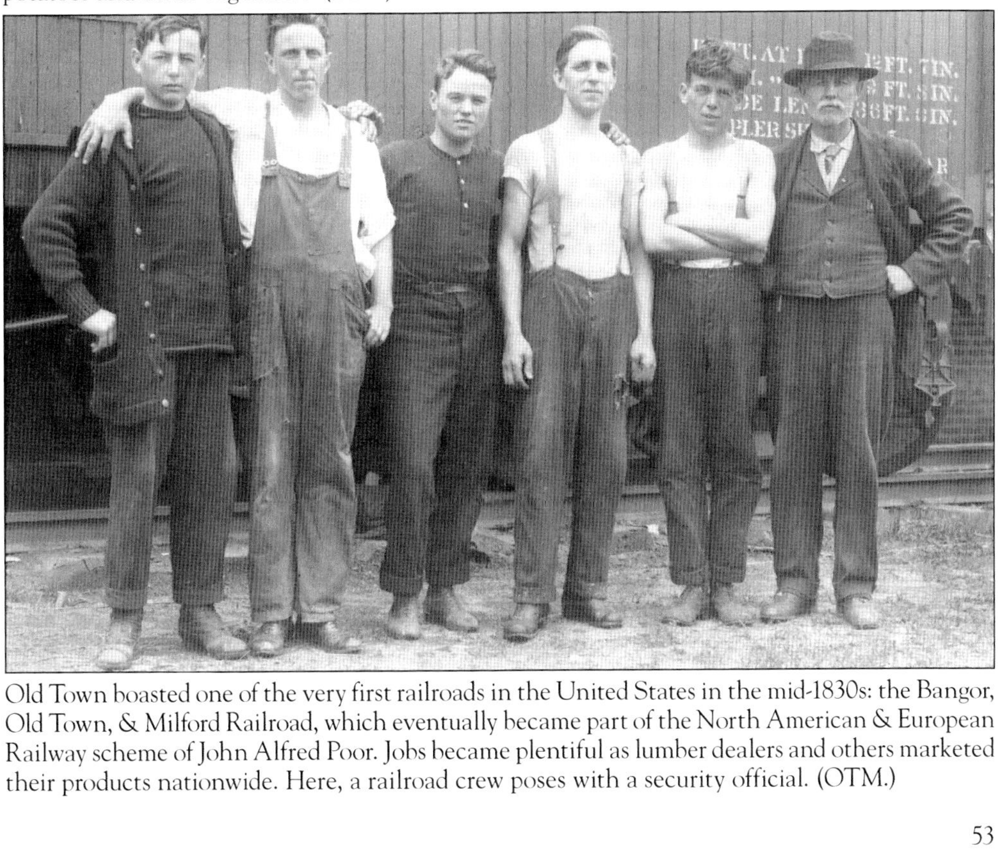

Old Town boasted one of the very first railroads in the United States in the mid-1830s: the Bangor, Old Town, & Milford Railroad, which eventually became part of the North American & European Railway scheme of John Alfred Poor. Jobs became plentiful as lumber dealers and others marketed their products nationwide. Here, a railroad crew poses with a security official. (OTM.)

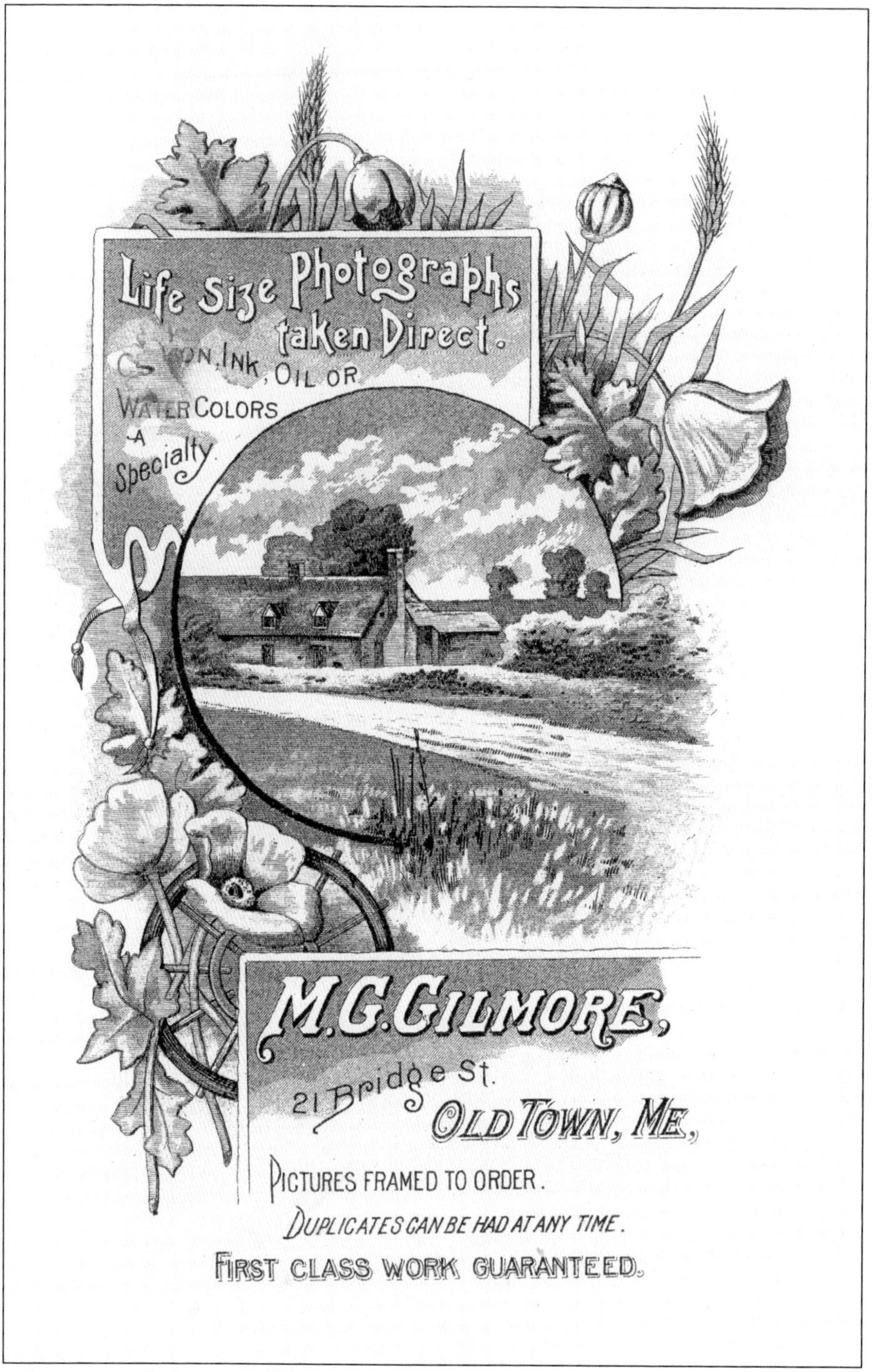

Throughout its early history, Old Town enjoyed an abundance of photographers, from M.L. Averill in the 1860s, to Almon B. Carr in the 1870s, to M.G. Gilmore in the 1890s. Gilmore produced a souvenir booklet of Old Town and Orono around 1900, billing himself as "Gilmore the Photographer." Shown here is the reverse of one of his many cabinet photographs as he advertises his skills with images, which he changed from time to time. (PRS.)

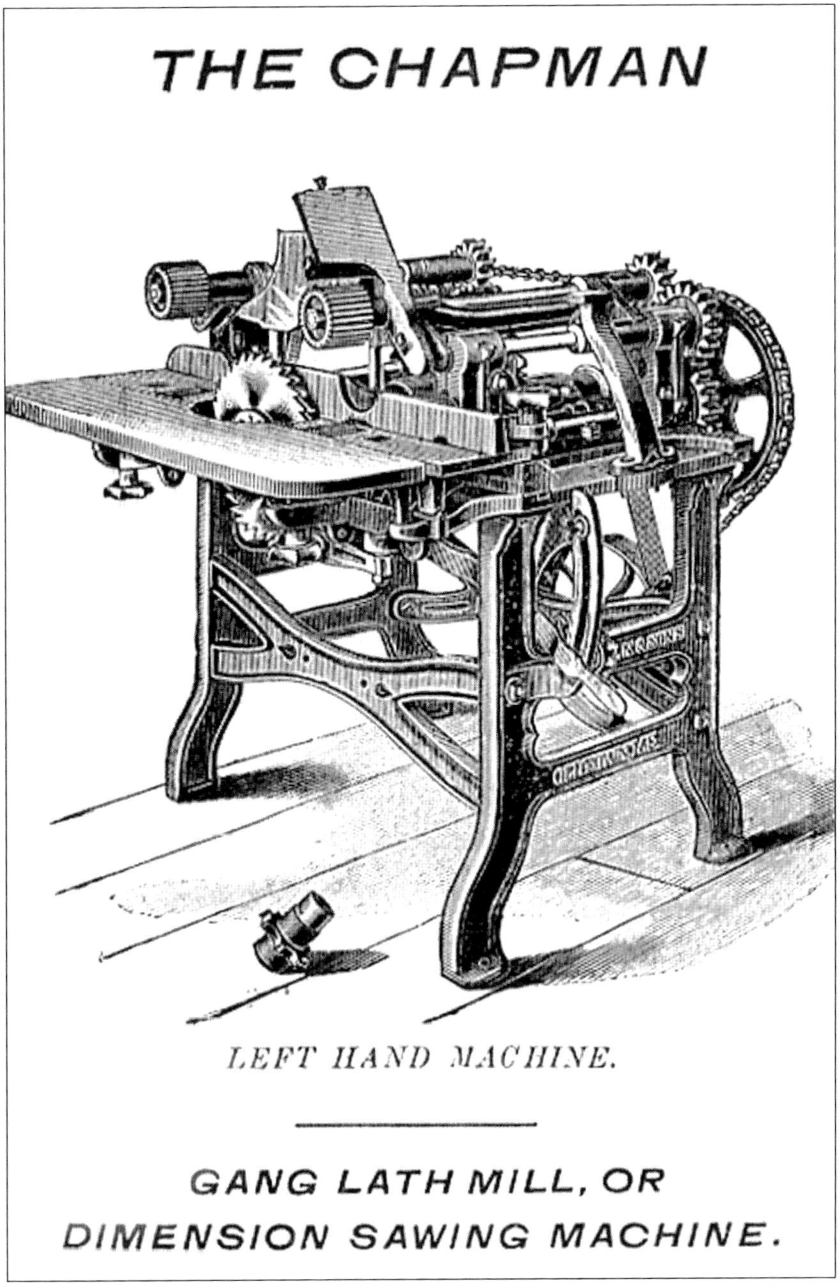

The Thomas M. Chapman Company began in Old Town in 1851 in multiple buildings on Water Street. Originally producing saw filing equipment for the lumber trade, the company patented the Chapman gang saw in 1883. Shown with two 10-inch saws, the device could be expanded to three saws with the adapter shown beside the base of the machine and to 14-inch saws as well. The operator lifted the handle at the front of the saw to depress the gears, shown at the top. Waterpower would pull the lumber through the saws, producing several pieces of finished product, such as spool bars to be turned into spools for cotton thread or laths for residential wall construction. Improvements in the Chapman allowed the addition of more saws. A left-hand machine refers to the placement of the saws on the left side. (PRS.)

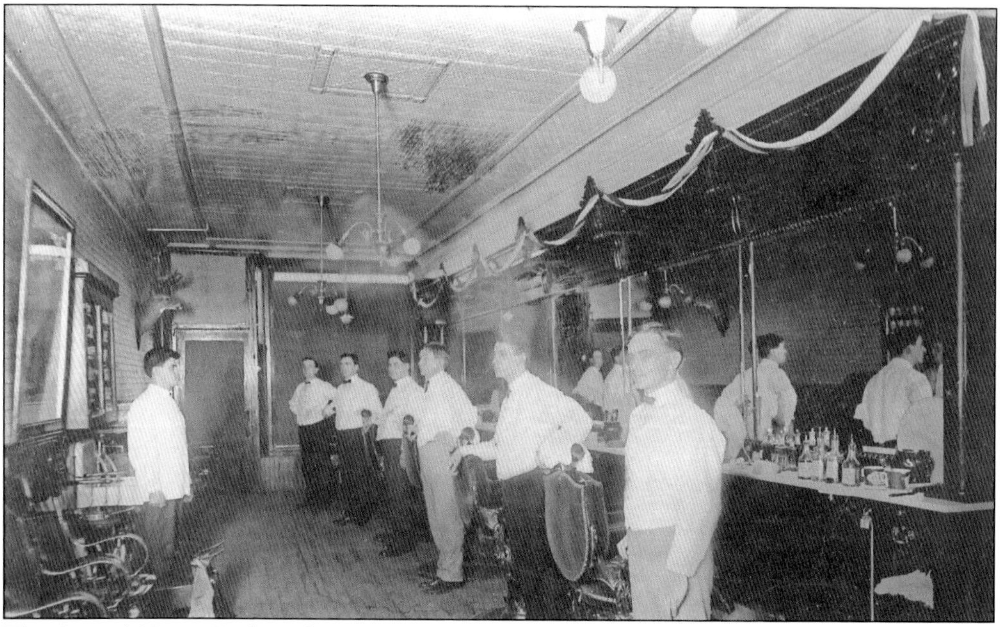

The Samuel Harris Barber Shop on Water Street offered top-notch grooming services to Old Town residents. Immaculately dressed barbers, attentive shoeshine boys, and a close shave were offered by Harris and his retinue. A mounted deer's head sent the signal to the male that this shop was a place to unwind and be taken care of. There were several barbershops in town besides Harris's. (OTM.)

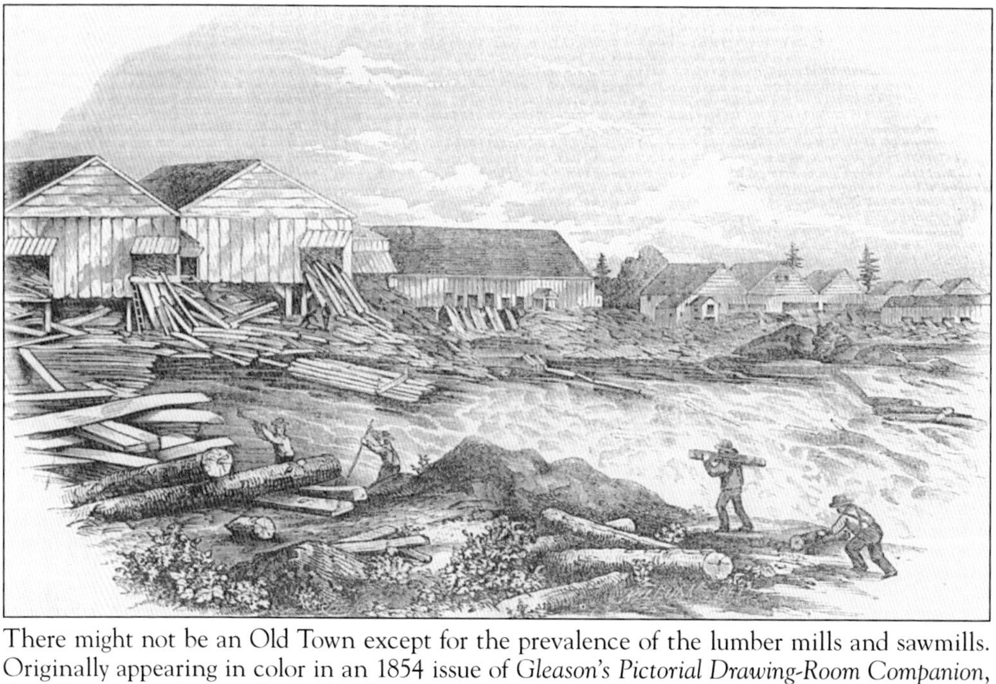

There might not be an Old Town except for the prevalence of the lumber mills and sawmills. Originally appearing in color in an 1854 issue of *Gleason's Pictorial Drawing-Room Companion*, this illustration depicts the mills of Gen. Samuel Veazie of Bangor. Located on the Penobscot River in the heart of town opposite Stillwater Avenue, mills of this sort all along the river put Old Town on the map. (OTM.)

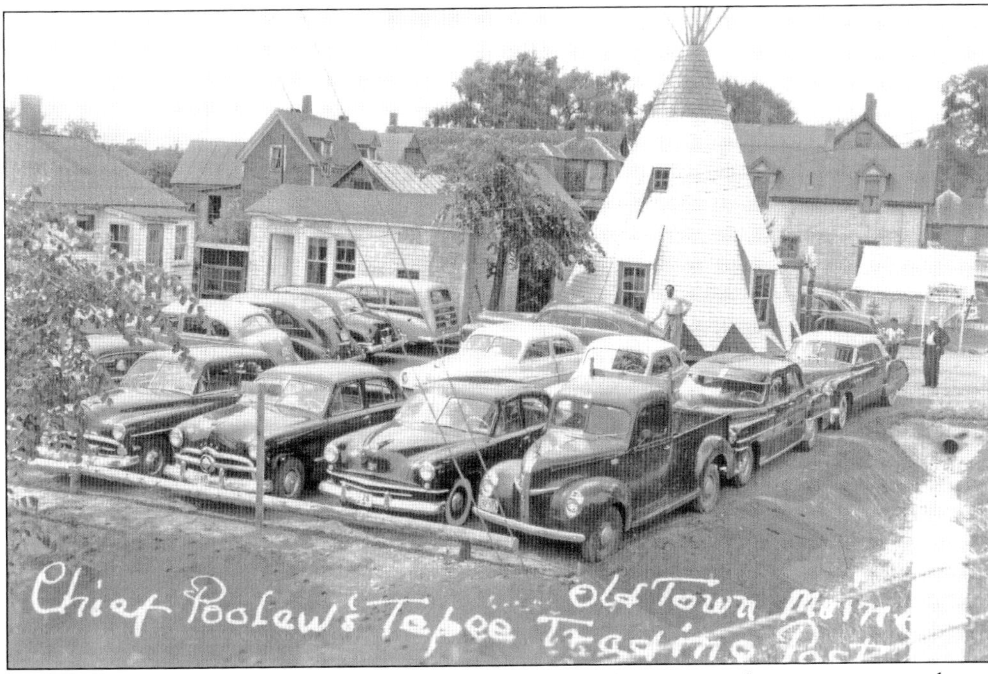

The first bridge connecting Indian Island to Old Town opened in 1951, resulting in an unprecedented increase interest in Chief Poolaw's Teepee. Life on the island had slowly improved, and its population had grown, but the Penobscot Nation was denied the right to vote. Lucy Nicolar Poolaw had returned from the entertainment circuit in the 1930s and fought valiantly both the bridge and voting rights for the Penobscot Nation. (MHPC.)

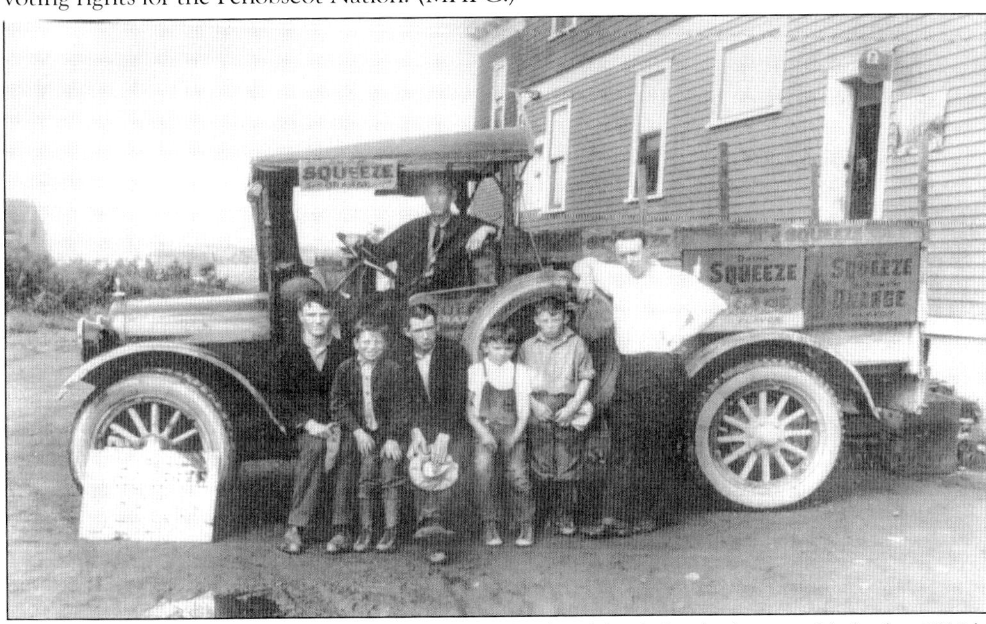

In 1922, Harold Spruce and Donald O'Keefe bought the old soft-drink plant established in 1910 by Mort Butterfield and called the Butterfield Bottling Company. Spruce, at the wheel, and O'Keefe, standing at the right, named soft drinks for themselves: the S&O'K brand. Neighborhood kids lapped it up, and the brand survived until demand dried up and the firm changed hands. (OTM.)

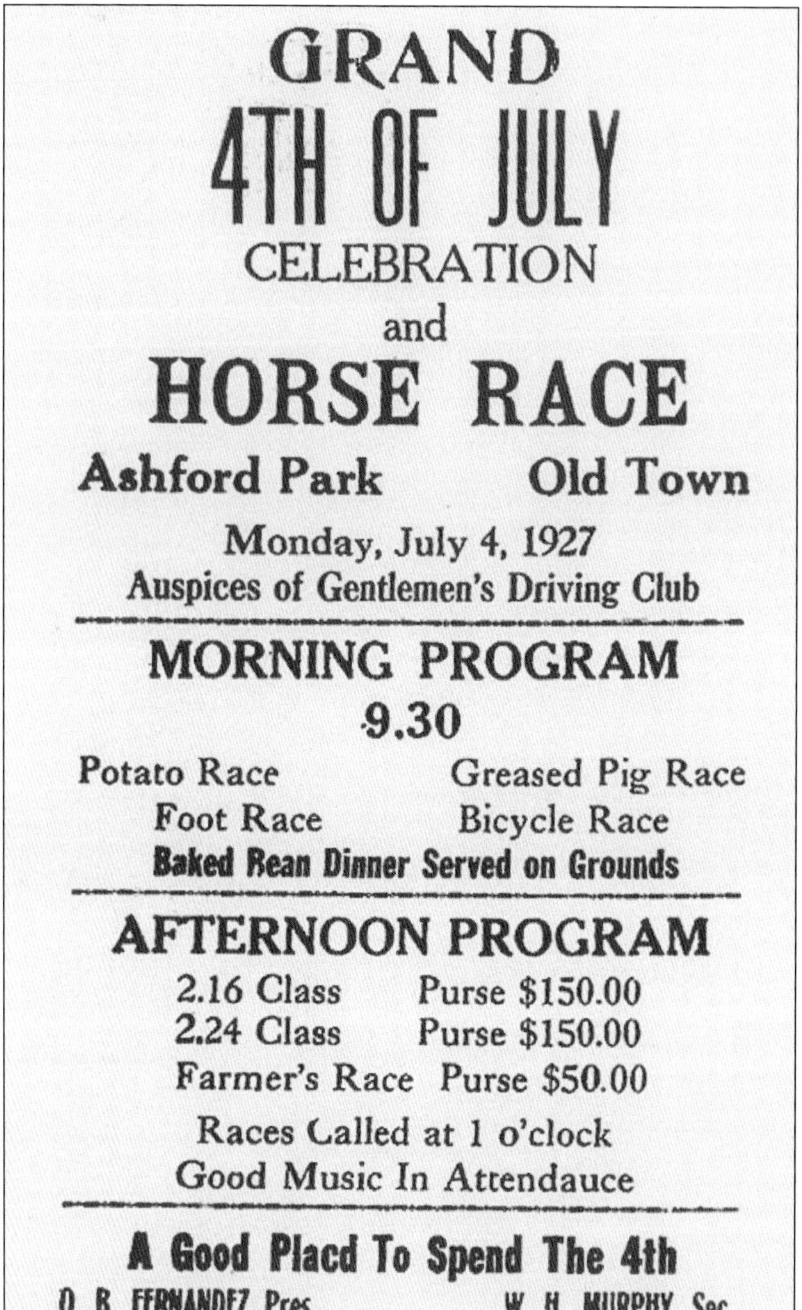

GRAND

4TH OF JULY

CELEBRATION

and

HORSE RACE

Ashford Park Old Town

Monday, July 4, 1927

Auspices of Gentlemen's Driving Club

MORNING PROGRAM

9.30

Potato Race Greased Pig Race

Foot Race Bicycle Race

Baked Bean Dinner Served on Grounds

AFTERNOON PROGRAM

2.16 Class Purse $150.00

2.24 Class Purse $150.00

Farmer's Race Purse $50.00

Races Called at 1 o'clock

Good Music In Attendauce

A Good Placd To Spend The 4th

O. B. FERNANDEZ, Pres. W. H. MURPHY, Sec.

When the horse was king, the Pea Cove section of Old Town was the site of a trotting park. Erected in the mid-1920s by Ashford Carr, who came from Fredericton, New Brunswick, and sired a family of 10 children, the park was popular with area residents. Each Fourth of July, special events, including horse racing, took place. At other times, the park hosted turkey and chicken shoots sponsored by civic groups. Ashford's sons and sons-in-law were sometimes responsible for dismantling and setting up the merry-go-round in other towns for their local fairs. Orman Fernandez was the proprietor of the movie theaters in town. (PRS.)

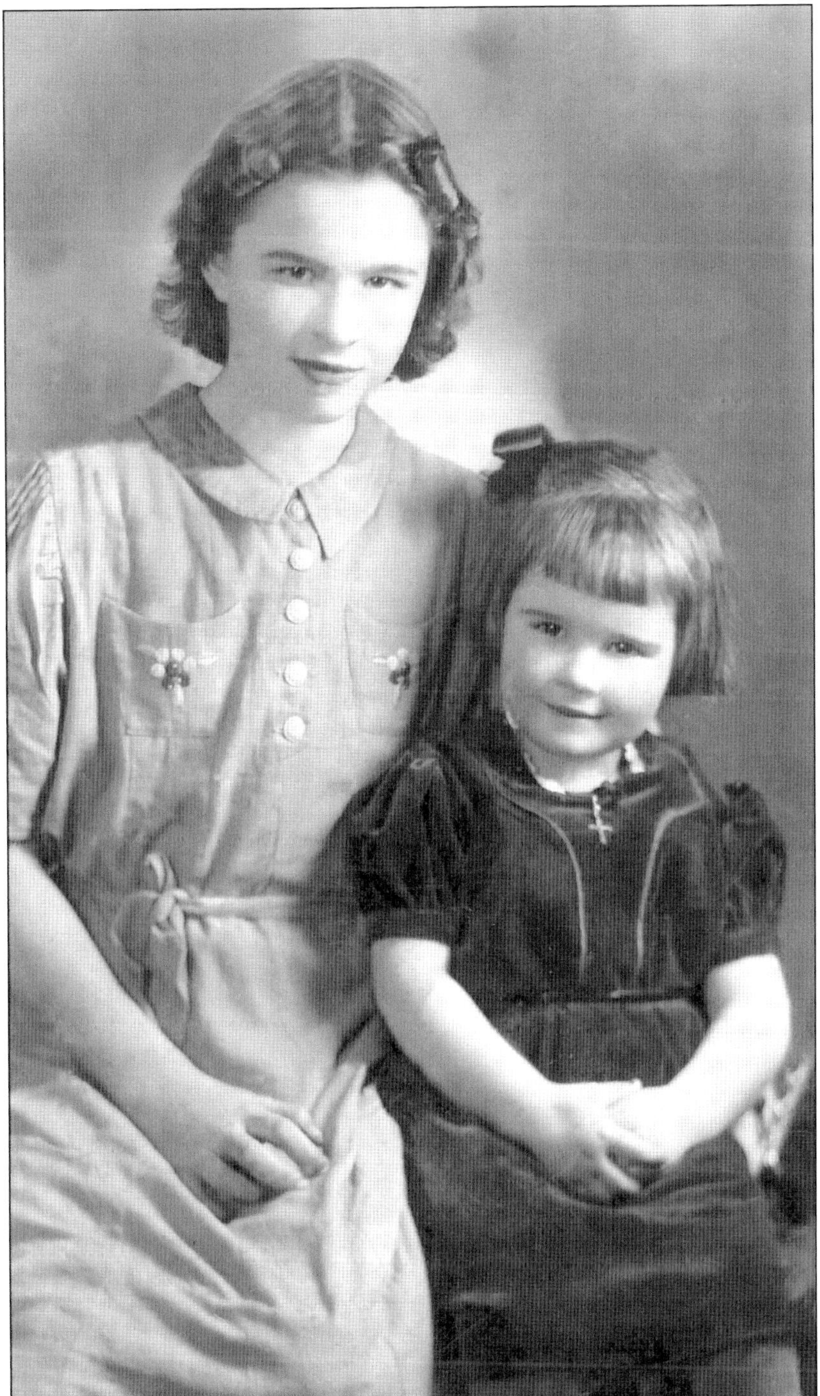

On the left is Ashford Carr's daughter Hattie Perkins. The child is Marion Shirland of Costigan, who later married Hattie's cousin Maurice Carr. Hattie lived in Pea Cove with her sister Eliza Briggs and attended the one-room schoolhouse in town. She later lived resided in Old Town, Orono, and Bangor and raised two boys, Golden and Arthur, and two girls, Alice and Bessie. (RJV.)

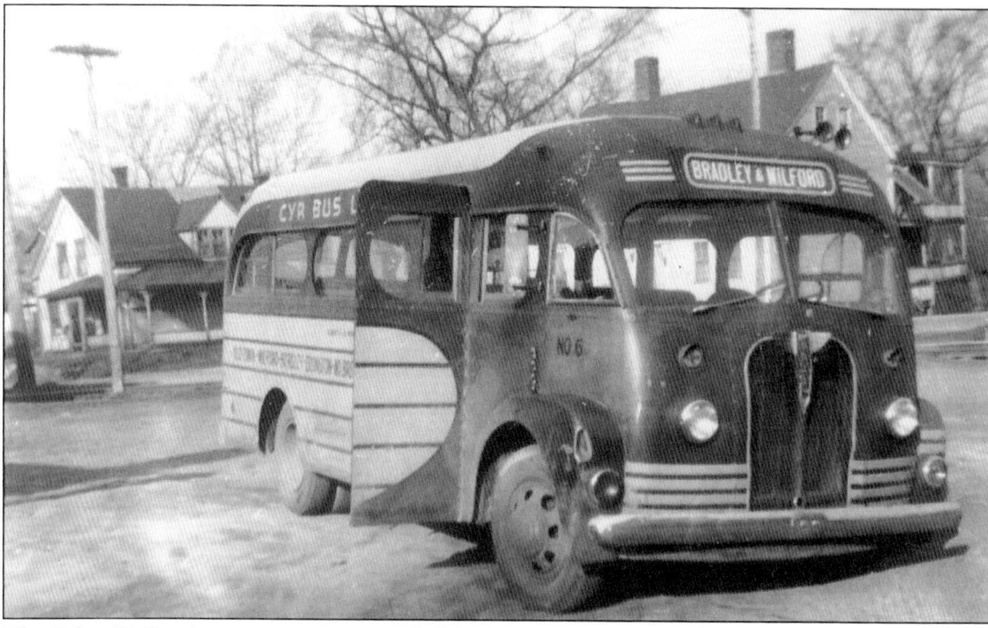

The John T. Cyr bus company expanded from trucks running short-haul routes around Old Town to a fleet of modern buses traversing much of the United States. John worked at the Jordan Lumber Company, while his brother Joseph worked at the Old Town Woolen Mill. In 1912, the two founded the company on French Island; it moved to larger quarters in 1980. (JSC.)

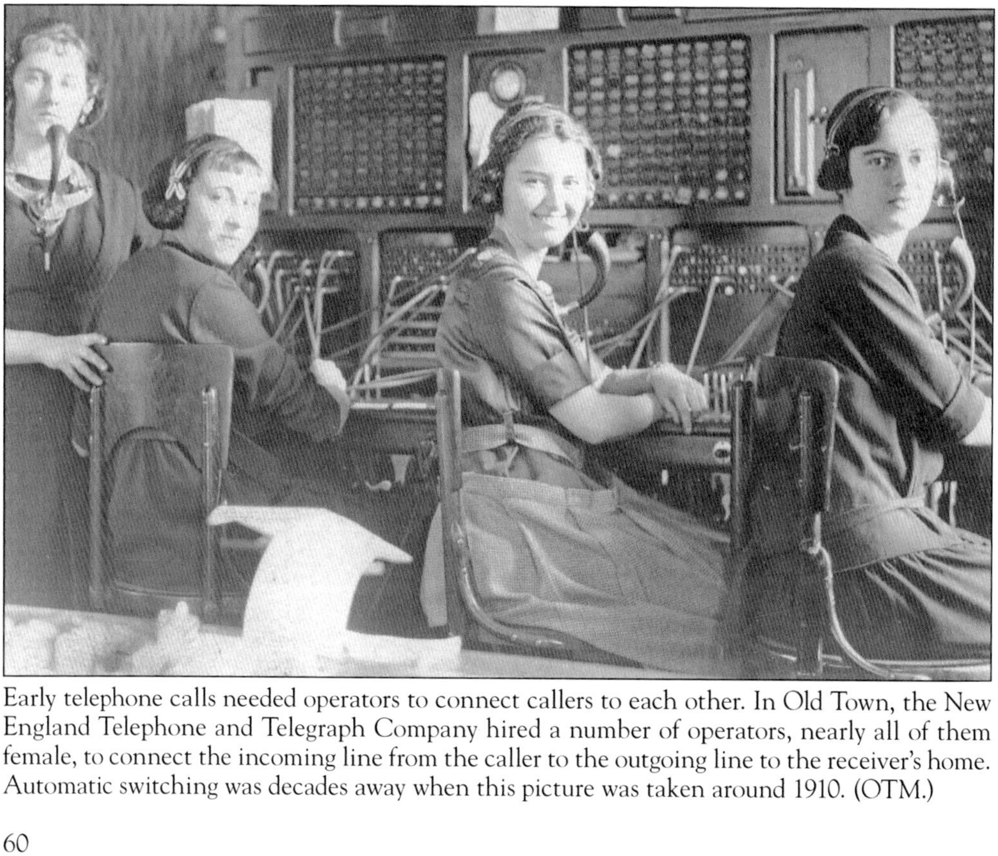
Early telephone calls needed operators to connect callers to each other. In Old Town, the New England Telephone and Telegraph Company hired a number of operators, nearly all of them female, to connect the incoming line from the caller to the outgoing line to the receiver's home. Automatic switching was decades away when this picture was taken around 1910. (OTM.)

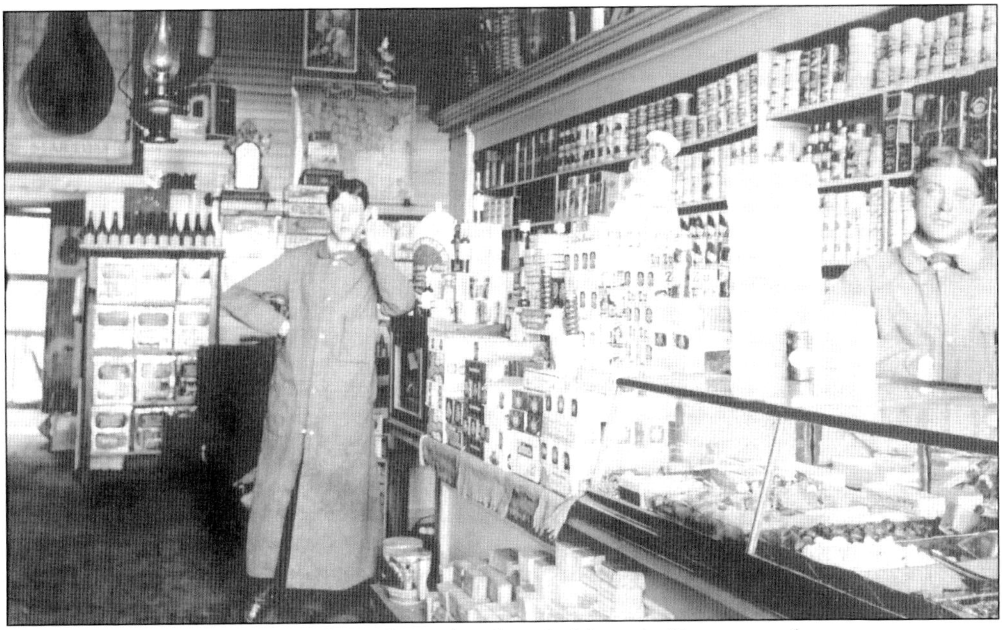

Chester M. Stevens is shown here dressed in his clerk's garb. He operated a grocery store on North Main Street that burned in 1924. His uncle, Charles O. Stevens, had operated a similar store farther up North Main in the Ounegan Block, which burned a year earlier. The interior of the latter business is shown here when Chester clerked for his uncle Charles, who may be the person on the right. (OTM.)

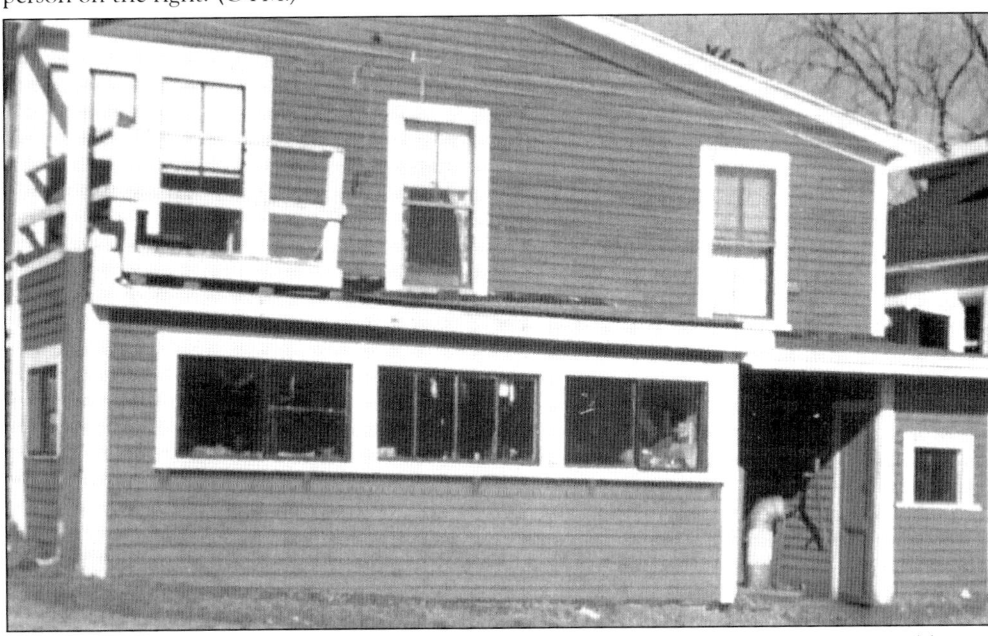

On French Island, businesses started small and were community friendly. No one could guess that in this small house, the famous LaBree's Bakery would be born in 1948. Soon, the company built a larger facility on Bodwell Street, baking thousands of donuts daily. A familiar sight on Sundays following church services was scores of families trekking to LaBree's for its famous donuts. (BLB.)

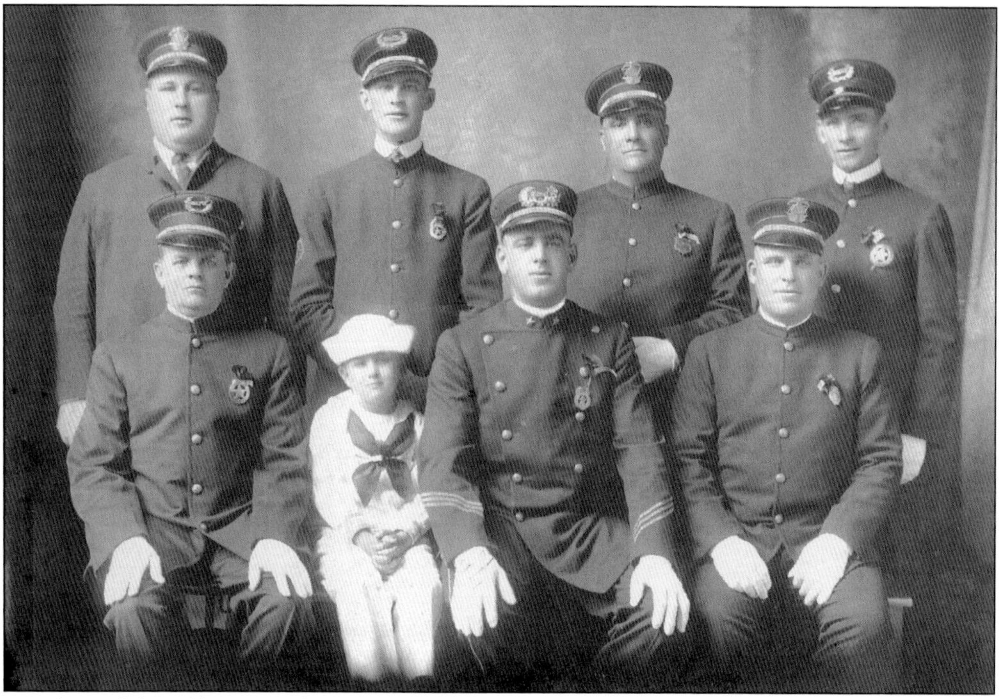

Members of the Old Town Police Department are shown in this image, taken May 30, 1923. They are, from left to right, (first row) Cornelius McCarthy, Charles Willett's son, Charles Willett, and Merritt Towle; (second row) Lewis Cyr, Dana Whidden, Ben Fortier, and Fred Curneil. (OTM.)

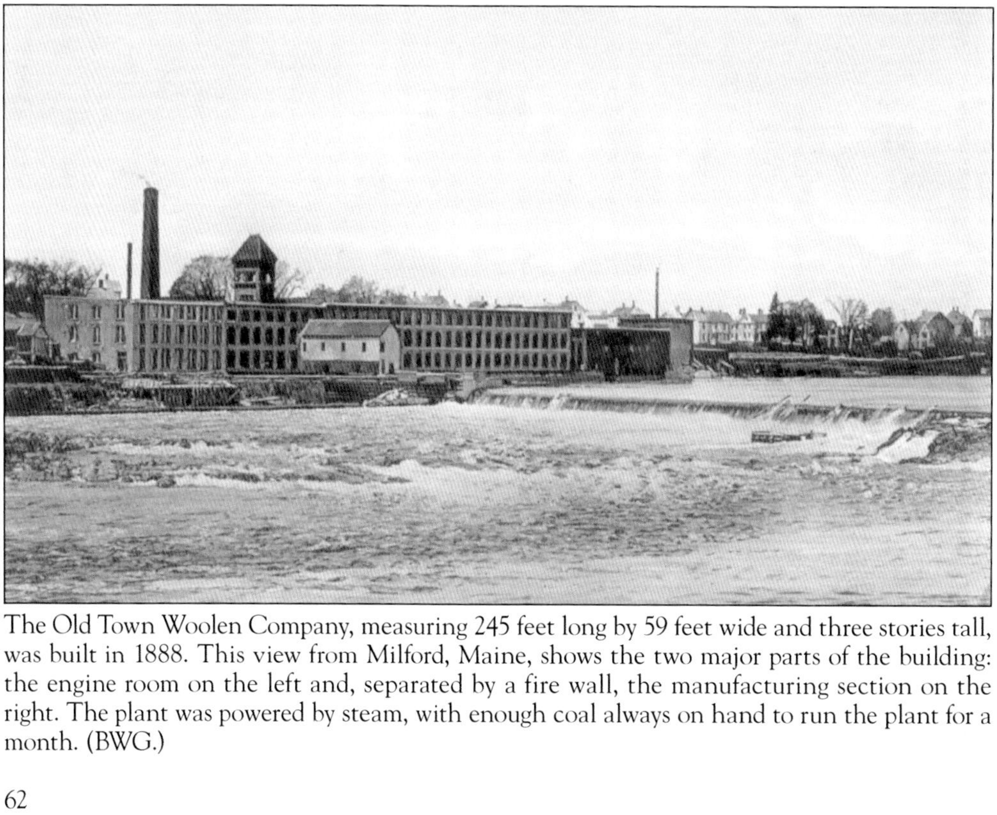

The Old Town Woolen Company, measuring 245 feet long by 59 feet wide and three stories tall, was built in 1888. This view from Milford, Maine, shows the two major parts of the building: the engine room on the left and, separated by a fire wall, the manufacturing section on the right. The plant was powered by steam, with enough coal always on hand to run the plant for a month. (BWG.)

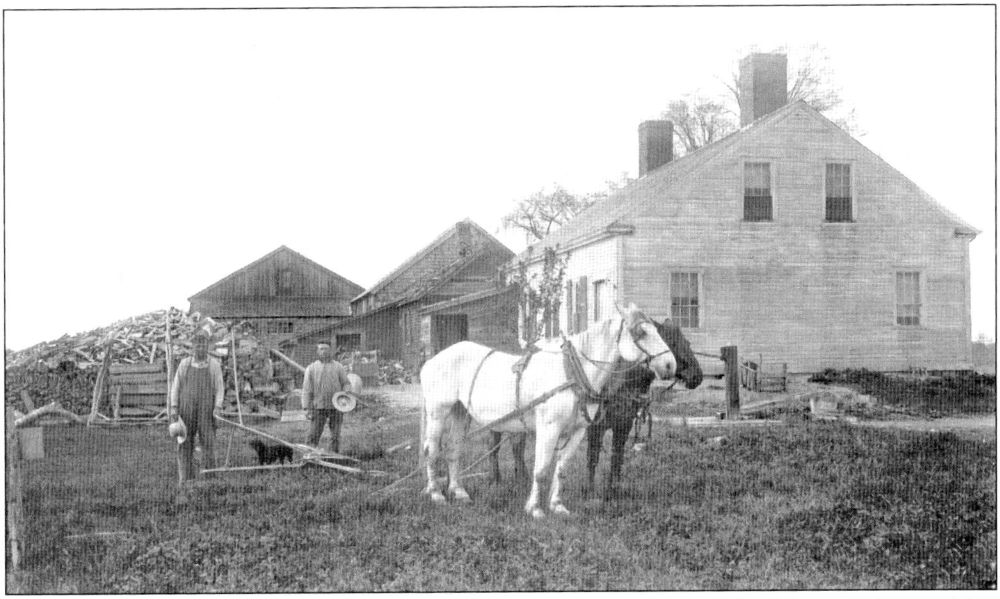

Agriculture flourished on the outskirts of town, with farmers producing hay, fruits and vegetables, and meats for the markets in town. Here, a team of horses is rigged to begin the tilling of the fields to prepare for planting. The huge supply of firewood may indicate that this farmer cut firewood in the winter to sell to his neighbors. (MHPC.)

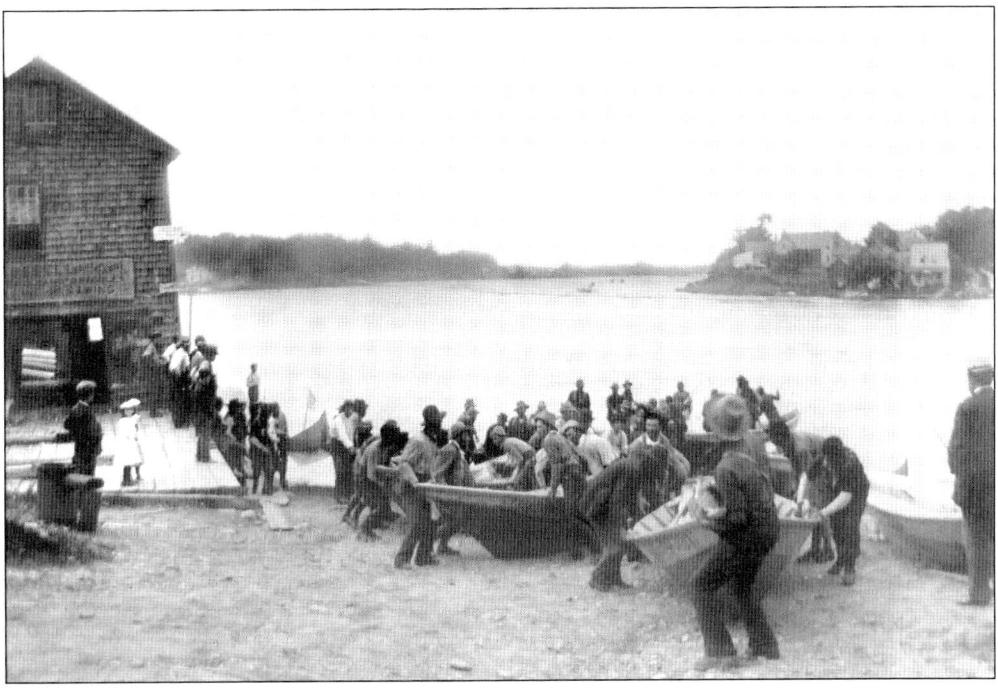

Shown here is a c. 1900 view of the Penobscot River with a log boom in the background and Indian Island to the right. River drivers pull their bateaux ashore at the end of their shift. The former Carleton boat shop is on the left. The sign on the building indicates that it is now the Bussell boat and canoe shop. This scene was located just above where the present bridge to Indian Island now sits. (OTM.)

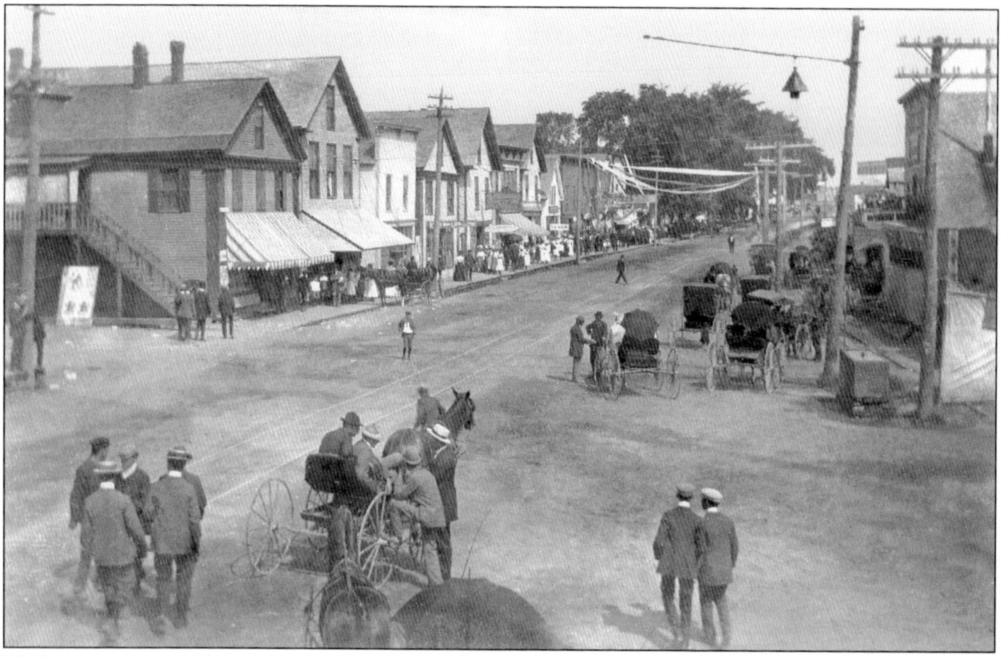

Trolley tracks run along North Main Street at Middle Street as a celebration takes places in Old Town. Residents bring out their finest chaise carriages. Along the street, Fred Godfrey sells his stoves alongside a lunchroom and a laundry. The Old Town Canoe Company is just up Middle Street across the railroad tracks. The top story of the Old Town Woolen Company can be seen in the right background. (BWG.)

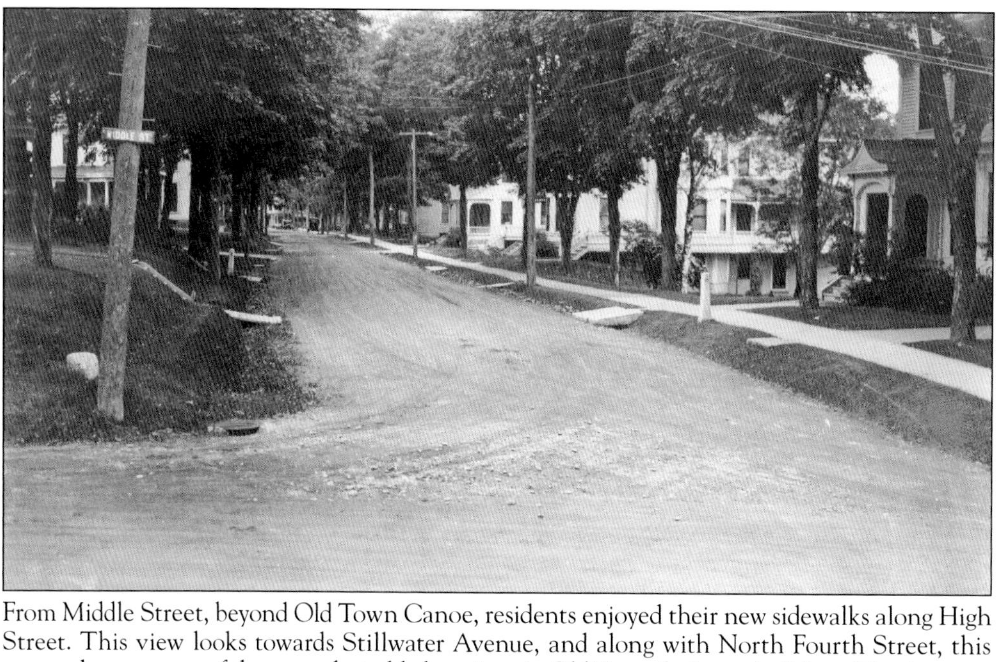

From Middle Street, beyond Old Town Canoe, residents enjoyed their new sidewalks along High Street. This view looks towards Stillwater Avenue, and along with North Fourth Street, this avenue became one of the more desirable locations in Old Town for home building. The drainage system installed here eliminated muddy streets, and the mature hardwood trees provided shade on a hot summer day. (BWG.)

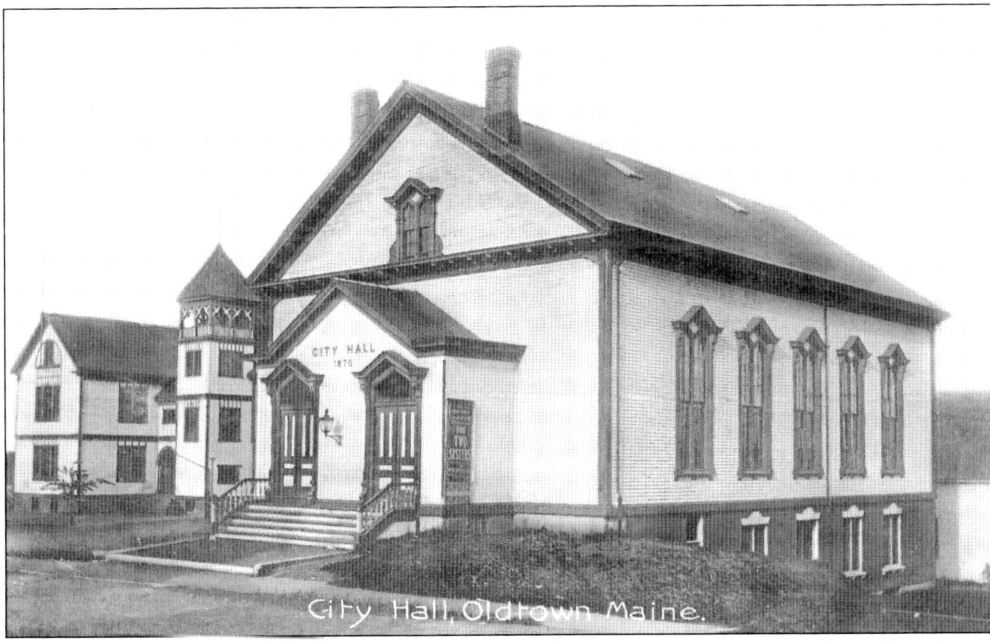

Construction of a new city hall was approved in 1850, but funding was not available. The solution was found in 1870 when the federal government paid bounties to the town for each of its soldiers who signed up to fight in the Civil War. Built for $12,000, the building was located at the corner of North Brunswick and Middle Streets. (BWG.)

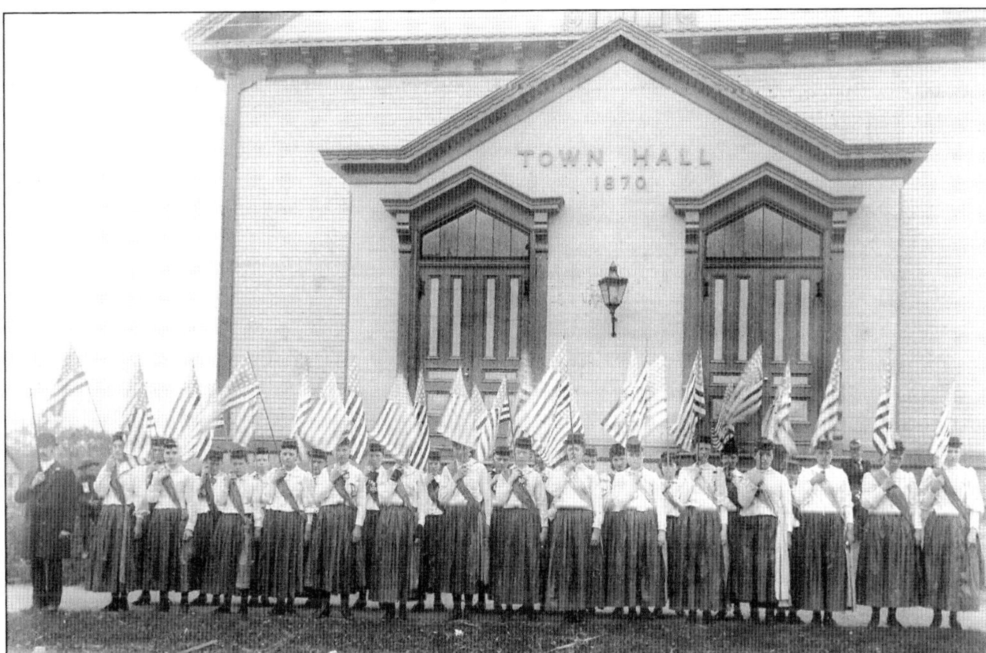

Following its construction, the new city hall served a variety of community functions, from patriotic displays to a venue for traveling theater groups. At a practical level, city government was housed here as well, from the aldermen and councilors to the building inspectors, tax collectors, and city clerks. (OTM.)

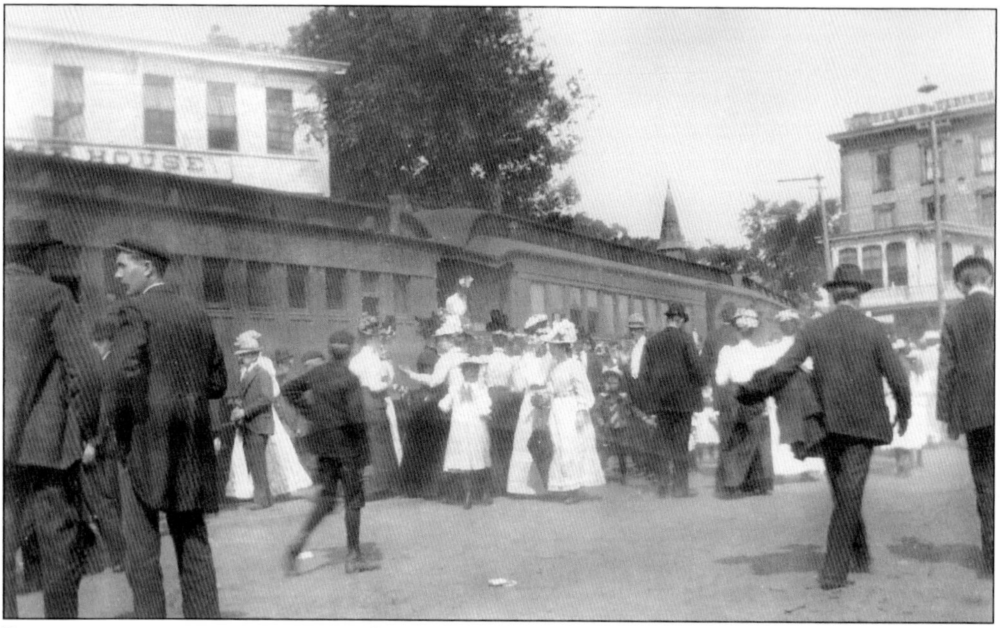

Passenger trains were common in the 1890s, with the city being served by the Maine Central Railroad, the Bangor & Aroostook Railroad, and others. Nineteen trains picked up and discharged passengers daily; the one seen here was used for a gala occasion in which men, women, and children display the height of fashion. The Bridge House on Water Street is at the left, with its name partly visible. (BWG.)

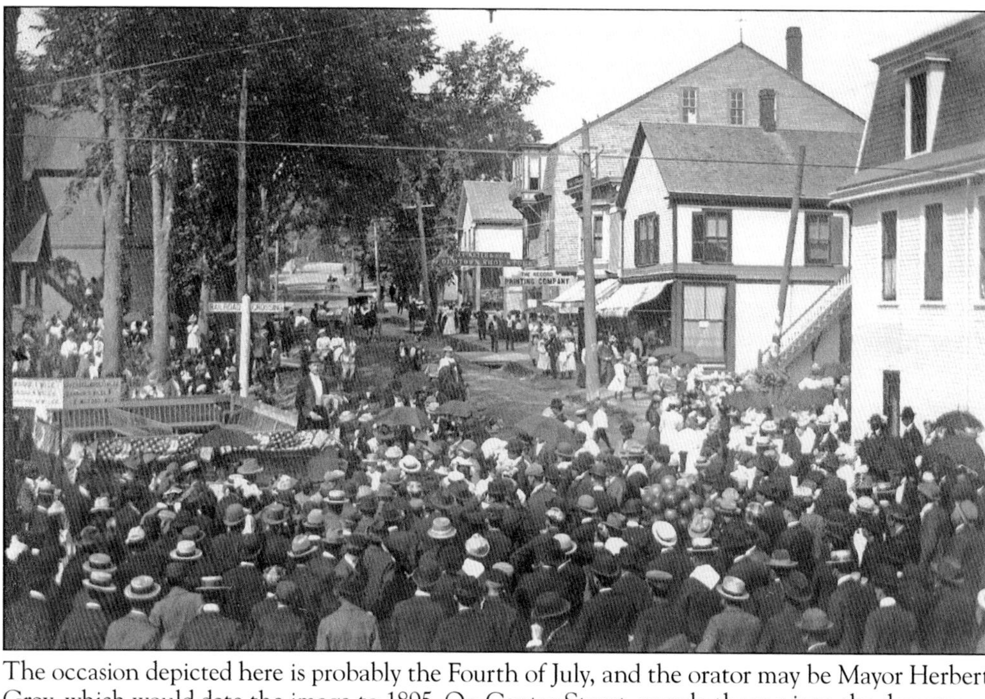

The occasion depicted here is probably the Fourth of July, and the orator may be Mayor Herbert Gray, which would date the image to 1895. On Center Street, people throng into the downtown area. Seen on the right are the corner of the Folsom Block, the Record Printing Company, and one of the shoe outlets of Justin L. Keith, who also manufactured footwear. (OTPL.)

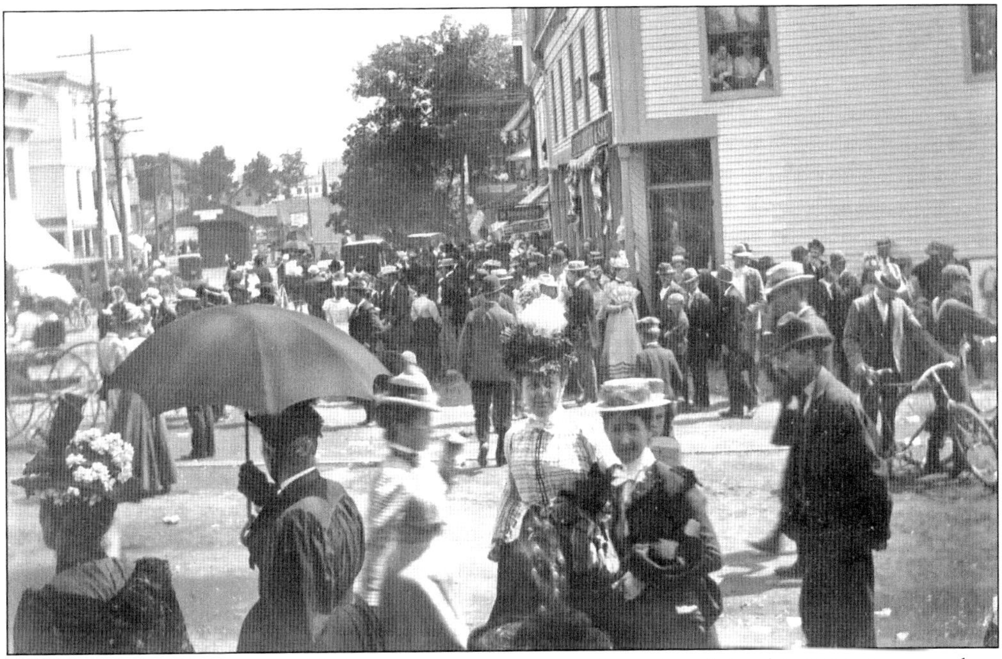

Occasions to celebrate the Old Town community were enjoyed by all. In this 1890s image, taken at the same time as the previous image, people mill about in Folsom Square in their finest dress. Spectators enjoy the excitement, and windows are filled with onlookers in the Bradbury Block on the right where Dr. A.P. Bradbury kept his office. (OTPL.)

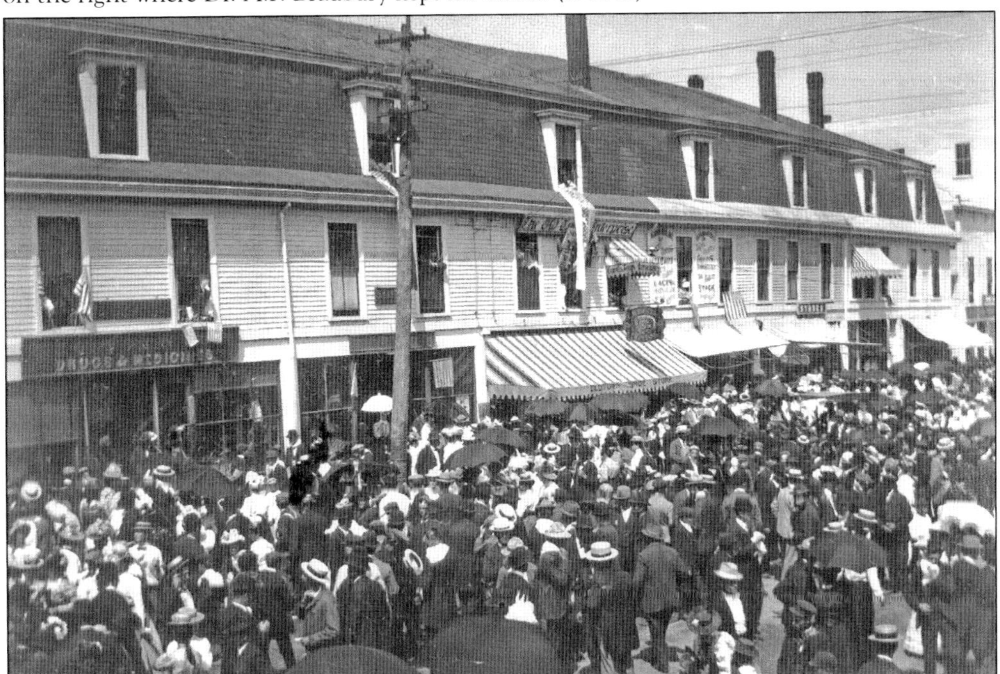

The Fourth of July celebration spills over onto North Main Street in front of the Folsom Block where the Folsom brothers kept their drugstore. Also seen in the office of the *Old Town Enterprise* is a second shoe shop, operated by Justin L. Keith, and the stove shop of E.A. Blanchard. (OTPL.)

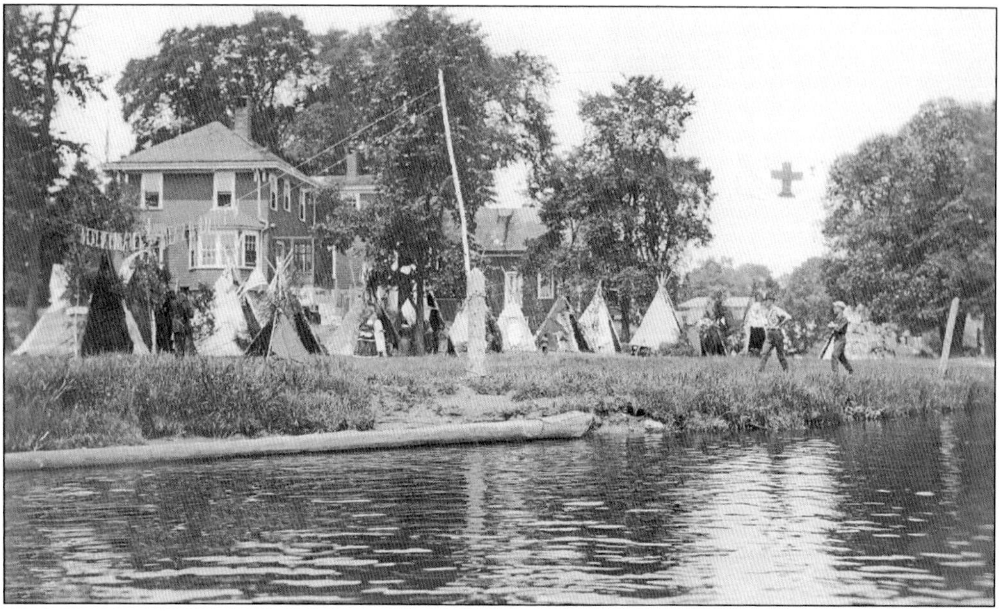

Community celebrations were enjoyed by the Penobscot Nation on Indian Island from time to time; the one seen here dates to June 1921. With the coming of the automobile, members of the Penobscot Nation packed up their finely crafted baskets in the summer and headed to popular tourist spots on the coast of Maine to sell their wares. (PRS.)

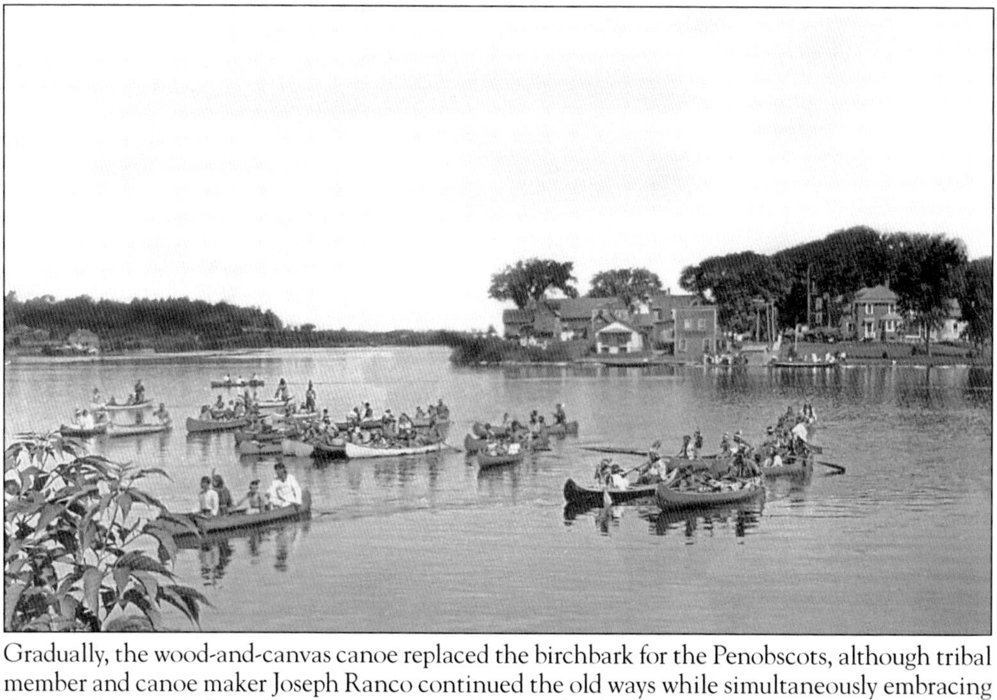

Gradually, the wood-and-canvas canoe replaced the birchbark for the Penobscots, although tribal member and canoe maker Joseph Ranco continued the old ways while simultaneously embracing the new. Here, tribal members enjoy a trip to the mainland. Canoe makers in town were diligent in crediting the Penobscot for their influence on their products. (PRS.)

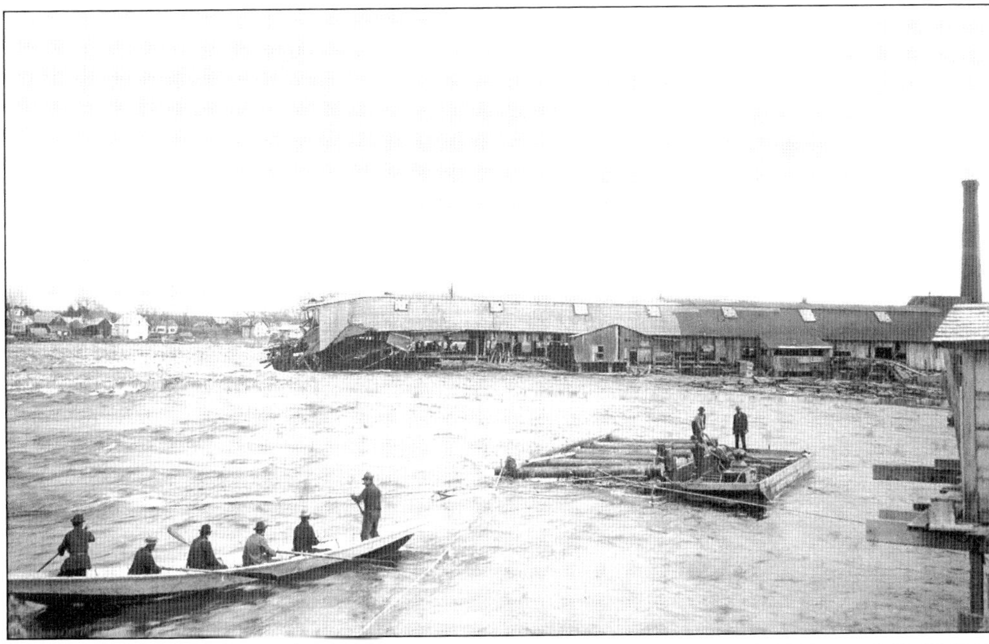

Facing death was common for sawmill workers who worked on the river. The men rarely lost their lives. In 1901, the sawmill of the Penobscot Chemical Fibre Company was heavily damaged by high water and dangerous debris. Here, men in a bateau struggle to prevent further damage amidst the swirling waters. (OTPL.)

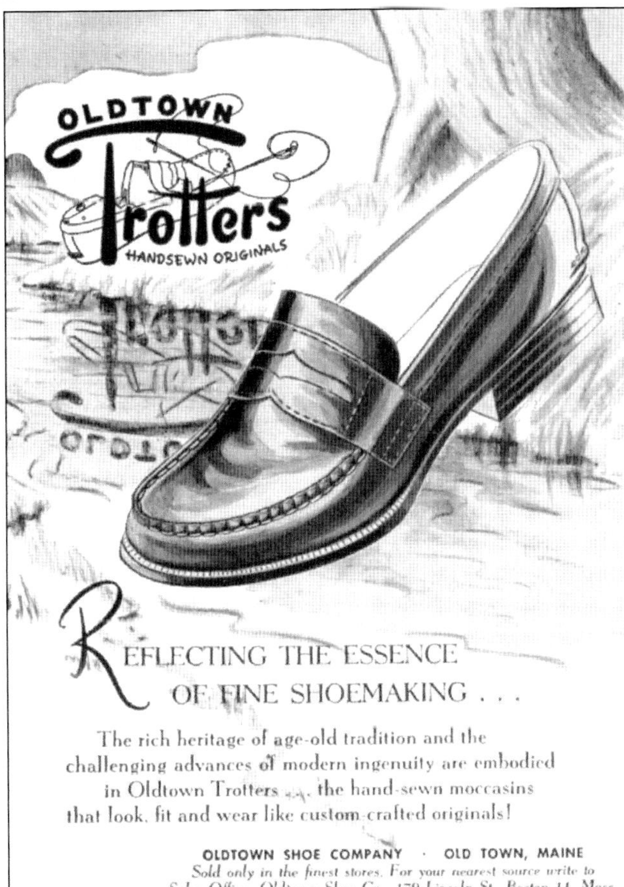

When the Old Town Woolen Mill closed, the Old Town Shoe Company moved in. It featured casual styles for women with the famous Old Town Trotter brand, first produced in 1925. Marketing strategies often included references to the Penobscot Nation and their heritage in making footwear. In 2000, the Phoenix Footwear Group of Carlsbad, California, acquired the Trotter brand and others, such as H.S. Trask and Royal Robbins. The company maintains a distribution facility in Old Town across North Main Street from the old Penobscot Shoe Company. (PRS.)

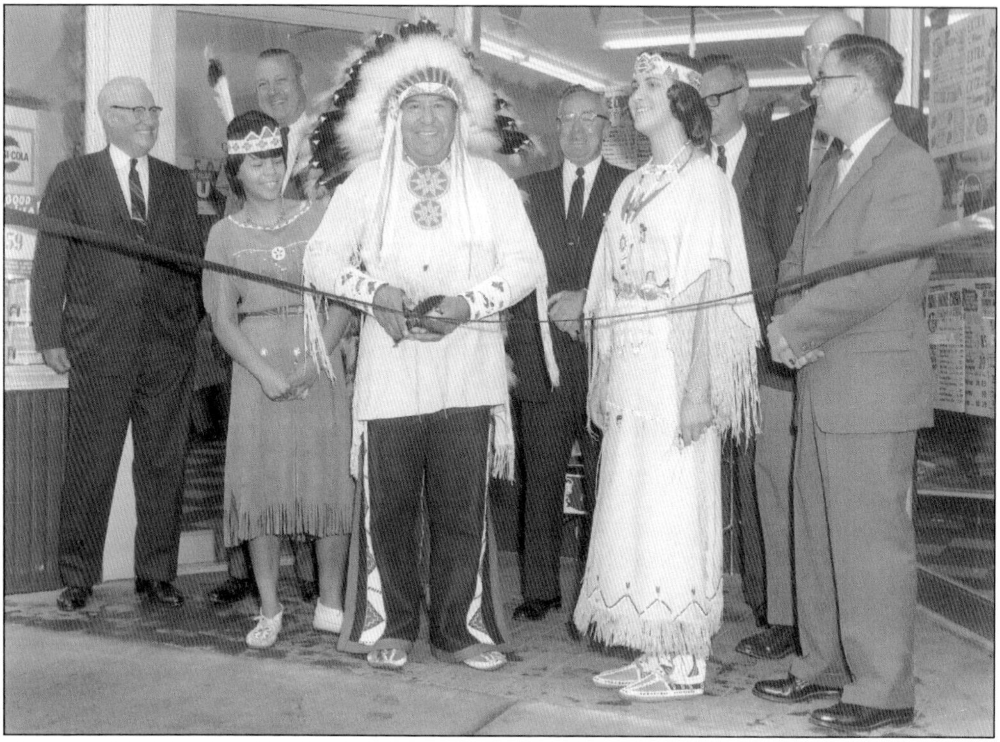

The remodeled A&P on North Main Street held a grand reopening in 1964. Pictured in the front row, from left to right, are Deanna Pehrson, Chief Bruce Poolaw, and Lucie Marie Anderson of the Penobscot Nation, and J. Lester Melanson, store manager. In the back row, left to right, are H.E. Barnes, O.J. Baker, and Reid Appleby, from the A&P, and city councilors John Bouchard and Joseph Sewall. (BHP.)

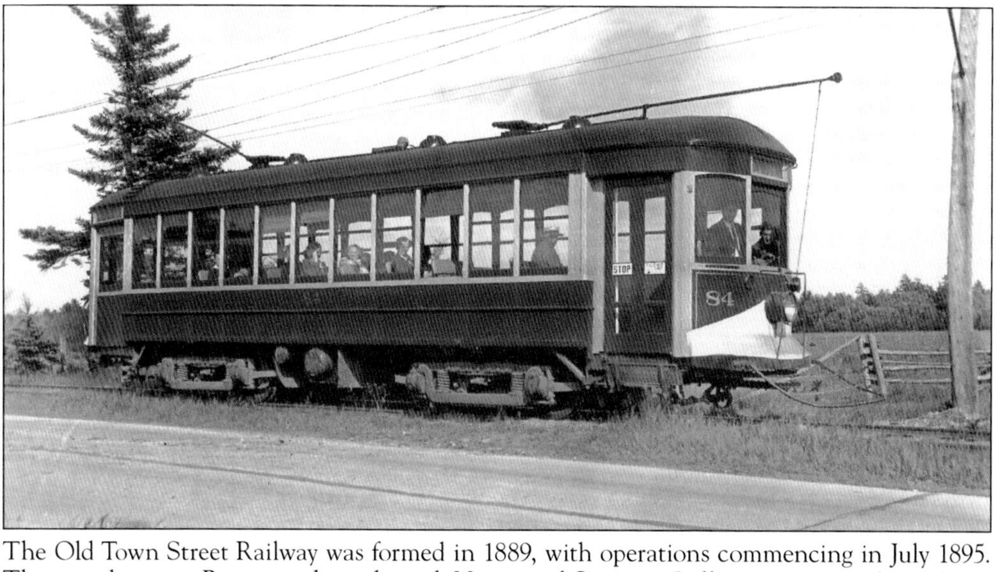

The Old Town Street Railway was formed in 1889, with operations commencing in July 1895. The route began in Bangor and ran through Veazie and Orono to Stillwater Avenue, shown here, to Boutin's Corner on North Main Street, and then to Jameson Street. Changing its name from time to time, the railway ended its run in 1945, leaving only two such trains in Maine. (PRS.)

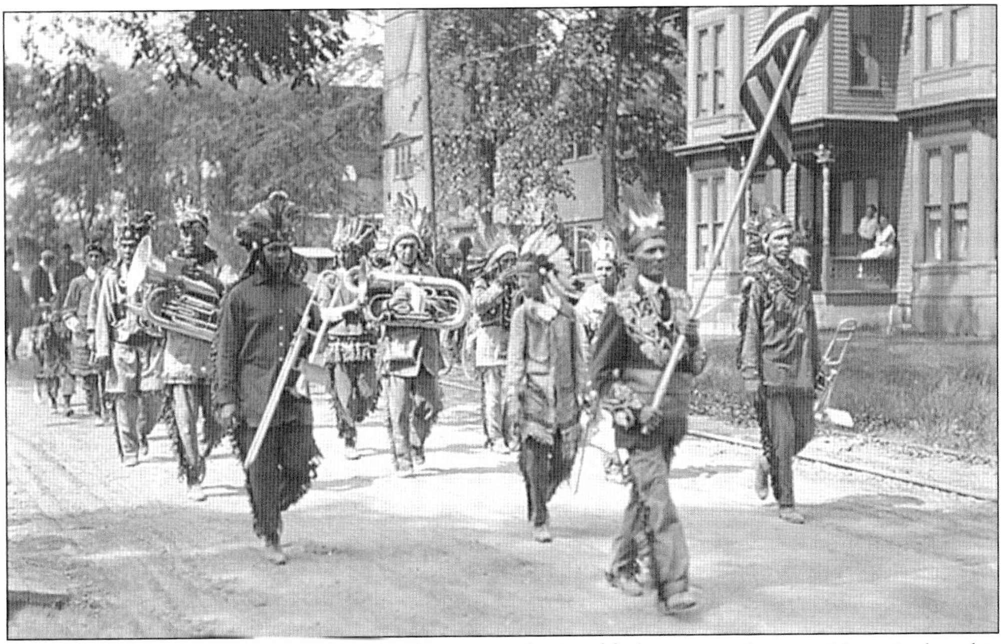

The Penobscot Nation founded musical groups, which added spice to the city. Here, its band is shown marching toward Great Works on South Main Street around 1915. Cultural assimilation was an evolving concept—Maine sent many young tribal members to out-of-state vocational schools, such as the Carlisle Indian Industrial School in Pennsylvania. (PRS.)

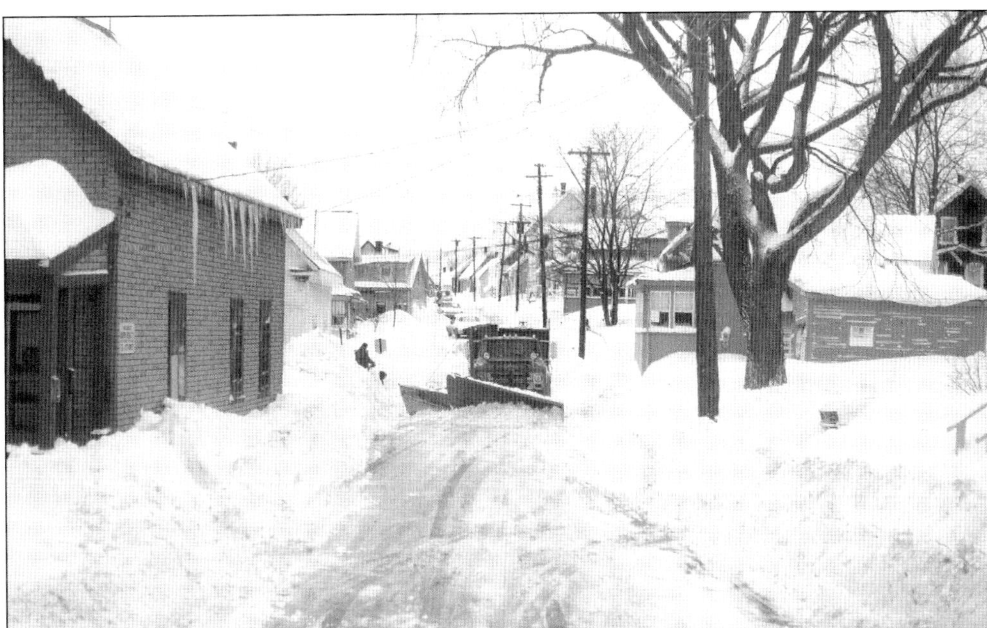

Winters could be tough in Old Town, as the community was often paralyzed by heavy snowfalls. On French Island, shown here in the 1970s, a snowplow executes a second run at pushing back the snowbanks, a task made more difficult by the island's narrow streets and closely built houses. (PWT.)

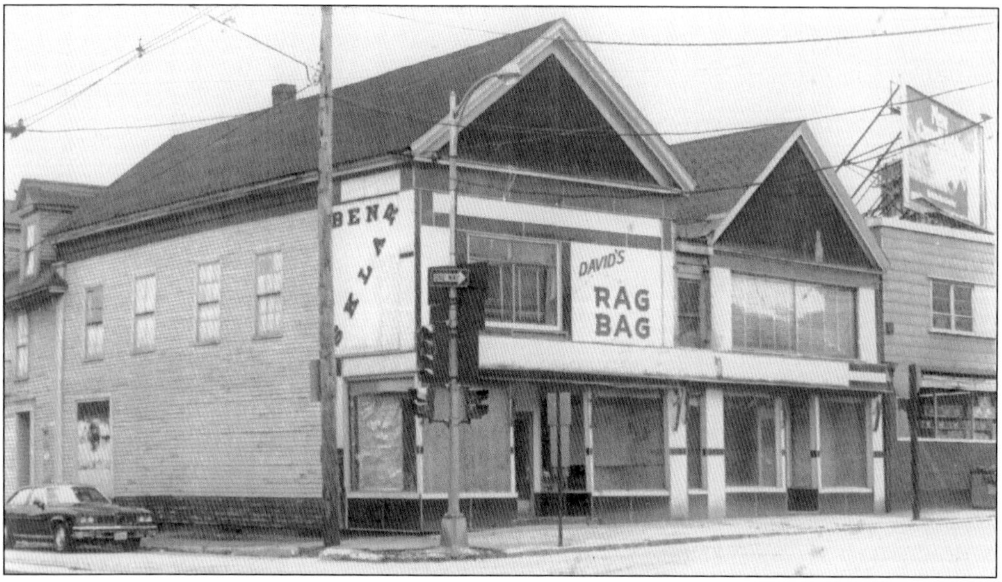

Ben Sklar's was an important part of Old Town's heritage for decades but faced challenges from more modern stores, urban decay, and the nonstop expansion of shopping centers in Bangor, easily accessible by modern highways. His son David Sklar tried valiantly to hang on at this Center Street location, but time conspired against him in the 1970s. (CLM.)

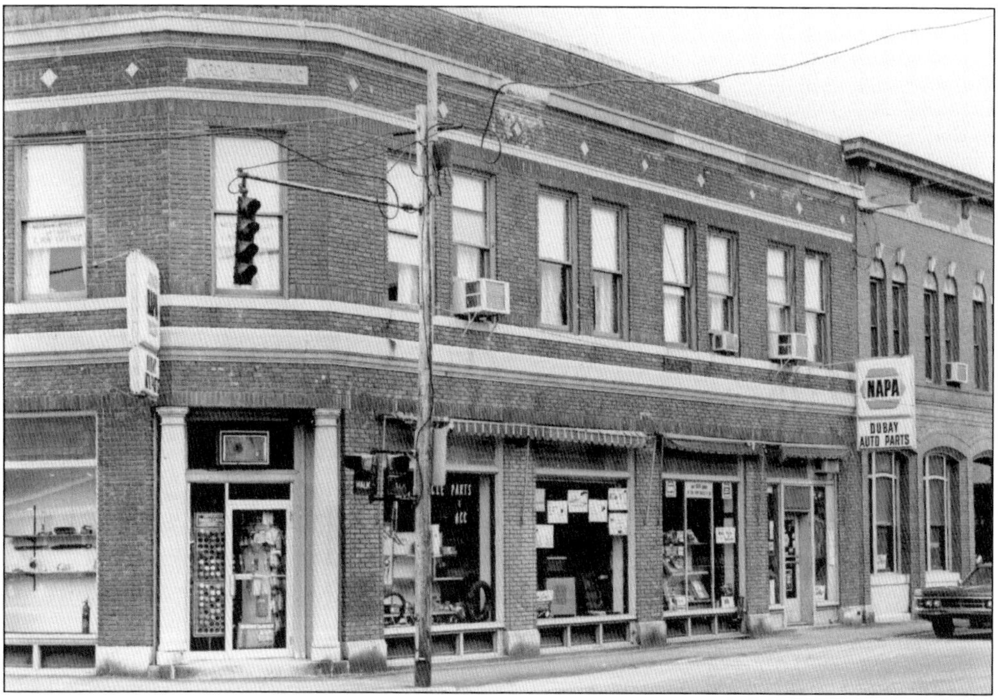

Located on Water Street, Jordan Lumber became the city's largest lumber dealer. Beginning in the early 1900s, Moses L. Jordan took over the wooden buildings of the T.M. Chapman Sons Company when the latter moved across the Penobscot. When the Jordan buildings burned, they were rebuilt of brick. In 1911, Jordan bought a powerful Stevens-Duryea automobile, reflecting the prosperity of the period. (CLM.)

Four

Schools and Churches

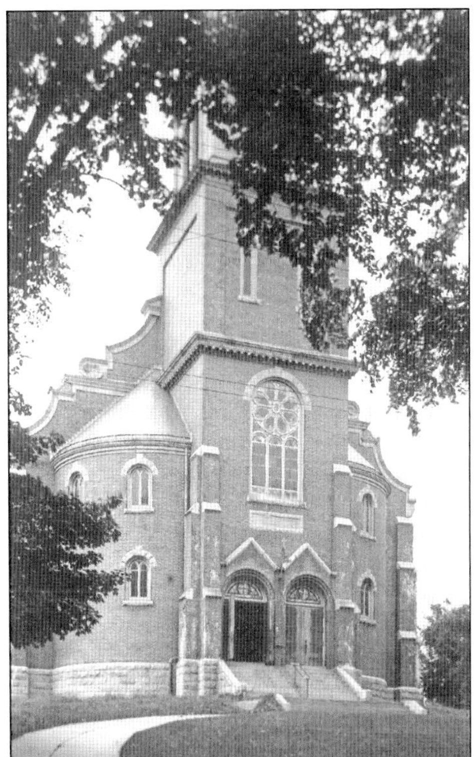

St. Joseph's Catholic Church was constructed in 1903 on South Main Street to replace another church moved from Great Works to Water Street, almost directly across from the location of St. Joseph's. The original move from Great Works was prompted in part by heavy winter snows and impassable muddy roads in the spring. Construction of St. Joseph's took several years, with the first documented services occurring in 1906. (CLM.)

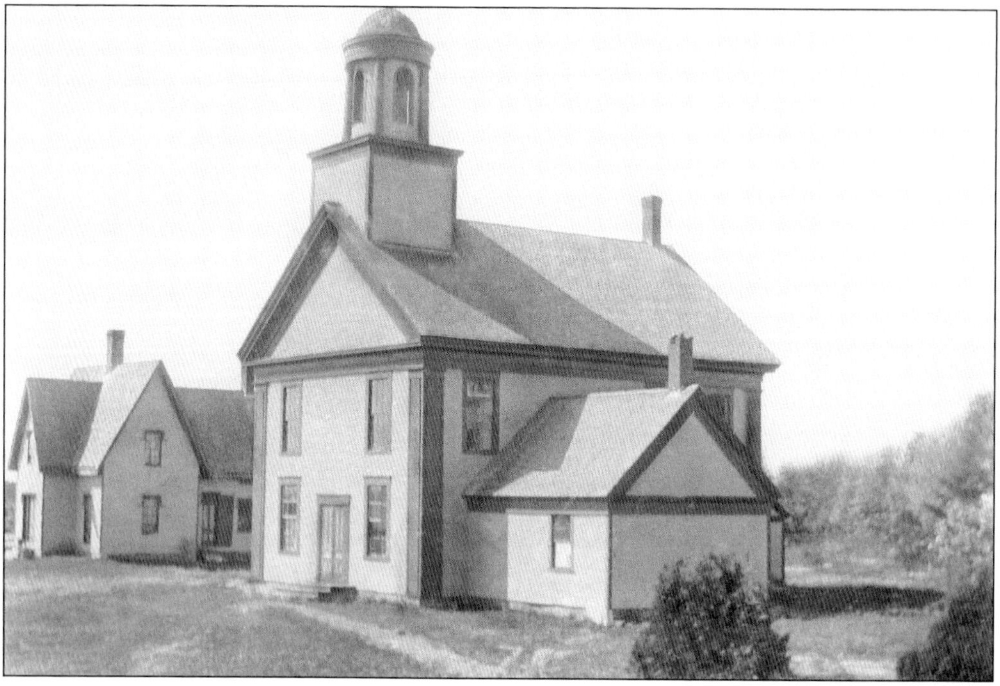

Union Academy was built on Academy Hill in 1847 to address growing educational needs. It then became a private school serving the intermediate grades. The academy finally found its role in the 1880s as Old Town's first high school. The school burned in 1900, forcing students into city hall. The background building was used as a boardinghouse and the headmaster's house and was later used by the Anchorage Hotel. (MHPC.)

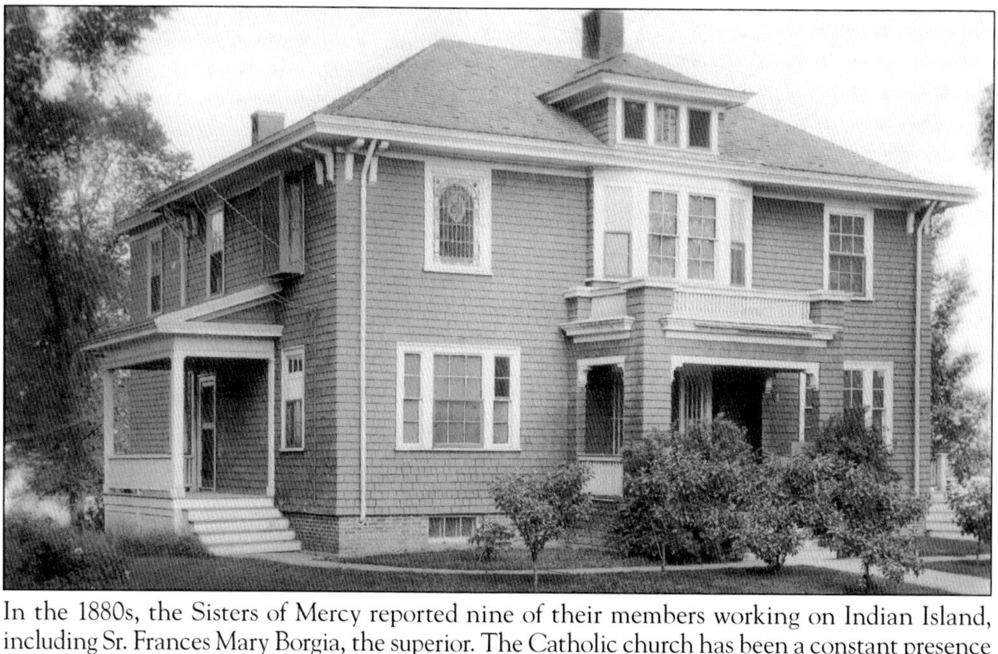

In the 1880s, the Sisters of Mercy reported nine of their members working on Indian Island, including Sr. Frances Mary Borgia, the superior. The Catholic church has been a constant presence on Indian Island since the 1680s. The convent was built in 1910 by George H. Wilbur of Old Town following the architectural plans of C. Parker Crowell of Bangor, Maine. (PRS.)

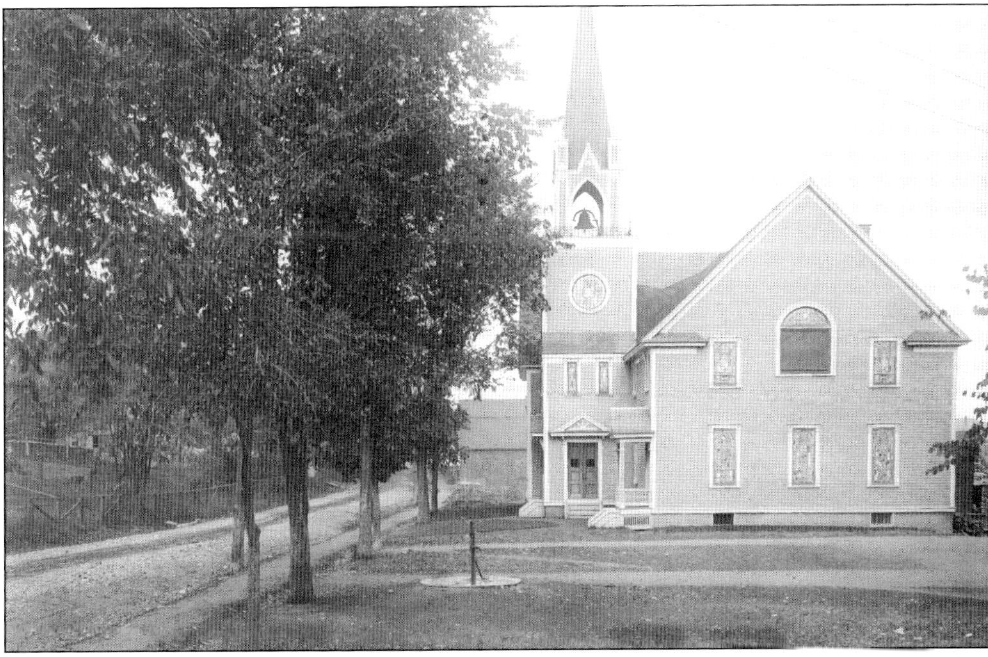

The Methodist church is shown on Brunswick Street in the 1920s. From the initial organizing efforts of Rev. Benjamin Bryant in the 1830s, a church was erected on the County Road (South Main Street). Outgrowing this building, the congregation erected a larger church that burned in 1853, as did its replacement in 1905. The Methodists moved to Stillwater in the late 1960s. (PRS.)

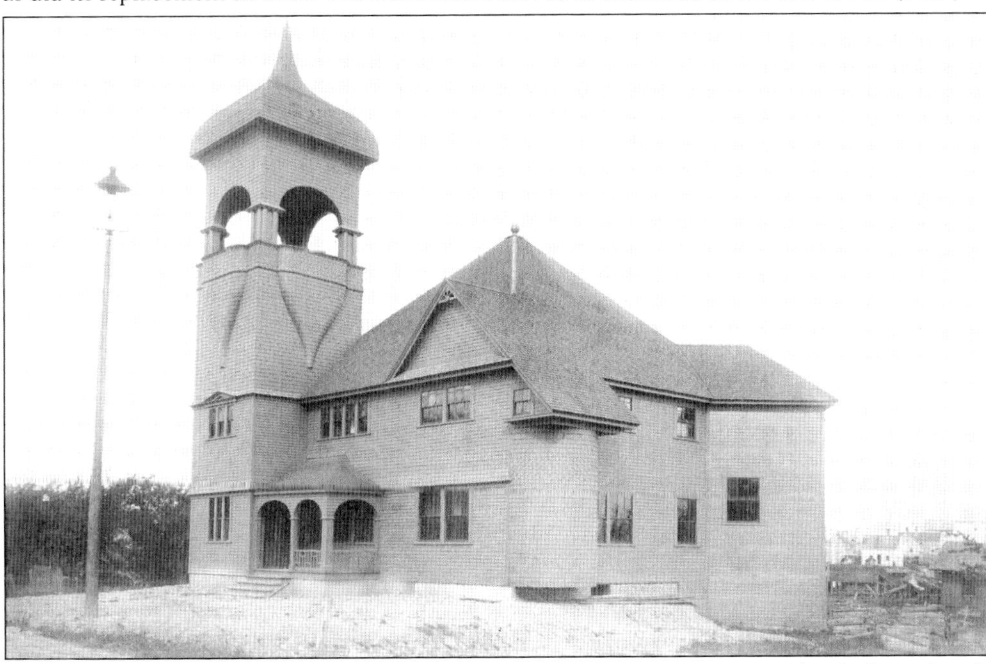

The Universalist church on South Main Street was built in 1846, just south of where the old Bickmore Company building stands today. In 1925, the Reverend Harriet B. Robinson reported that the congregation consisted on 85 members, up from just 45 two years earlier. Similarly, Sunday school attendance increased by more than a third in that period of time. (MHPC.)

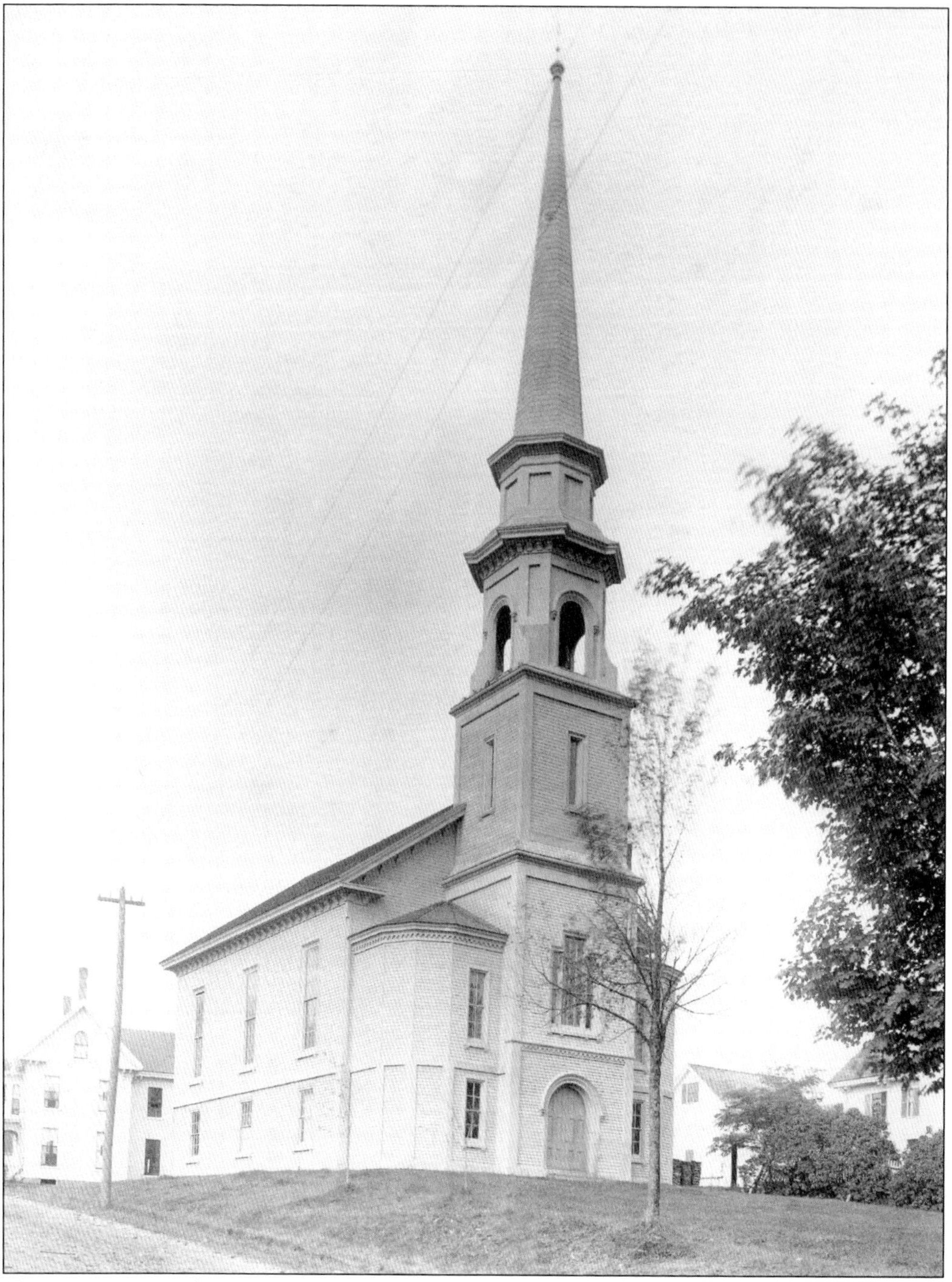

The Congregationalists were in Old Town before the 1830s. Organized by the Reverend Joseph C. Lovejoy, the first church was built in 1832 at the corner of Center and Brunswick Streets. This church burned in the so-called Lincoln Fire of April 19, 1865. Pictured here, a successor church was built the next year at the same location. Sporadically without a minister, services at the church languished over the years, and the church fell into disuse. The YMCA's first programs were held in the church vestry in the 1940s. The Congregational church was razed in June 1959 due to structural safety concerns following several failed inspections by city officials. (MHPC.)

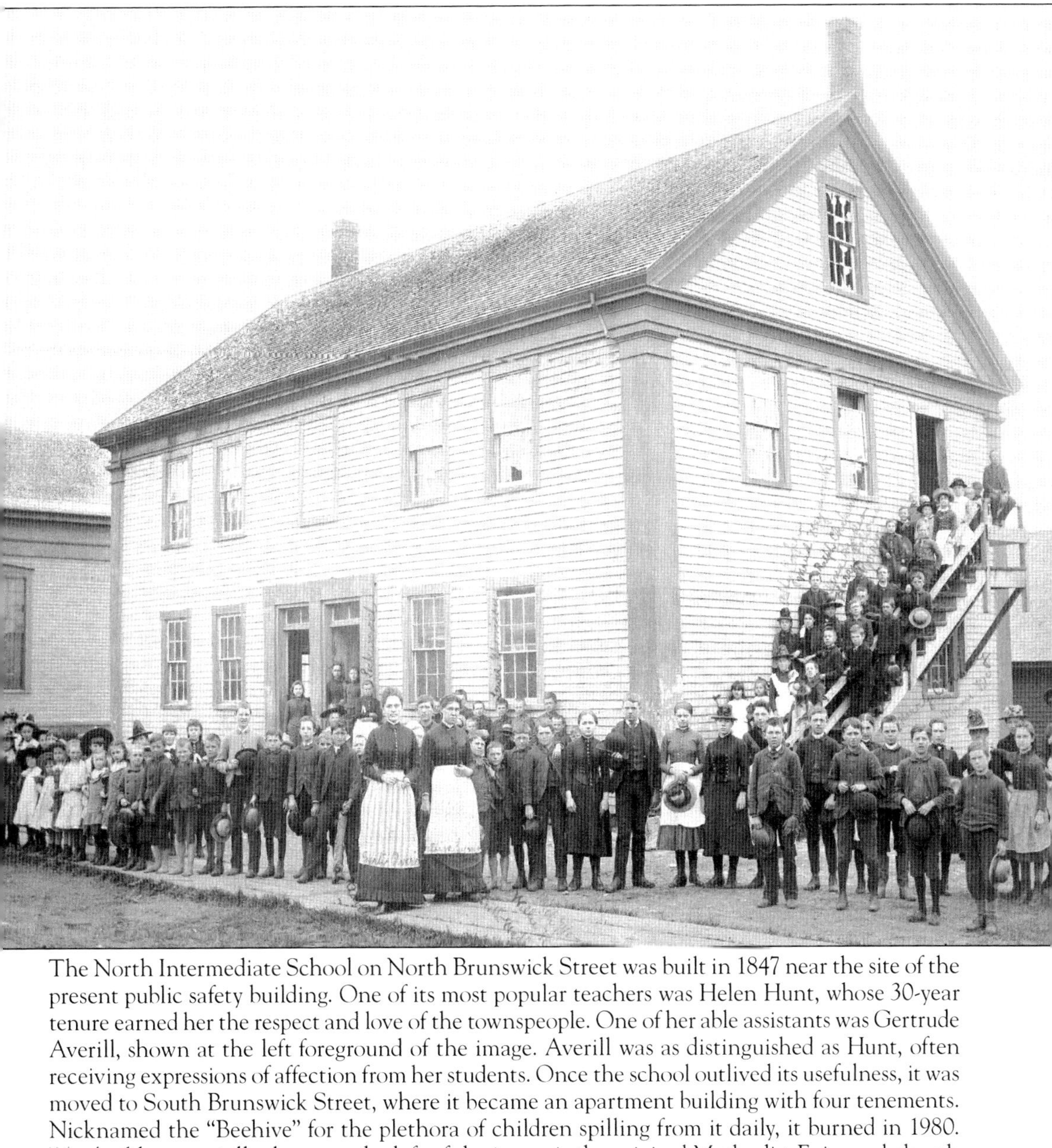

The North Intermediate School on North Brunswick Street was built in 1847 near the site of the present public safety building. One of its most popular teachers was Helen Hunt, whose 30-year tenure earned her the respect and love of the townspeople. One of her able assistants was Gertrude Averill, shown at the left foreground of the image. Averill was as distinguished as Hunt, often receiving expressions of affection from her students. Once the school outlived its usefulness, it was moved to South Brunswick Street, where it became an apartment building with four tenements. Nicknamed the "Beehive" for the plethora of children spilling from it daily, it burned in 1980. The building partially shown at the left of the image is the original Methodist Episcopal church on North Brunswick Street in Old Town. (OTPL.)

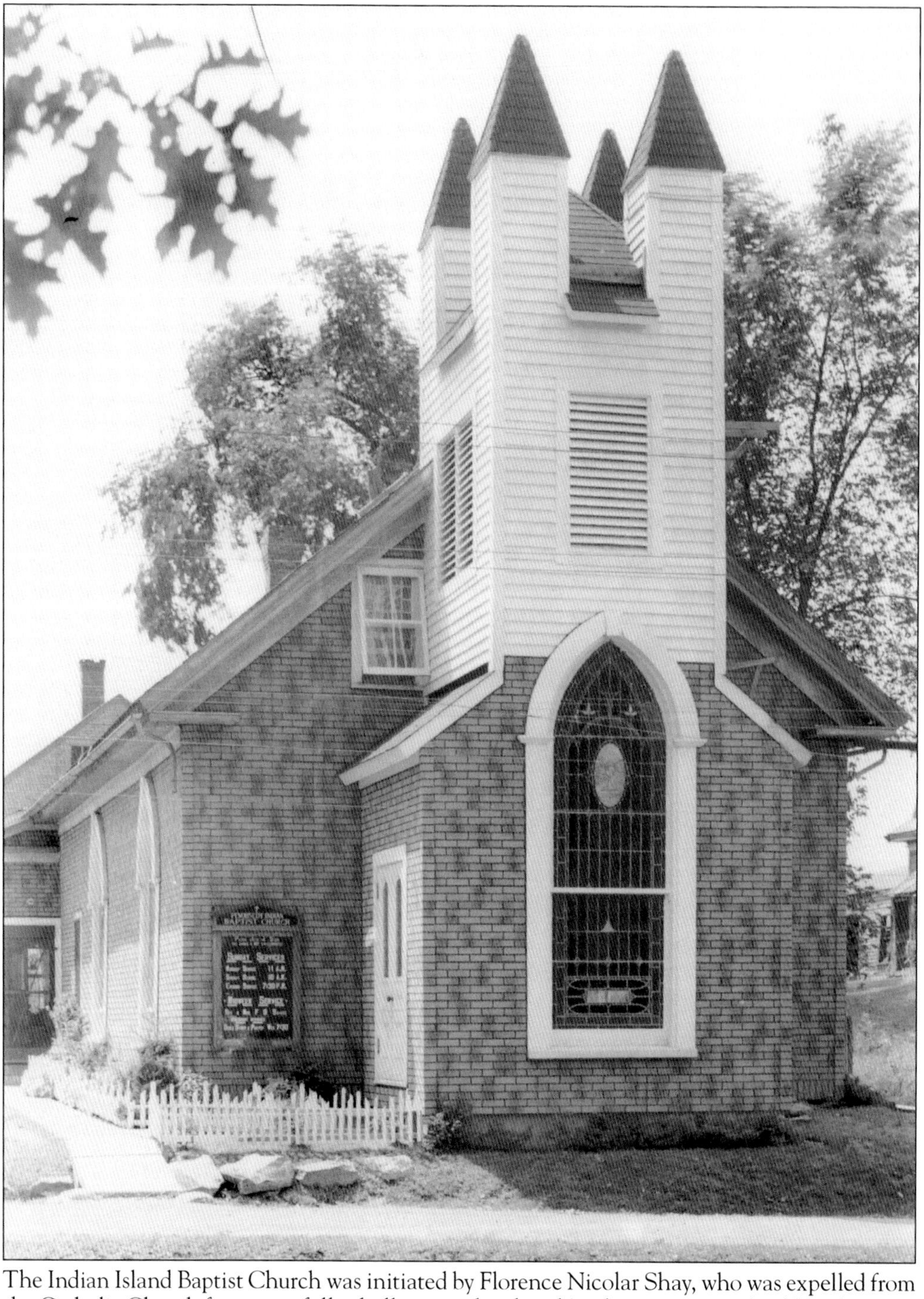

The Indian Island Baptist Church was initiated by Florence Nicolar Shay, who was expelled from the Catholic Church for successfully challenging the church's religious-oriented public education curriculum. Maine passed a law in 1931 allowing the Penobscots to be educated in local schools. Florence was a lifelong advocate for the Penobscots. She was highly educated and experienced in the ways of the world. With her husband, Leo Shay, she had four sons, who were all drafted into the service during World War II. (PRS.)

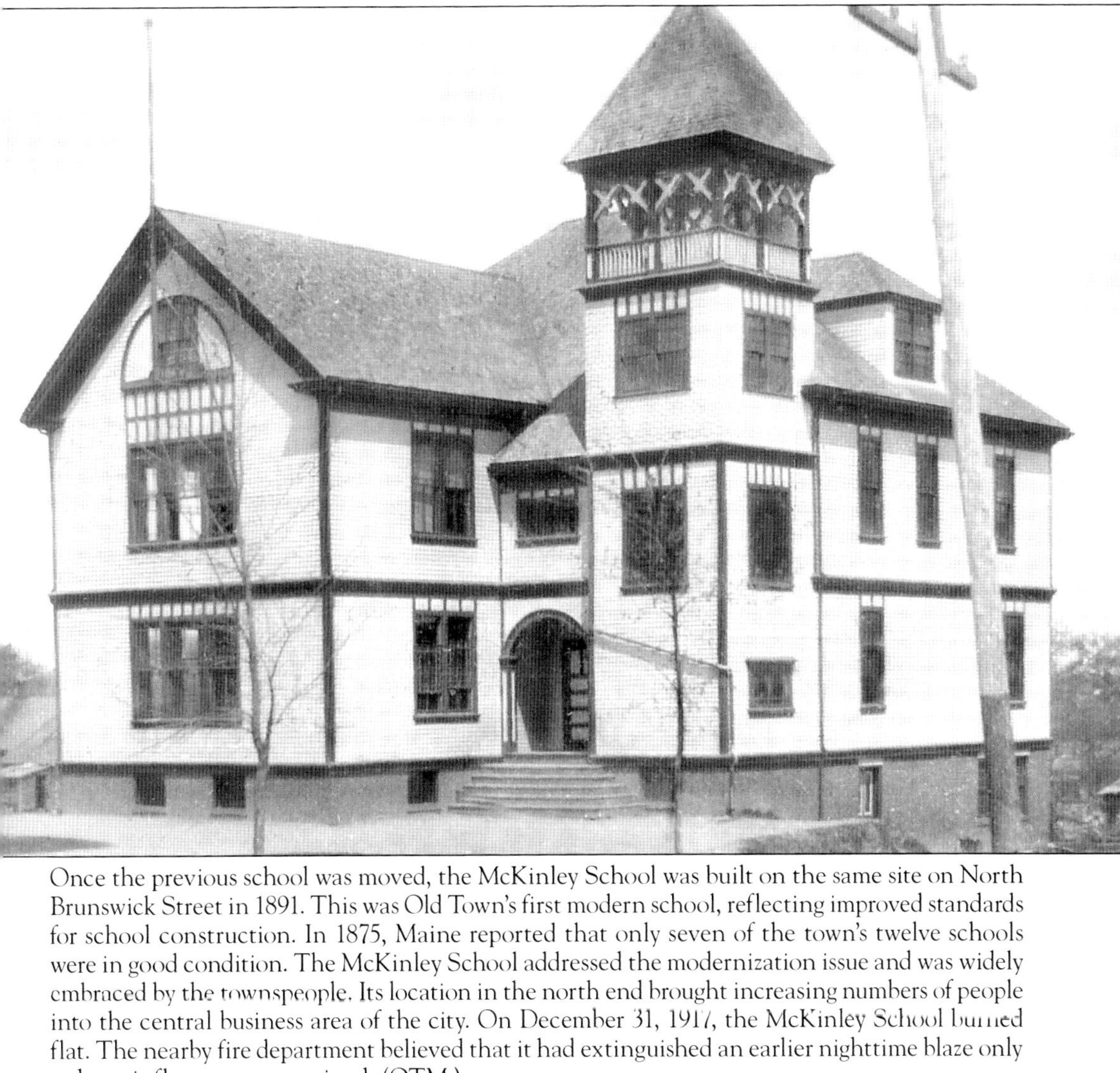

Once the previous school was moved, the McKinley School was built on the same site on North Brunswick Street in 1891. This was Old Town's first modern school, reflecting improved standards for school construction. In 1875, Maine reported that only seven of the town's twelve schools were in good condition. The McKinley School addressed the modernization issue and was widely embraced by the townspeople. Its location in the north end brought increasing numbers of people into the central business area of the city. On December 31, 1917, the McKinley School burned flat. The nearby fire department believed that it had extinguished an earlier nighttime blaze only to have it flare up unrestrained. (OTM.)

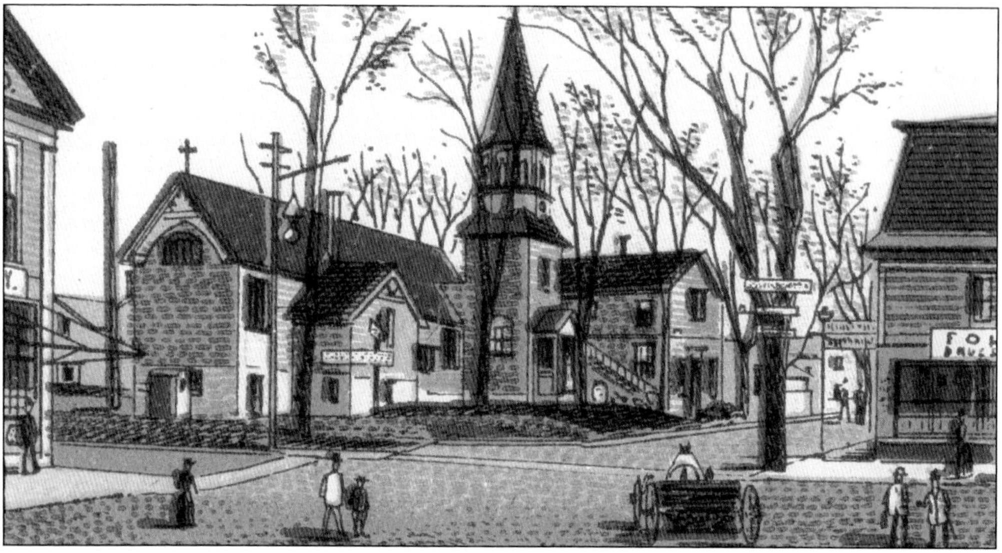

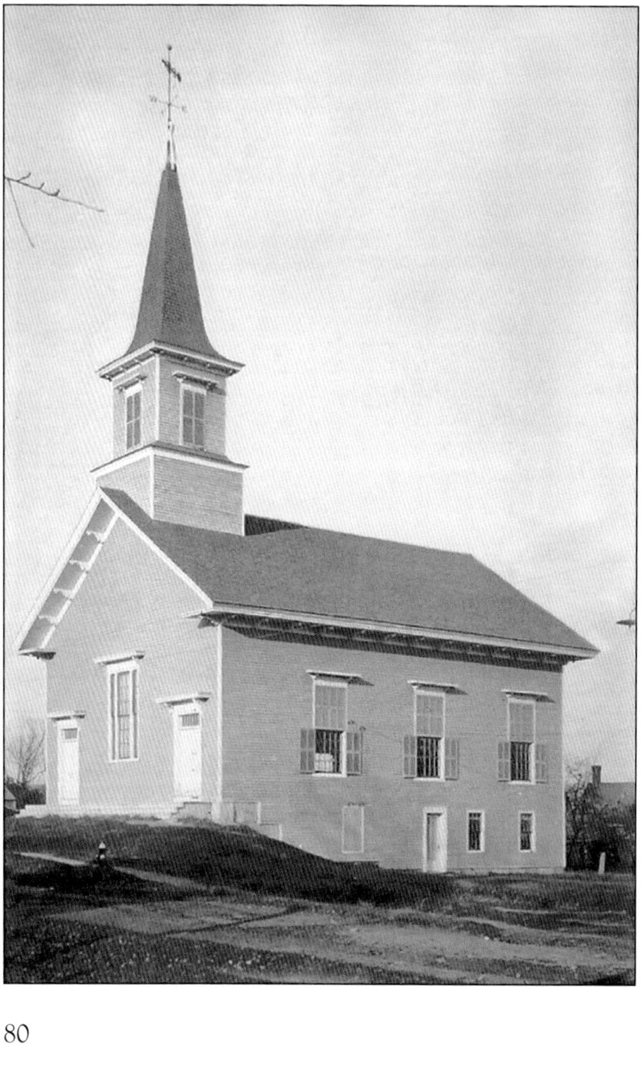

The Church of St. James was organized in 1845 in Milford, Maine, with Bangor's Rev. John West officiating. Congregants had earlier met at the Wadleigh School in Old Town and, in 1847, returned to this city. In 1852, the St. James Episcopal Church was erected and is shown here after it was remodeled. Old Town photographer M.G. Gilmore immortalized the surroundings of the church in his unique crayon style. The church is listed in the National Register of Historic Places. (OTM.)

The Stillwater Union Church was built on Bennoch Road before 1855 by Baptists and Universalists, later joined by Congregationalists and Methodists. Once the Universalists withdrew, the church became known as the Stillwater Federated Church. (PRS.)

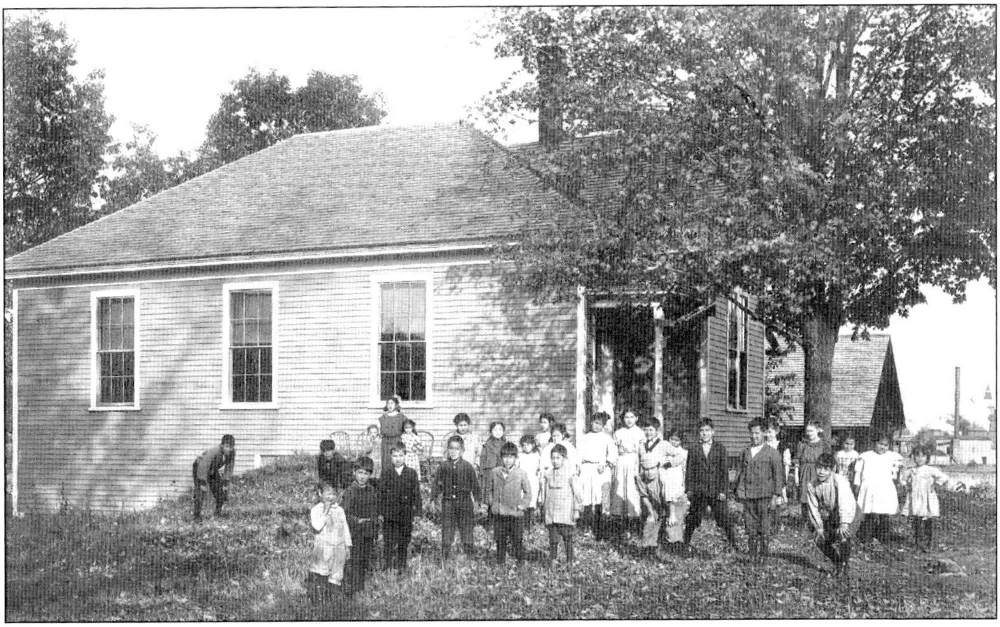

Following Maine's separation from Massachusetts, the Penobscots became wards of the state by treaty. The first efforts to school the Indians came in 1823, when Josiah Brewer and a group of Bangor citizens established a school there for a few months. But Maine lacked resolve, and educational services lagged. When the Sisters of Mercy arrived in 1878, immediate results followed. Shown here is the Indian Island School around 1910. (MHPC.)

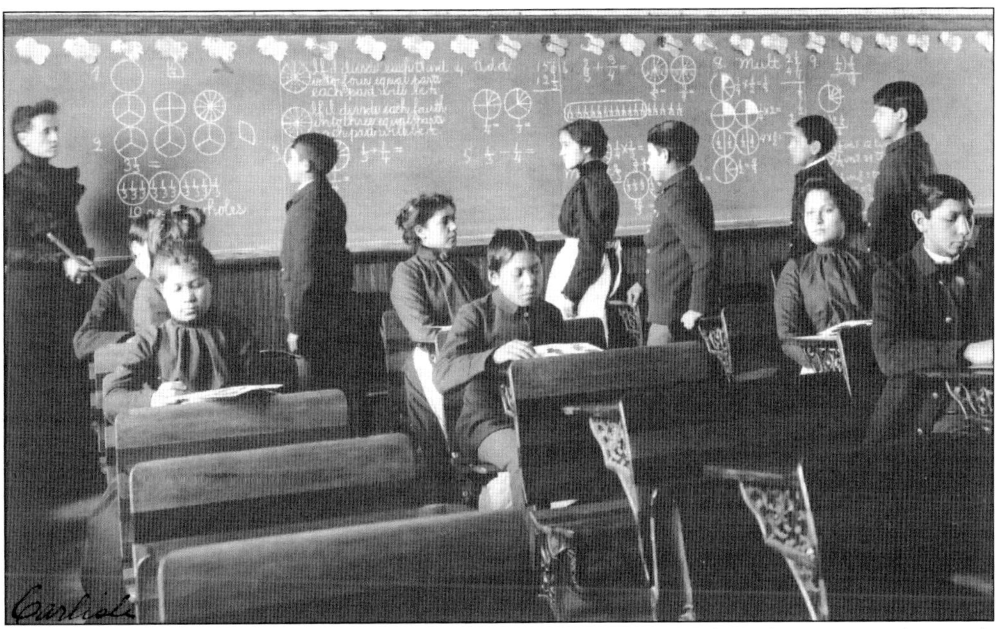

The tension in this classroom is palpable as Native American students line up to solve math problems. A by-product of the eugenics movement was the separation of Native Americans from their heritage. The government encouraged Penobscots to relocate to receive special training at schools such as the Carlisle Indian Industrial School in Pennsylvania, shown here around 1910. Most of them returned to Indian Island to immerse themselves in their native customs. (LOC.)

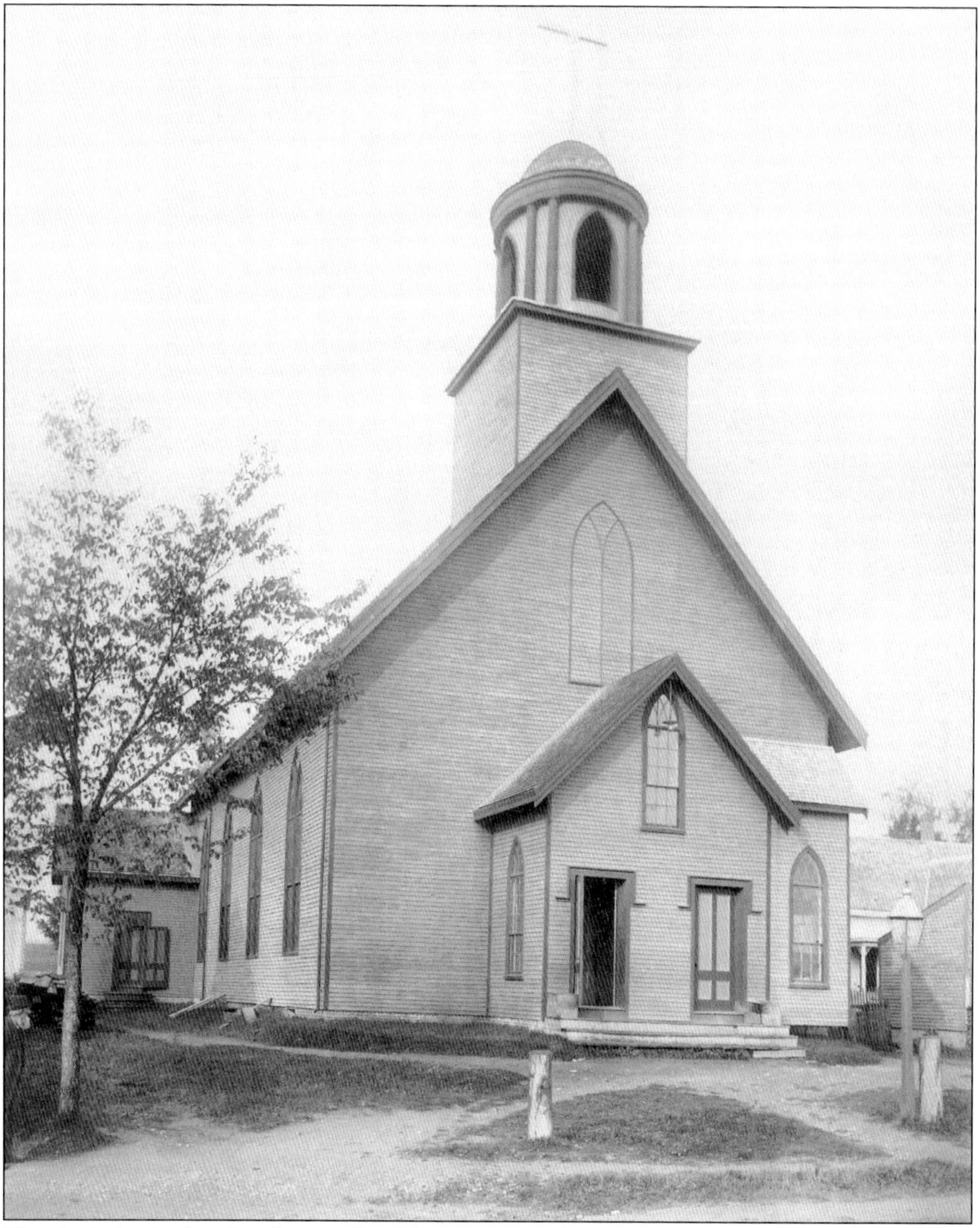

The Catholics built a church near the old cemetery on the New County Road (later called South Main Street) in Great Works in 1852. Demand grew over the succeeding years for services to be closer to the population center, as winter snows and muddy roads in the spring had become too much for parishioners to bear. In 1870, the church was moved to a location on Water Street facing the Penobscot River. In 1877, an addition was erected, making the church the largest used for worship in town. (MHPC.)

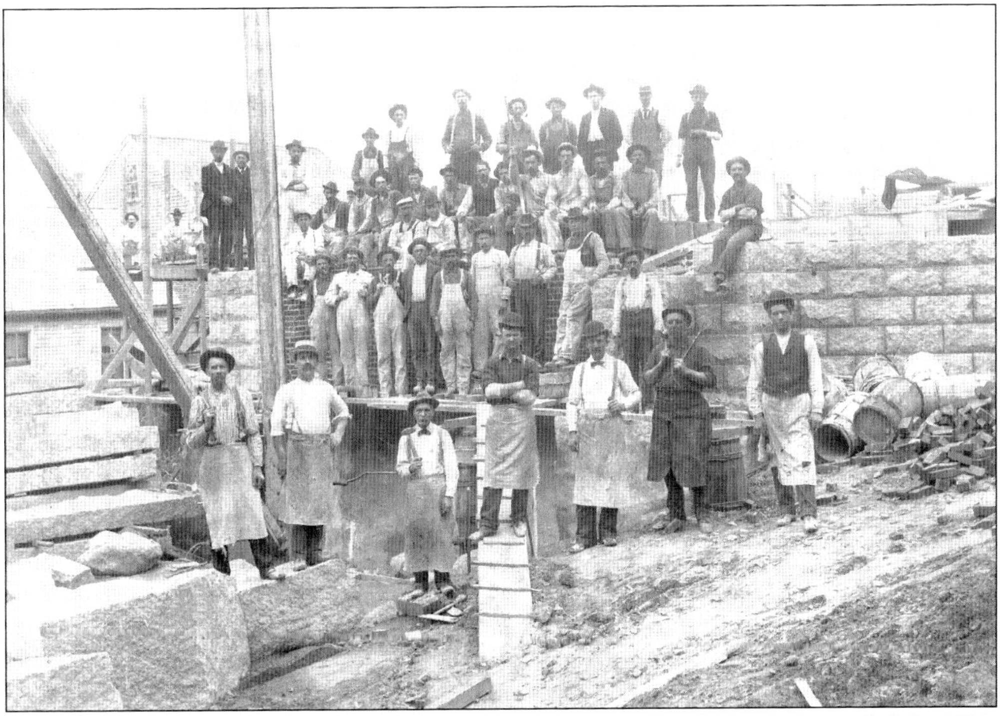

Even with the 1870s addition to the church, an even larger church was soon needed. In 1888, the *Old Town Enterprise* reported that the Catholic Society was planning the new church that was eventually built in 1903. French Catholic workers from Québec are shown building the foundation for St. Joseph. Québécois were heavily recruited to Maine by the paper and fabric mills. (MHPC.)

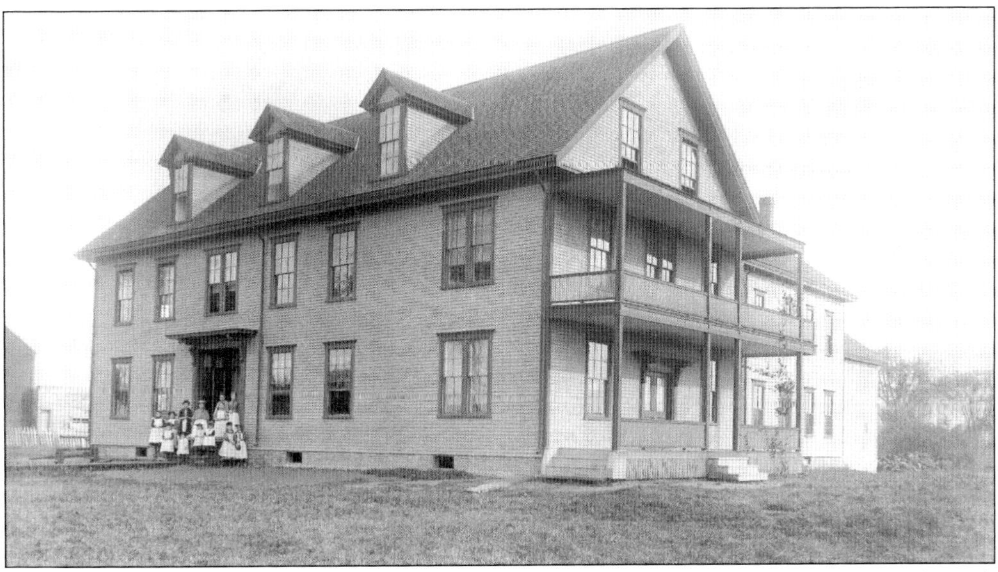

In 1885, the Catholic Church acquired a new property between South Main Street and South Brunswick Street bordered by Carroll Street. One of its first tasks was to erect a new convent school that year. Here, St. Joseph's School is shown soon after it opened with an enrollment of 120, taught by the Sisters of Mercy. (MHPC.)

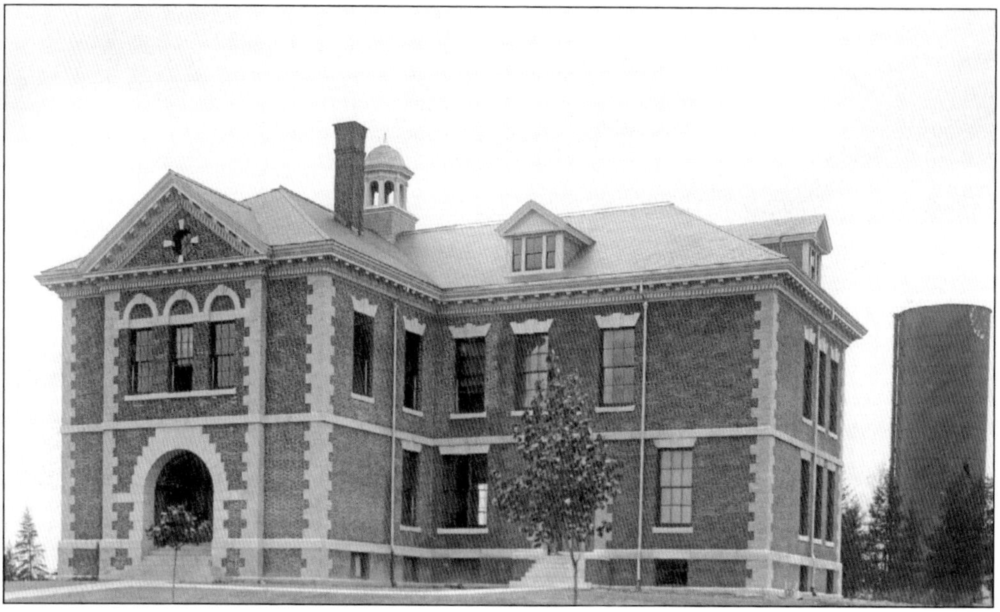

Soon after the Union Academy burned in 1900, a new high school was built on the same site. As with the McKinley School, the city again followed modern school recommendations with a multistory design and brick construction. Since the 1870s, the city had worked to eliminate semiautonomous ward schools in favor of city-controlled schools. (MHPC.)

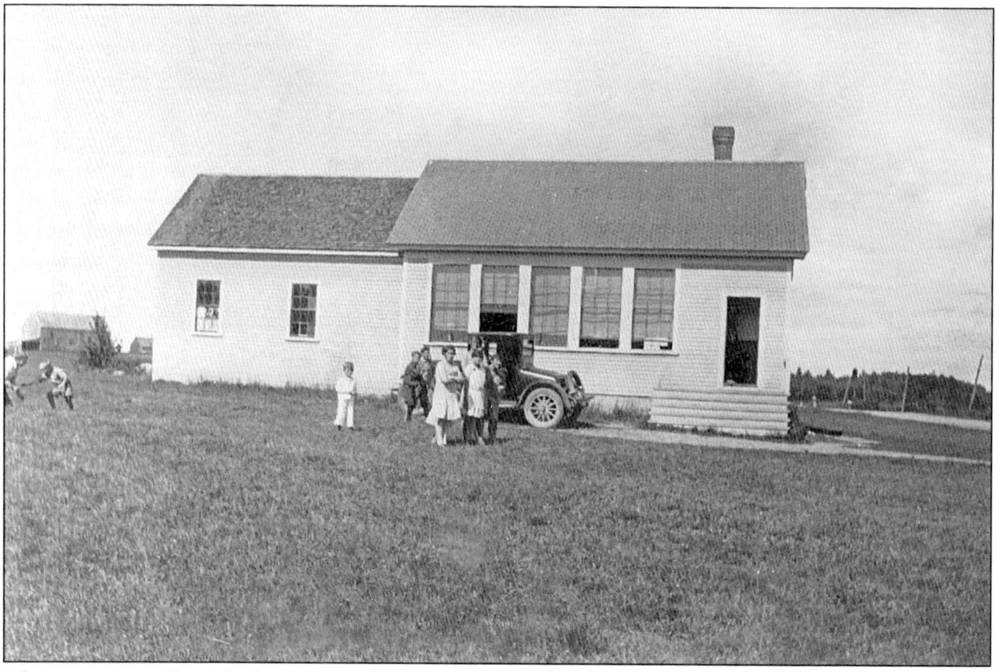

There were two French Settlement designations in Old Town: one on South Main Street toward Great Works and another around the Gilman Falls area. This is the French Settlement School on outer Gilman Falls Avenue. In the 1920s, two neighboring schools, West Old Town and Gilman Falls, were closed, with students transferred to this school. This school too was later closed and sold off in the mid-1940s. (CLM.)

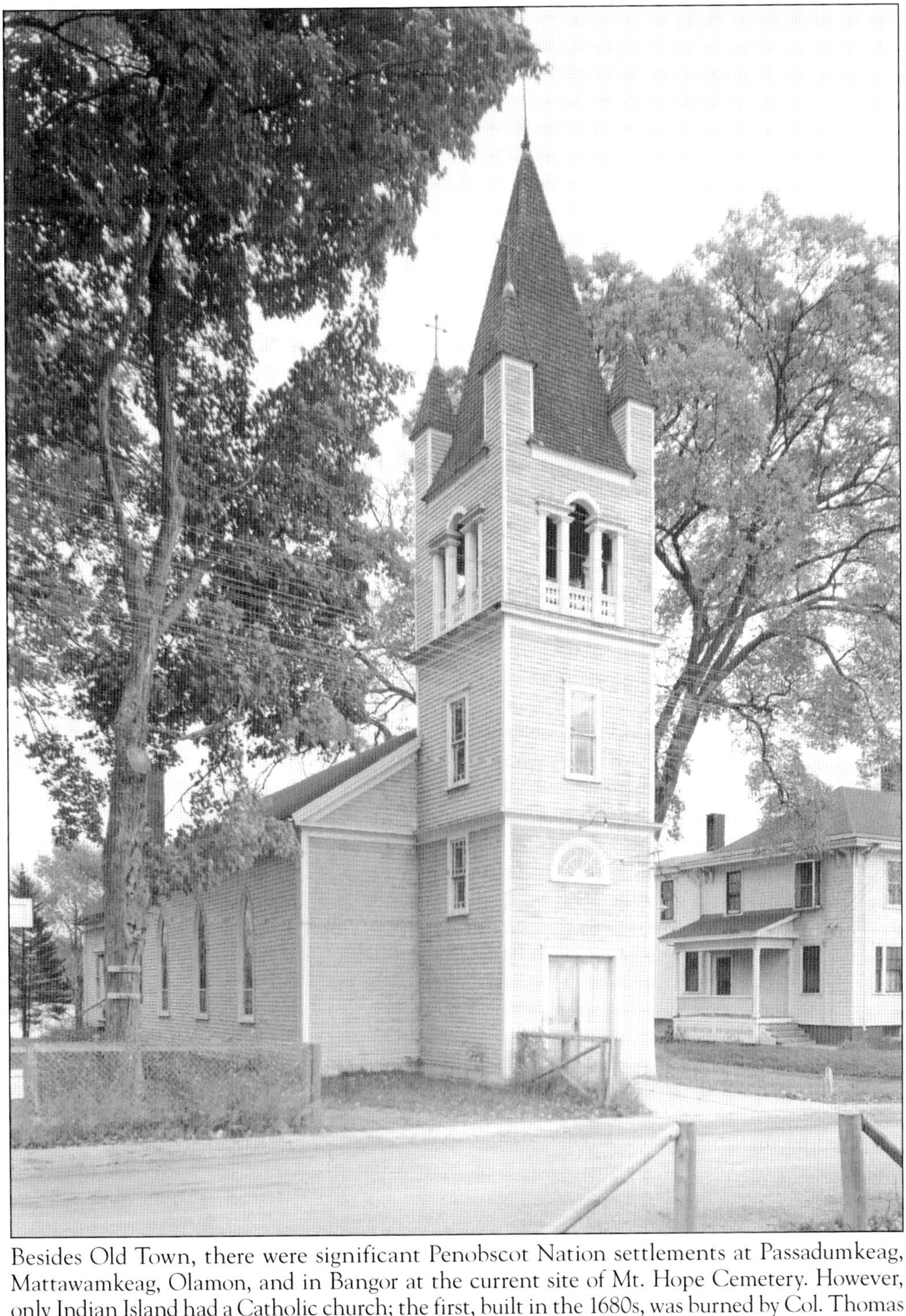

Besides Old Town, there were significant Penobscot Nation settlements at Passadumkeag, Mattawamkeag, Olamon, and in Bangor at the current site of Mt. Hope Cemetery. However, only Indian Island had a Catholic church; the first, built in the 1680s, was burned by Col. Thomas Westbrook in 1723 during Dummer's War. The church pictured here was built about 1834 and is now in the National Register of Historic Places. This church served the needs of the white settlers in Old Town for many years before another church was built in Great Works. (MHPC.)

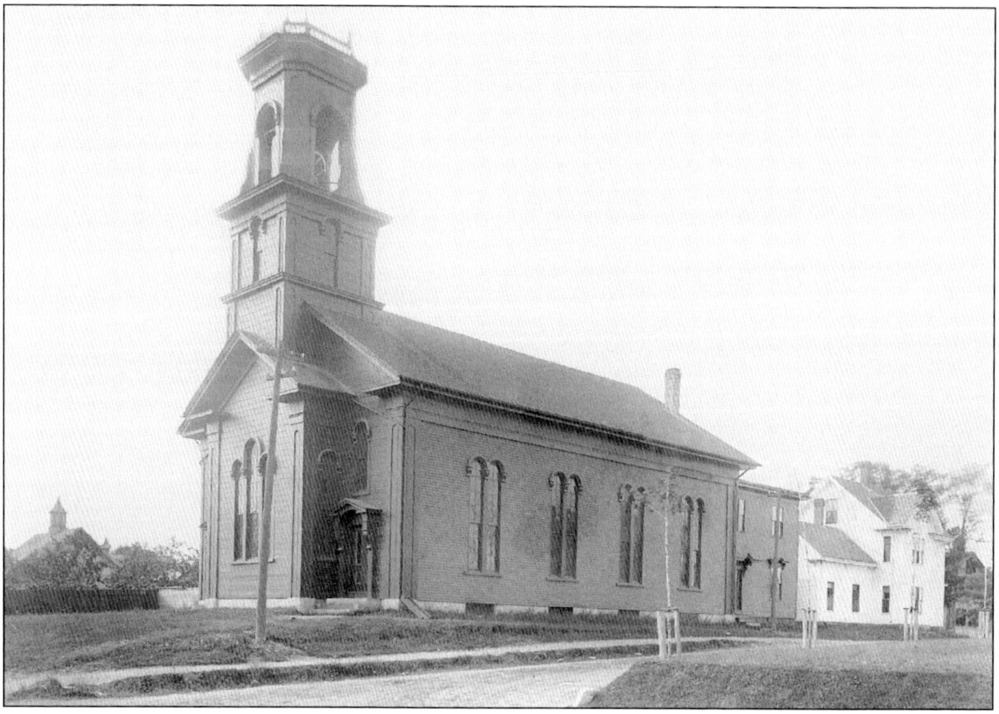

Early in the village's history, Charles Blanchard converted the old Lovejoy School on North Fourth Street into a Baptist church and meetinghouse. In 1854, a new church was built there. This church was among those lost to the Lincoln Fire of 1865. Undeterred, the Baptists built this church the next year, and it is still in use. (MHPC.)

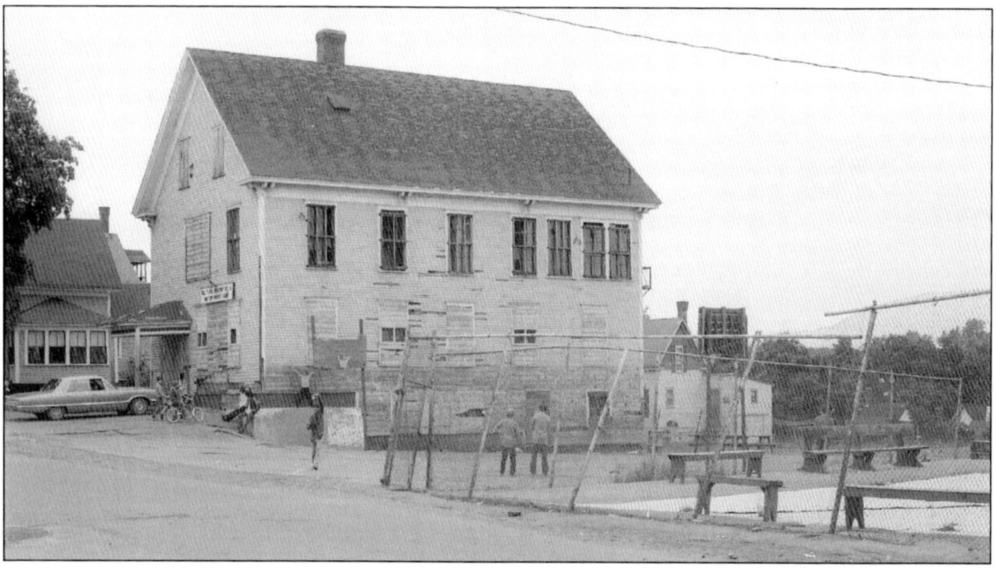

The Treat and Webster School, commonly called the French Island School, was built in 1902 and enlarged sometime later. Many of its students would later attend St. Joseph's School on South Main Street. Following its discontinuance as a public school in 1953, the former Treat and Webster building was used as a community youth center. Anna Wareing was one of the final teachers there. (PWT.)

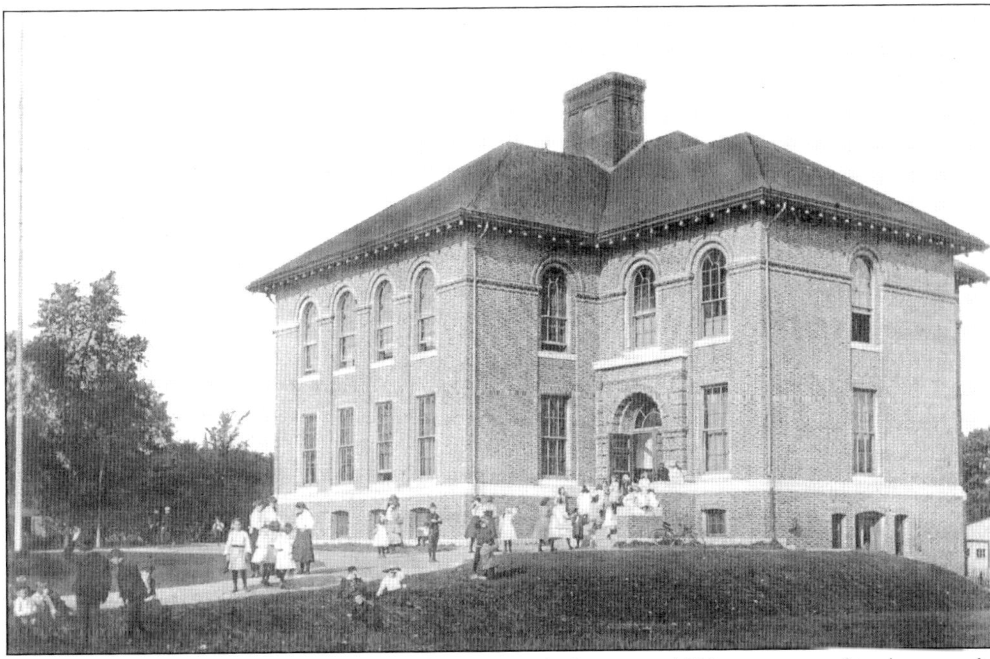

The Helen Hunt School, built on South Brunswick Street in 1903, was named in honor of a highly regarded teacher who taught in the old Brunswick Street School for 30 years. Originally an elementary school, Helen Hunt School later became a junior high school, then reverted to its original use once a new junior high school was built about 1963. (MHPC.)

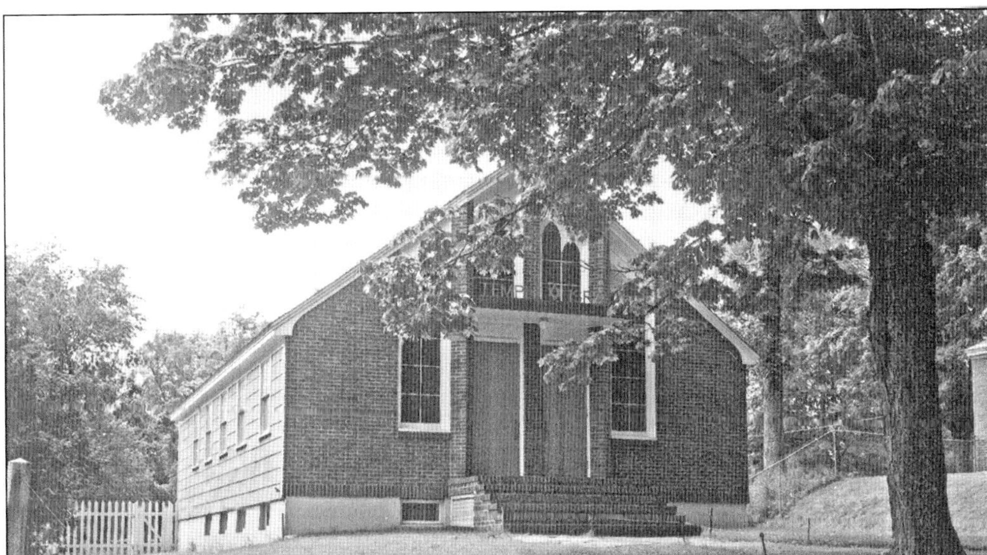

From Russia, Poland, and Germany, they came to Old Town: Nathan Shiro, Israel Cutler, Abe Epstein, Bernard Ginsburg, David Goldsmith, Sidney Hoos, and more. Religious services had been held in private homes for many years until 1955, when Old Town's Jewish community erected Temple Israel on Center Street. It is no longer in use as a temple. (OTM.)

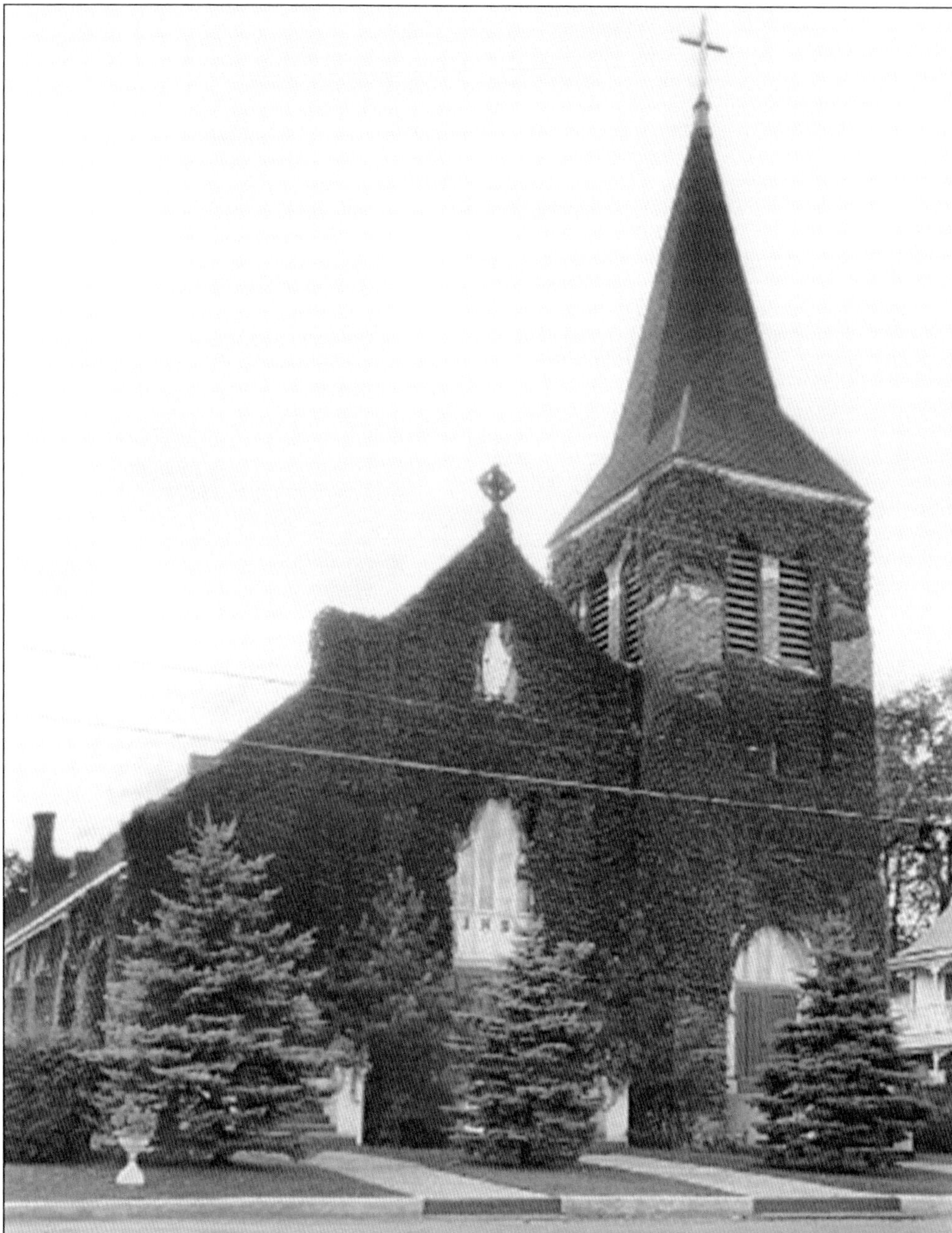

St. Mary's Catholic Church on South Main Street was erected in 1928 to serve the demands of the English-speaking population of the city. The plan to divide the church from St. Joseph's was approved at the highest levels of the diocese in Maine. Struggling under its debt during the prolonged Great Depression, the church labored on. Better times prevailed following World War II, but declining church attendance and dwindling finances forced a reexamination of the two-church concept. Facing its problems head-on, the Diocese of Portland initiated a process that ultimately led to St. Mary's closing in 1996. The building currently serves as headquarters for the Old Town Museum. (OTM.)

Five

Fire and Water

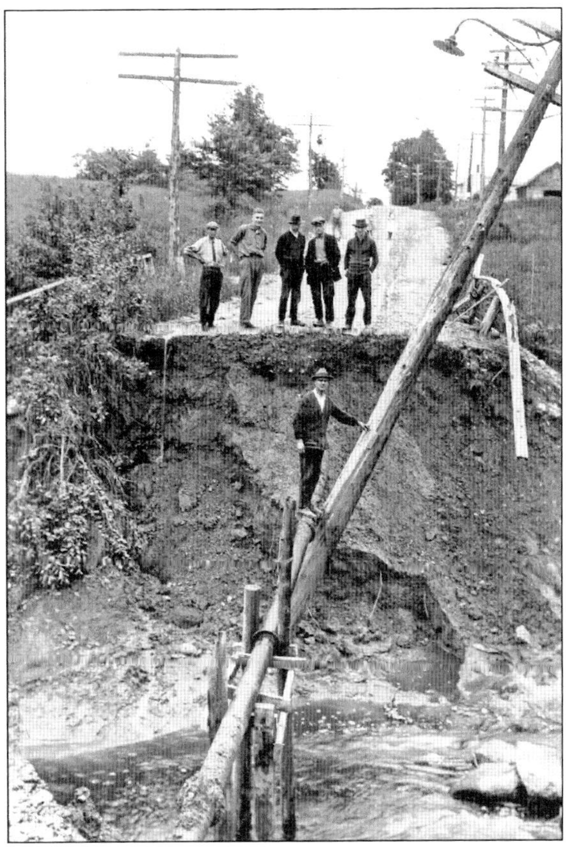

This washout on the Bennoch Road in Orono severed Stillwater from the town it was once part of. Fires and floods helped shape Old Town from its beginning. Still talked about today is the notorious Lincoln Fire of April 19, 1865, so-called because townspeople were exiting a tribute to the fallen president in the Congregational church on Brunswick Street just as the fire broke out. Destroying the nearby Rines Block, the fire went on to decimate parts of Brunswick, Center, Oak, and North Fourth Streets. The church was quickly consumed and the nearby Baptist church was lost as well but was soon rebuilt on the same lot. J.Y. Richardson's home was spared through the application of wet quilts to the roof. The town's fire department was practically nonexistent in those days. Days later, an even larger fire at Augusta prompted statewide outcries for modernized firefighting equipment. (OTM.)

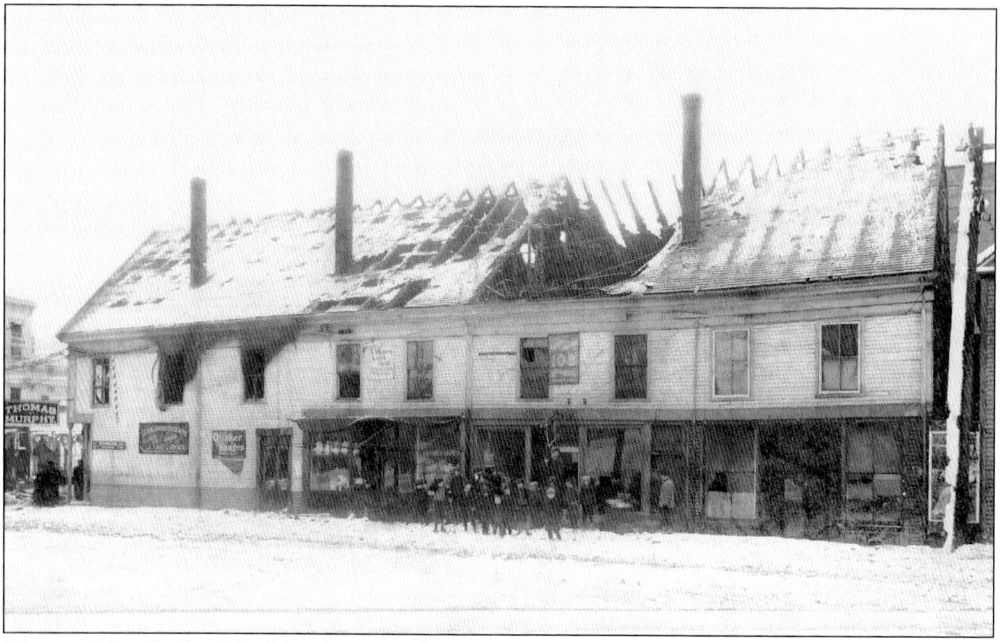

Thomas Murphy had died by the time this 1912 fire broke out in an upstairs apartment in the Bradbury Block along Center and South Main Streets. A defective chimney was faulted. The sale of the business was delayed as insurance claims were being settled. The peaked roof was removed at the city's urging, but later a third story was added. (MHPC.)

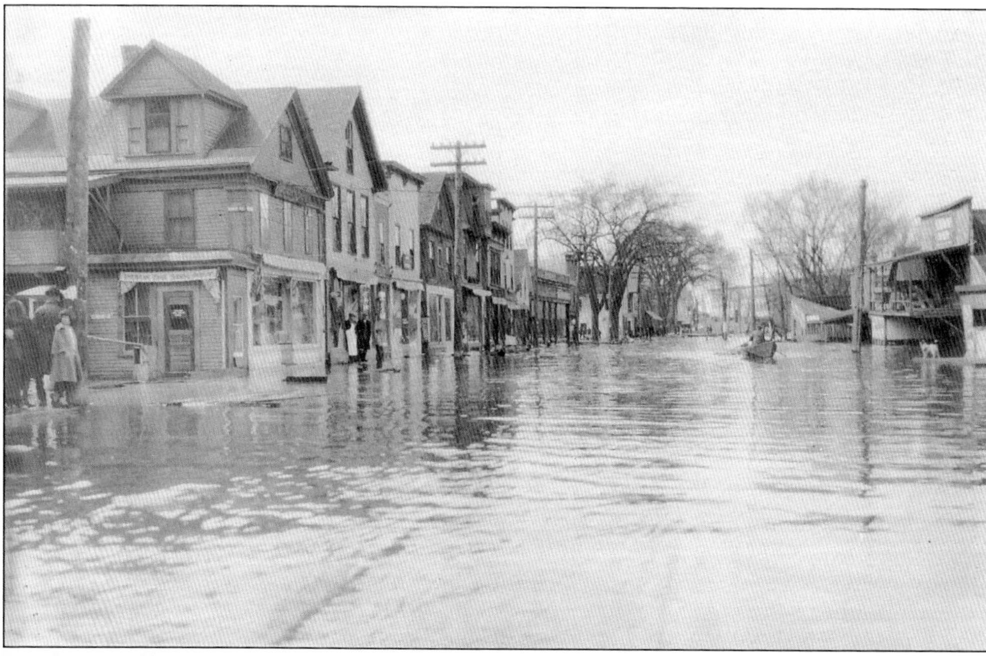

Residents and businessmen were dismayed at the spectacle of the mighty Penobscot overflowing its banks during late May 1923. This image shows North Main Street inundated at Middle Street. Shopkeepers at the Jordan Brothers confectionary shop watch intently while a boatman closes in to rescue a stranded dog across the street. (WAO.)

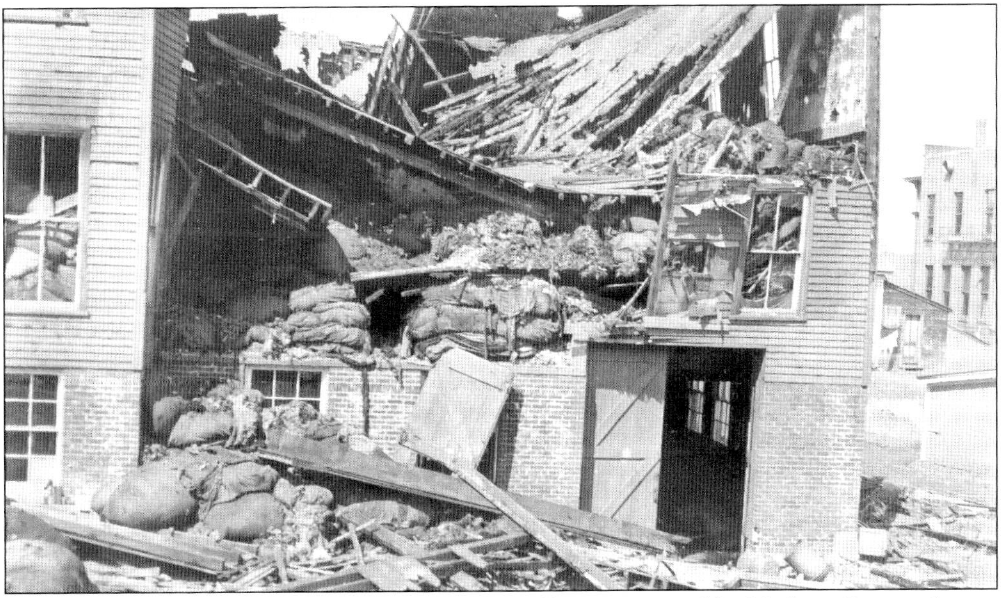

This building on Shirley Street behind the post office was owned by Herbert Gray and once housed the Bickmore Gall Cure Company and the Old Town Canoe Company. At the time of this fire on April 5, 1927, the building was being used to store some of the unsold products from the recently closed Old Town Woolen Mill. (OTPL.)

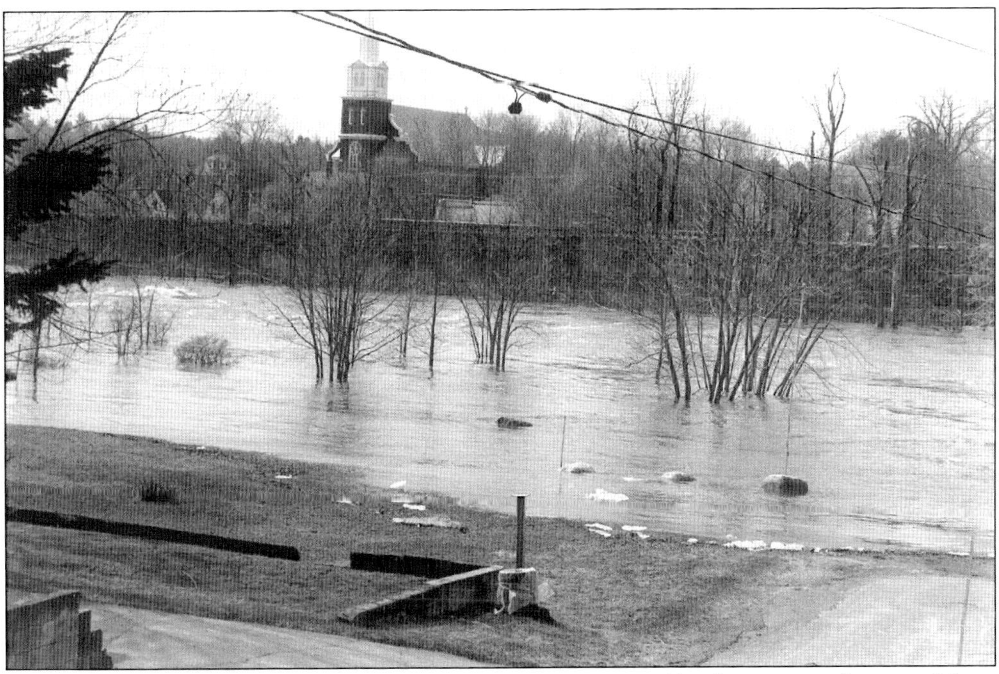

French Island lies within the channel of the Penobscot River itself and is perennially in peril from high water. This image shows a submerged Nadeau Street. Floods have become a way of life for river towns along Maine's major rivers, including the Penobscot, the Kennebec, the Androscoggin, and the St. John. St. Joseph's Catholic Church is across the water. (PWT.)

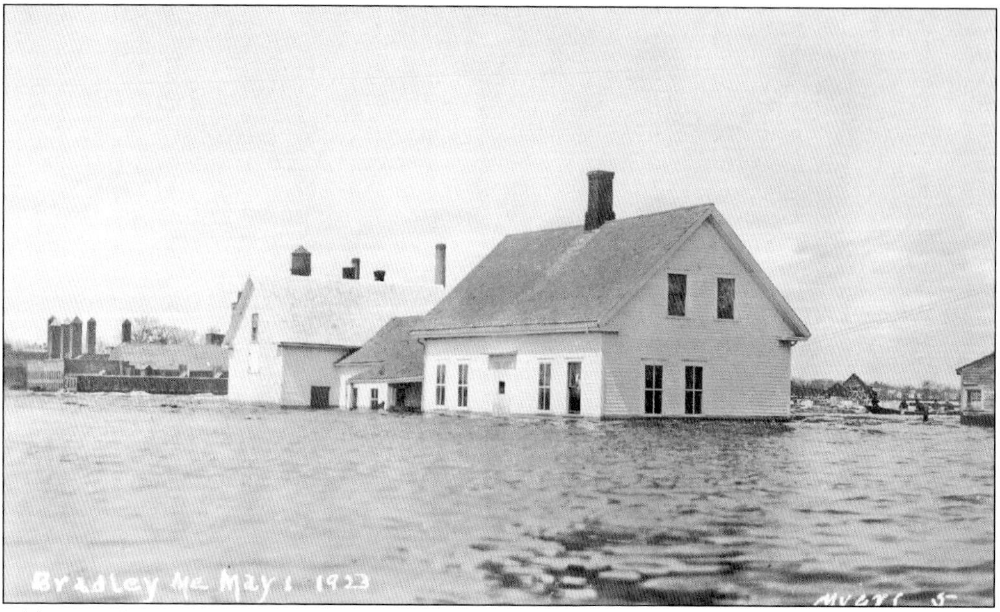

Old Town photographer Frank Myers took this photograph of a Bradley, Maine, residence stranded amidst surging floodwaters of the Penobscot River on May 1, 1923. The mills of the Penobscot Chemical Fibre Company can be seen in the left background. Torrential spring rains combined with a deep winter's snowpack often spells trouble for river towns. (OTM.)

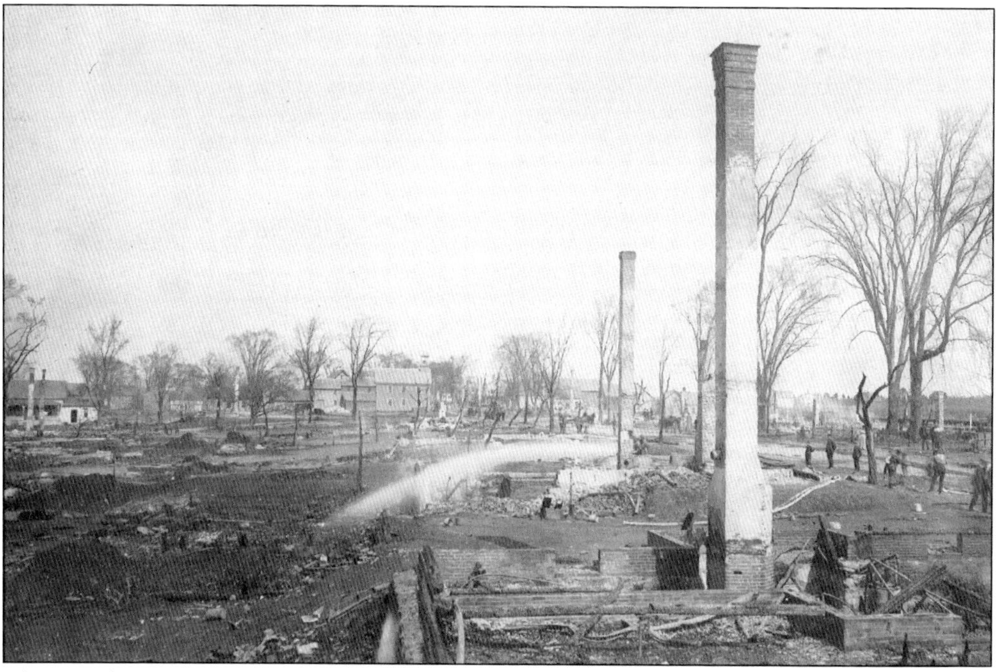

The utter destruction of this fire precludes its positive identification. Since the photographer, R.M. Howe, worked in the early 1900s, the image likely depicts the Stillwater fire of July 1, 1901. Three mills and a score of homes, most of them between Spring Street and Bennoch Road, were burned. Lack of cooperation from the nearby pumping station added greatly to the loss. (MHPC.)

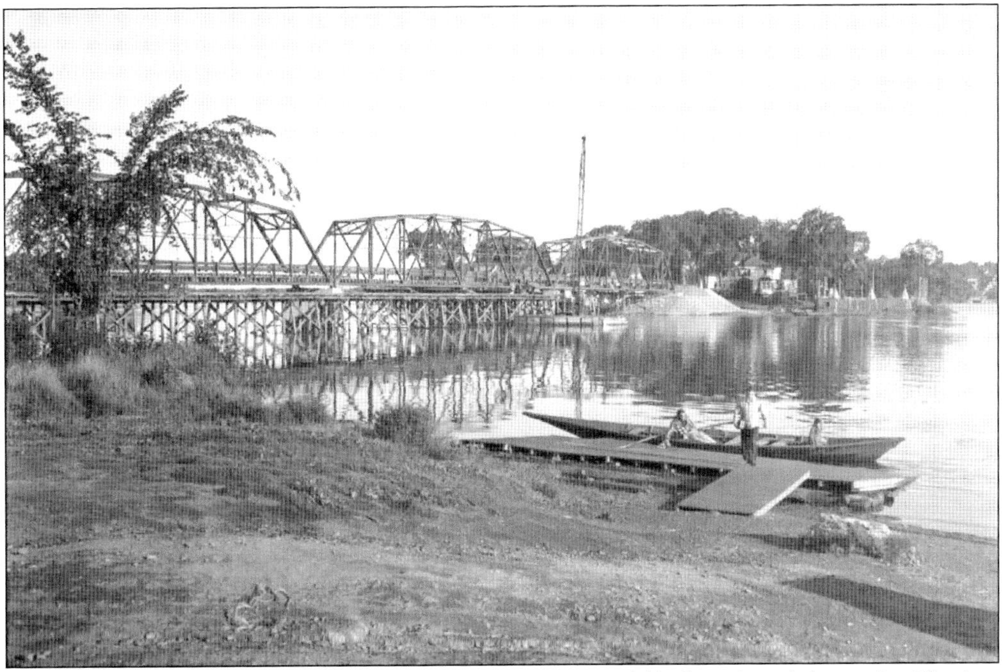

In this image from the early 1950s, the Penobscot River peacefully flows from left to right. The first bridge to Indian Island from North Main Street nears completion. The ferry operator pushes his bateau from the dock after discharging a young Penobscot student on his way to school. (BHP.)

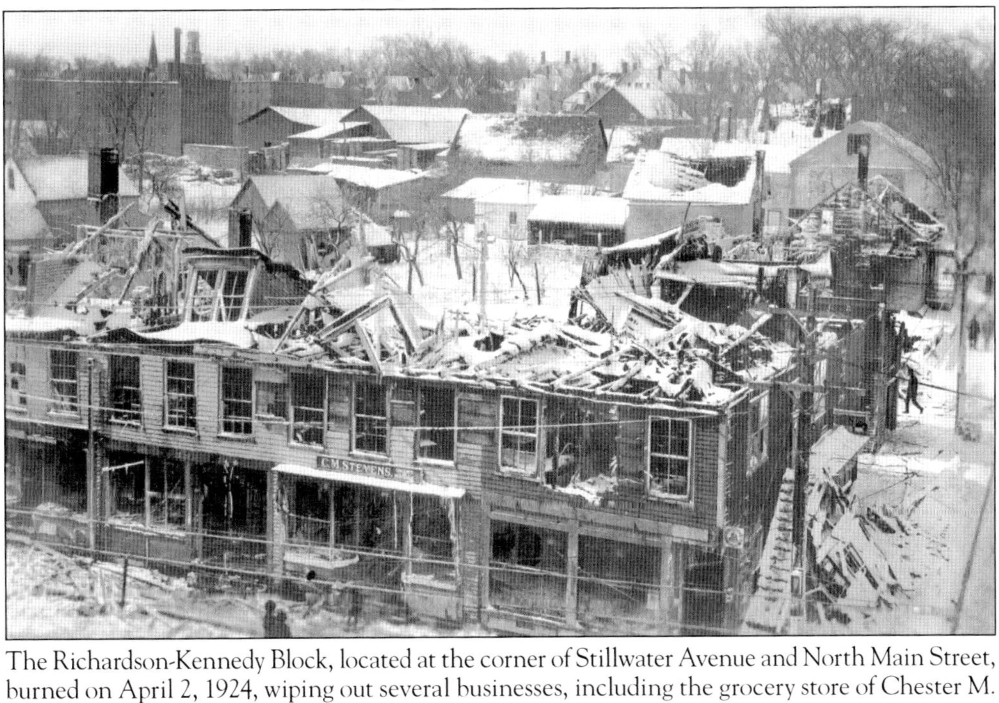

The Richardson-Kennedy Block, located at the corner of Stillwater Avenue and North Main Street, burned on April 2, 1924, wiping out several businesses, including the grocery store of Chester M. Stevens, and the fruit and candy store of Francis X. Boutin, shown beneath the telephone sign. The fire leapfrogged several residences and came perilously close to the storage sheds of the Old Town Canoe Company. (OTM.)

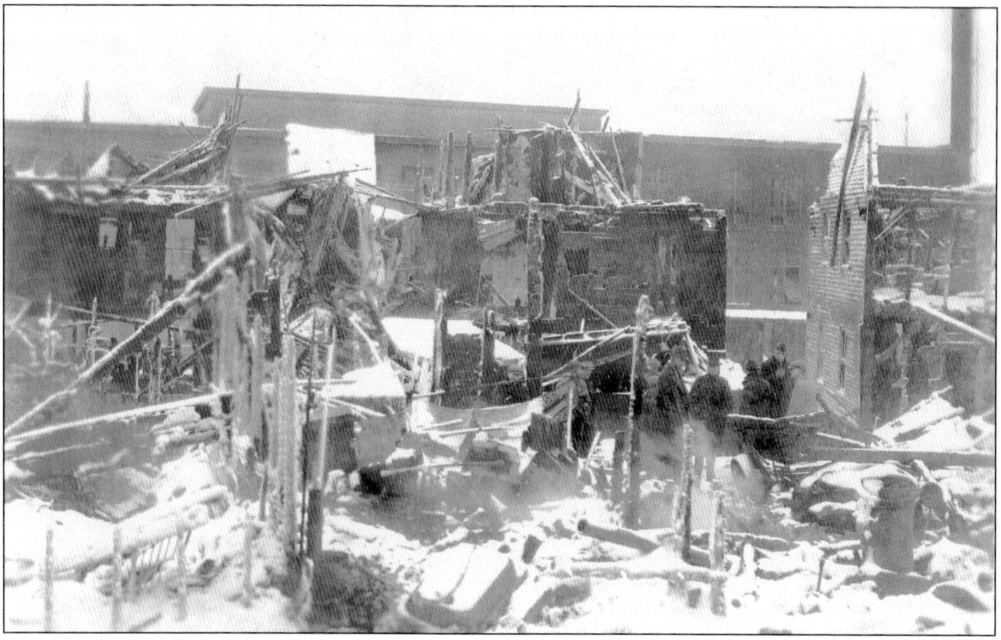

A second view of the April 2, 1924, fire shows its aftermath. Several men amble among the ruins, trying to make sense out of the calamity. Across North Main Street, the Ounegan Woolen Mill looms above the scene. Miraculously, the building was salvaged and still stands today. (OTM.)

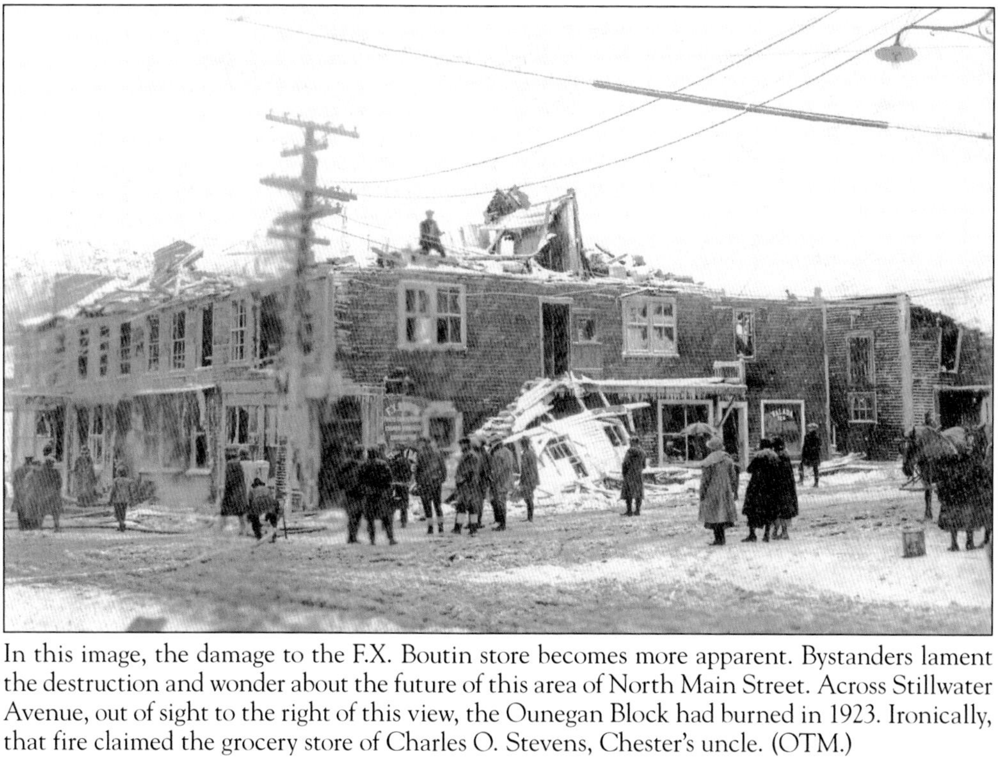

In this image, the damage to the F.X. Boutin store becomes more apparent. Bystanders lament the destruction and wonder about the future of this area of North Main Street. Across Stillwater Avenue, out of sight to the right of this view, the Ounegan Block had burned in 1923. Ironically, that fire claimed the grocery store of Charles O. Stevens, Chester's uncle. (OTM.)

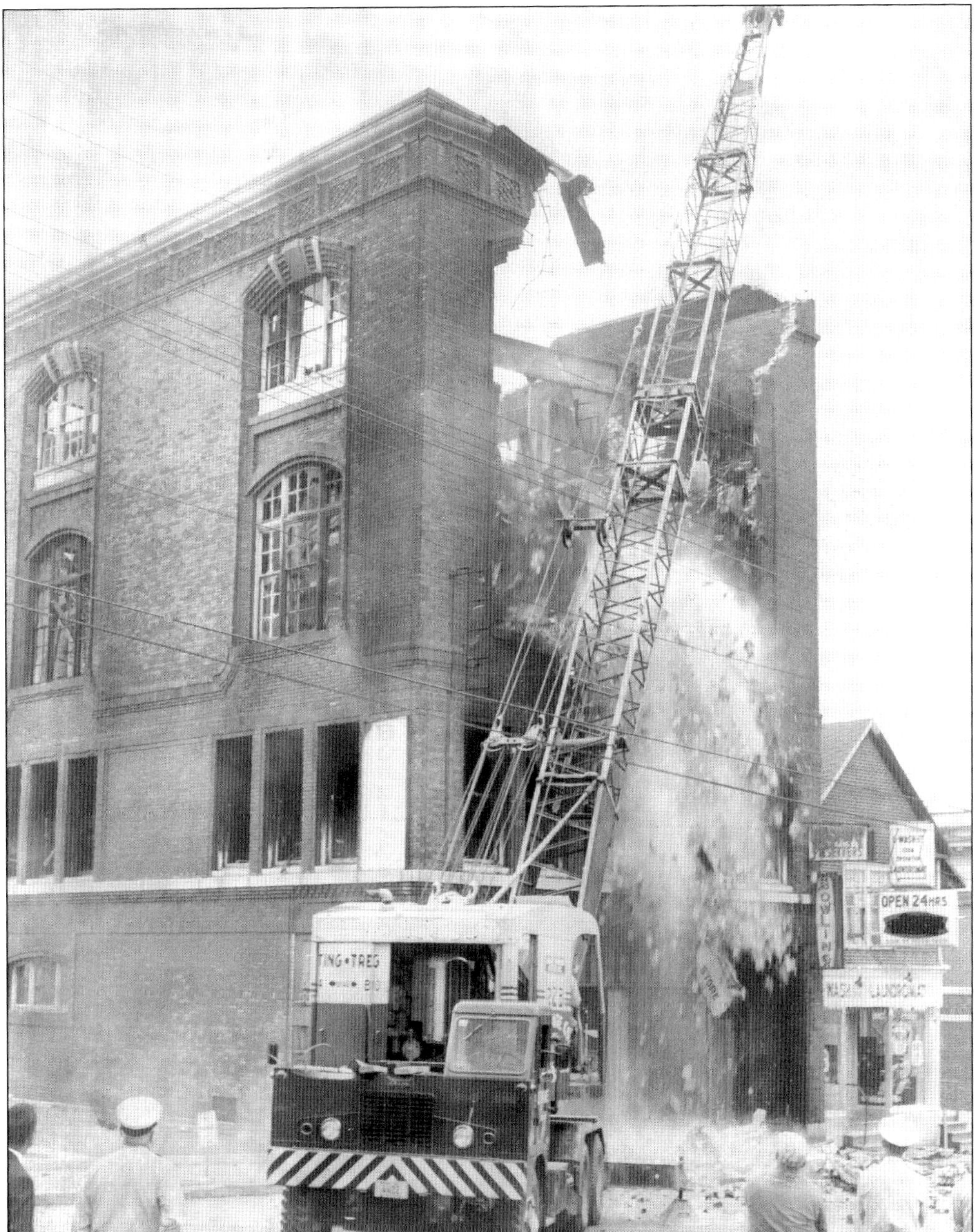

The durable Masonic Building stood on Center Street near the post office for decades before fire took its life on June 14, 1962. The hazards created by the weakened building were so perilous to people and property that the state fire inspector demanded the building's removal that day. Built around 1912, the structure was part of a building boom for the city, which also included a new post office, a new bank, and two new bridges. Times were good in 1912, with Old Town Canoe and the Bickmore Company enjoying national reputations and with two fabric mills, a paper mill, a pulp mill, and an abundance of railroad connections. (OTM.)

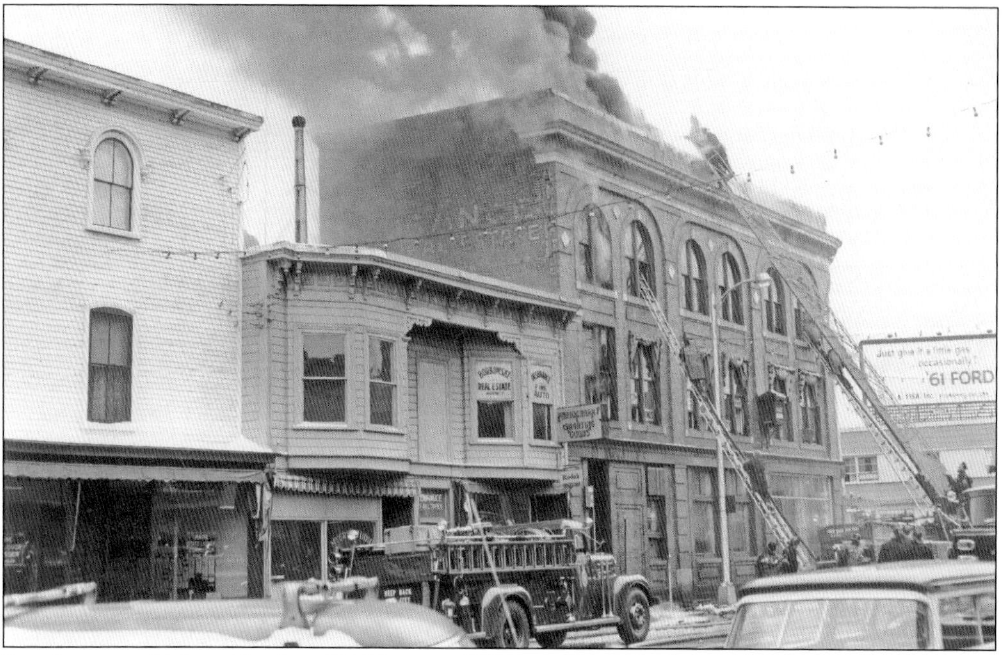

Fire threatened life and limb in Old Town on February 27, 1961, when a blaze broke out on the top floor of the Merrill Trust Building in the center of the business district. Simultaneously, alarms were sounded for the disappearance of a six-year-old boy. The worst was confirmed when he was found beneath the fire's rubble, fueling speculation about how the fire started. (OTM.)

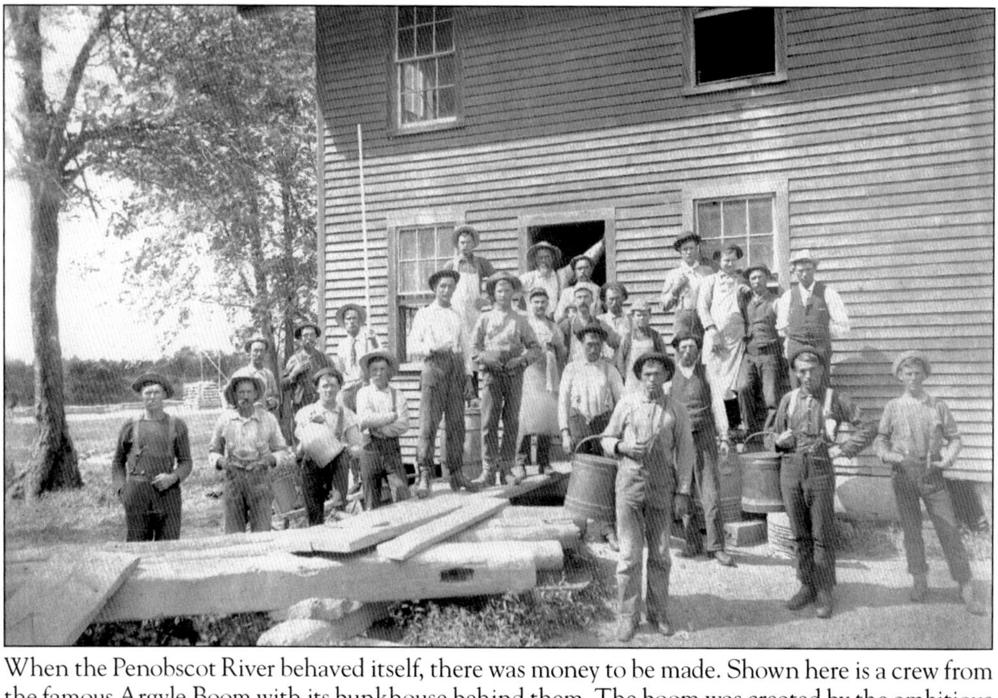

When the Penobscot River behaved itself, there was money to be made. Shown here is a crew from the famous Argyle Boom with its bunkhouse behind them. The boom was created by the ambitious Gen. Samuel Veazie in 1837 on his way to owning more than 100 sawmills on the Penobscot. The cribwork contained sorting pens used to tag logs to their various owners. (OTM.)

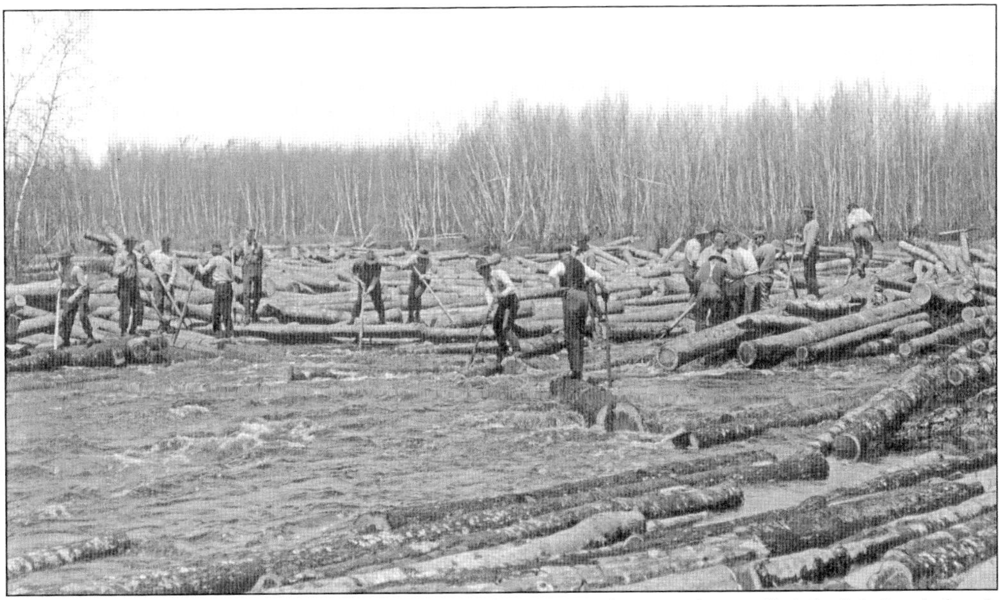

A score of men apply their skills in breaking up a logjam on what was then called the Medenekehunk Stream during high water in the spring of about 1910. River drivers prided themselves on their athletic skills and ability to stay on a log as it rolled and tossed about in the foamy waters. The Medenekehunk name is no longer in use. (OTM.)

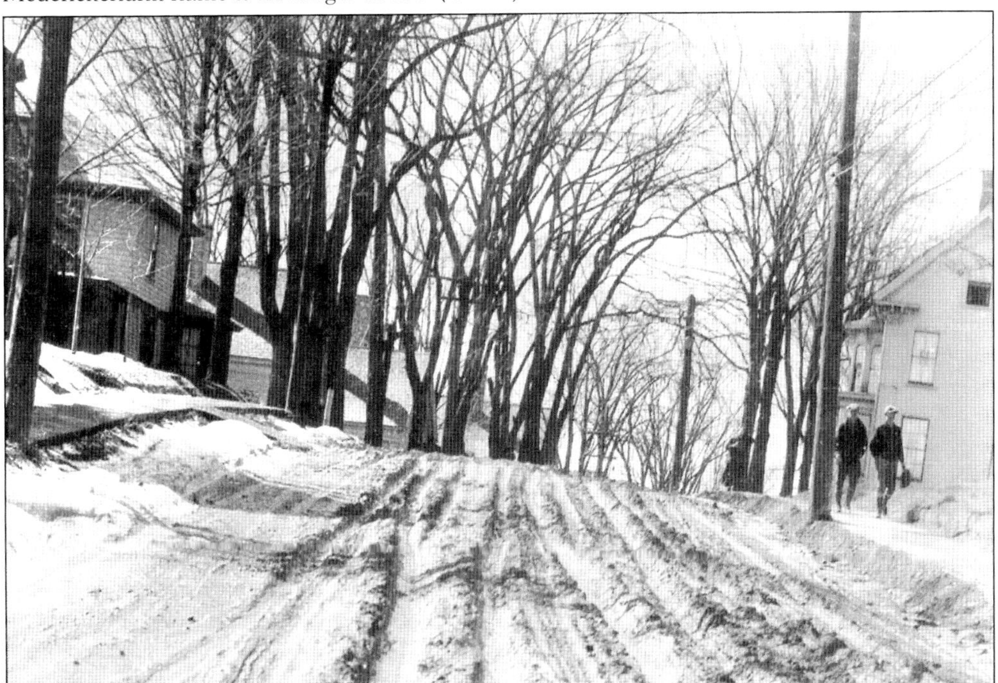

Perhaps no image better captures the need for highway improvement than this March 1925 photograph of Center Street during "mud season," that season in Maine between winter and spring. Fortunately, automobiles built back in the day were high off the ground and wore thin tires and wheels, which made getting stuck in the mud more difficult than with today's cars. (OTPL.)

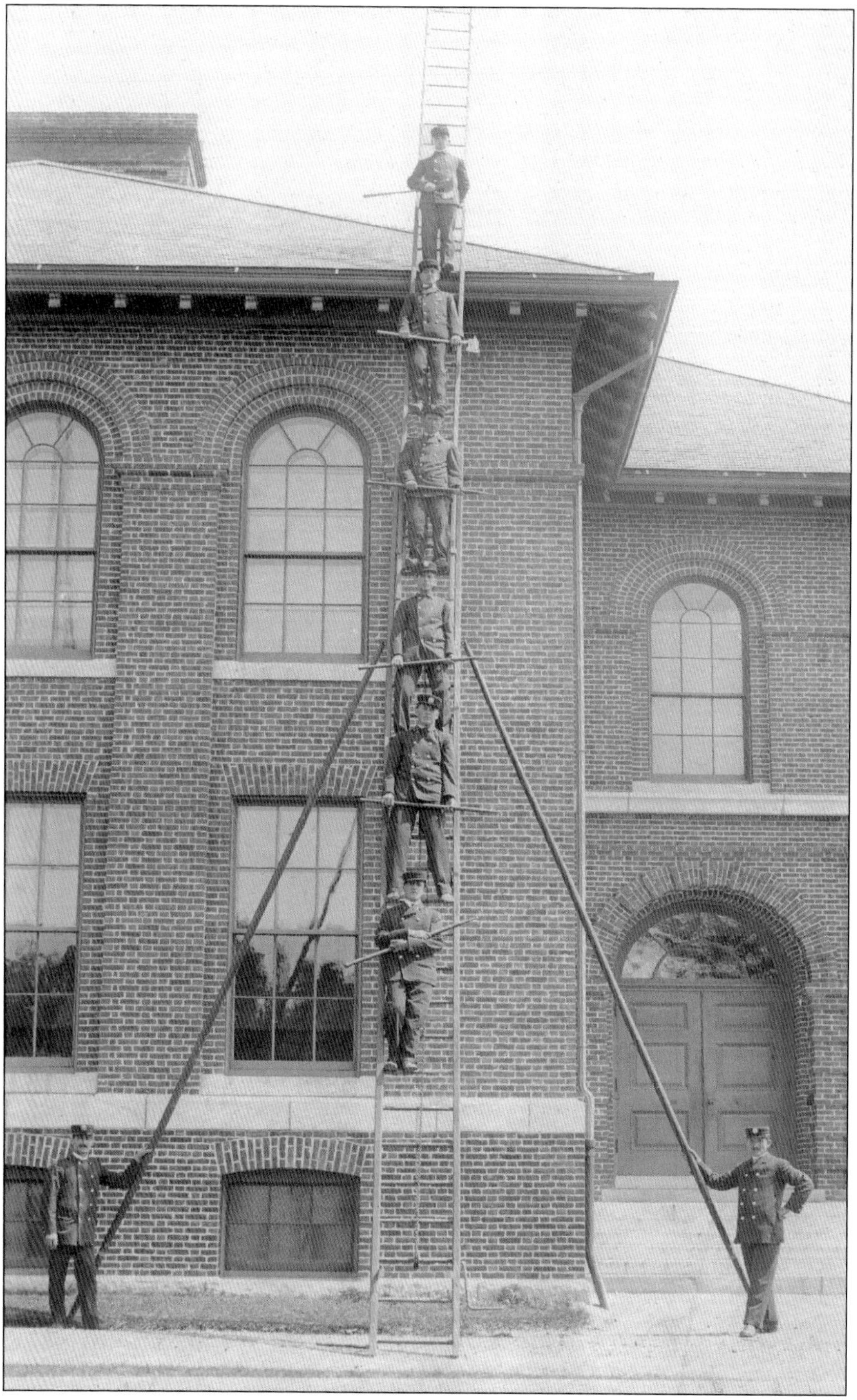

Firemen at the Helen Hunt School demonstrate that students are in good hands during a fire emergency. Taken just a few years after the school opened July 12, 1915, the photograph seems to imply that the new brick schools in town were inherently less prone to fire than those made from wood. (OTM.)

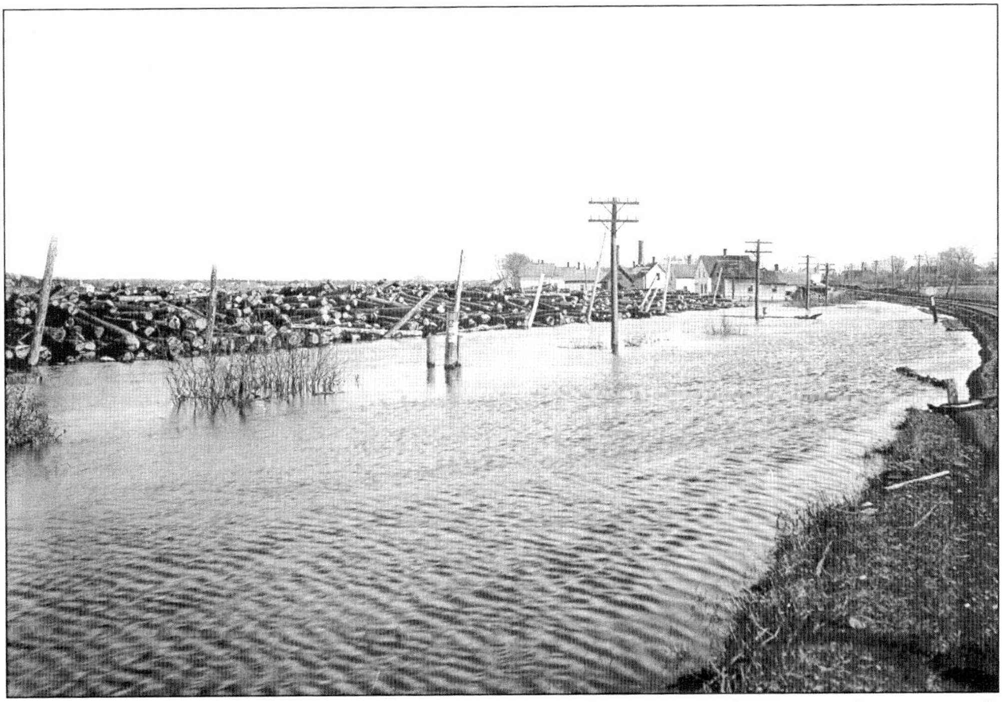

The disruption to Old Town's business flow is shown in this image. In this image taken just south of the Penobscot Chemical Fibre Company, the tracks of the Maine Central Railroad are in danger of being weakened by the rising floodwaters. The Penobscot River is out of sight in this image but lies to the left of the log piles. (OTPL.)

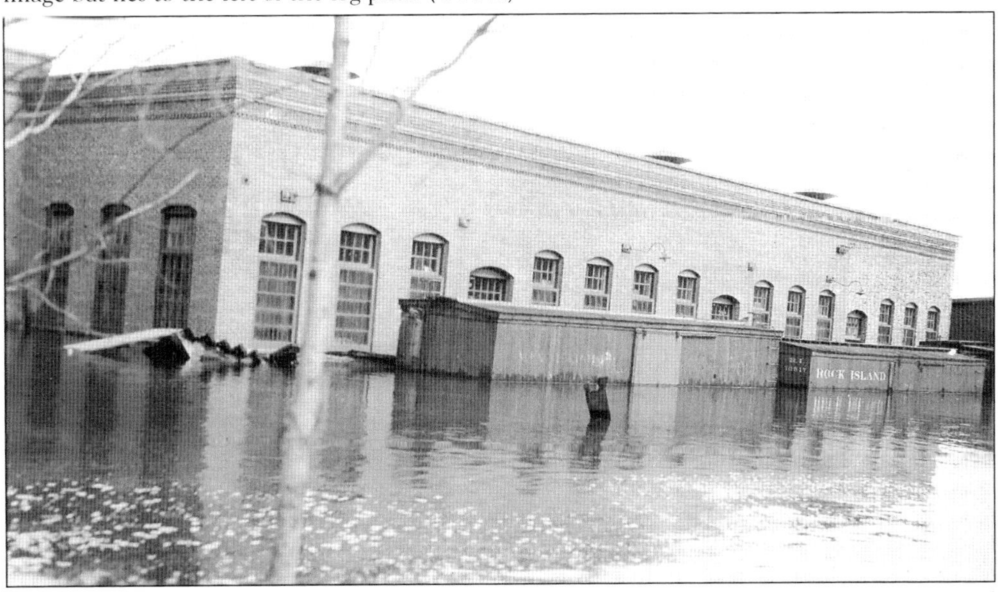

The Nekonegan Paper Company's plant just south of the Ounegan Woolen Mill was completed late in 1900, providing jobs for more than 200 people. Situated next to the Penobscot River, it was subject to its whims. The mill is shown here in 1923 during one of the worst floods in Old Town's history. Locals later called the building the "Pie Plate" when its product line shifted to pressed plates. (OTM.)

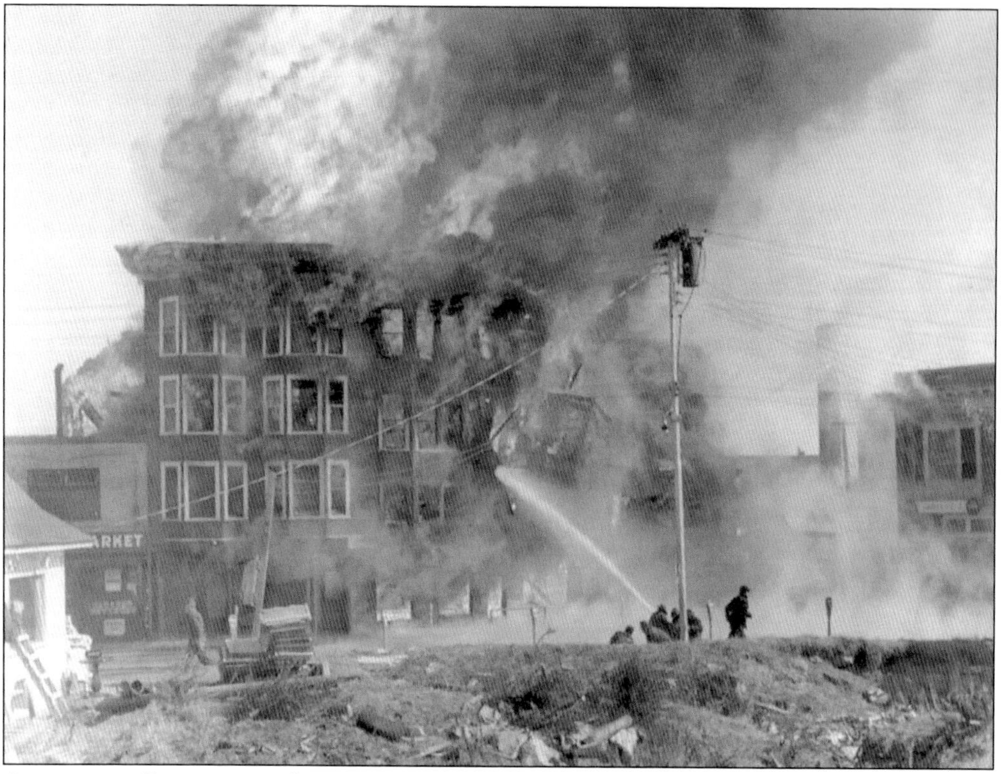

A cement wall separating the two structures spared the Fransway Hotel when the Thomas P. Murphy furniture store burned in 1913, but in 1953, the hotel burned in a spectacular blaze that destroyed nearby businesses and took more than 80 firefighters to contain. Thirty-seven people were left homeless by the fire, with significant water damage to several businesses, including Sklar's. (BHP.)

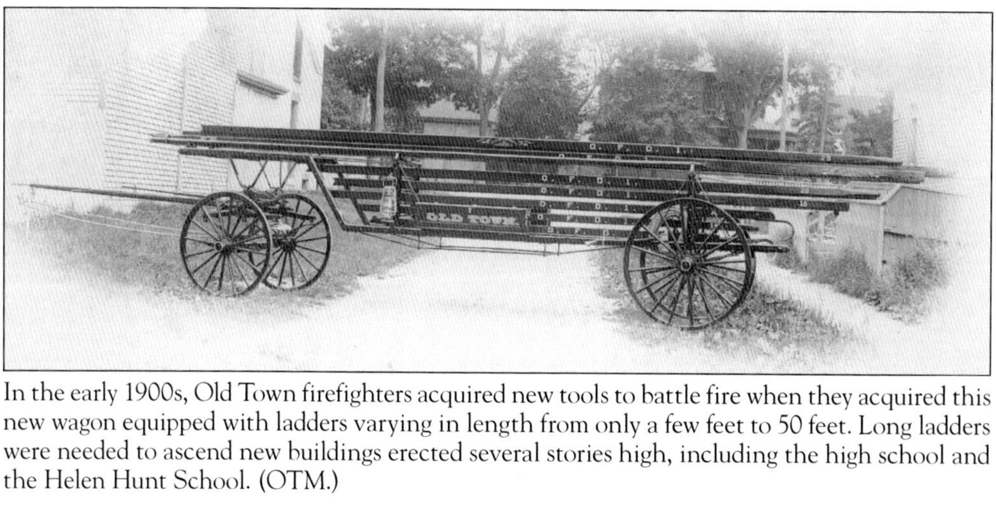

In the early 1900s, Old Town firefighters acquired new tools to battle fire when they acquired this new wagon equipped with ladders varying in length from only a few feet to 50 feet. Long ladders were needed to ascend new buildings erected several stories high, including the high school and the Helen Hunt School. (OTM.)

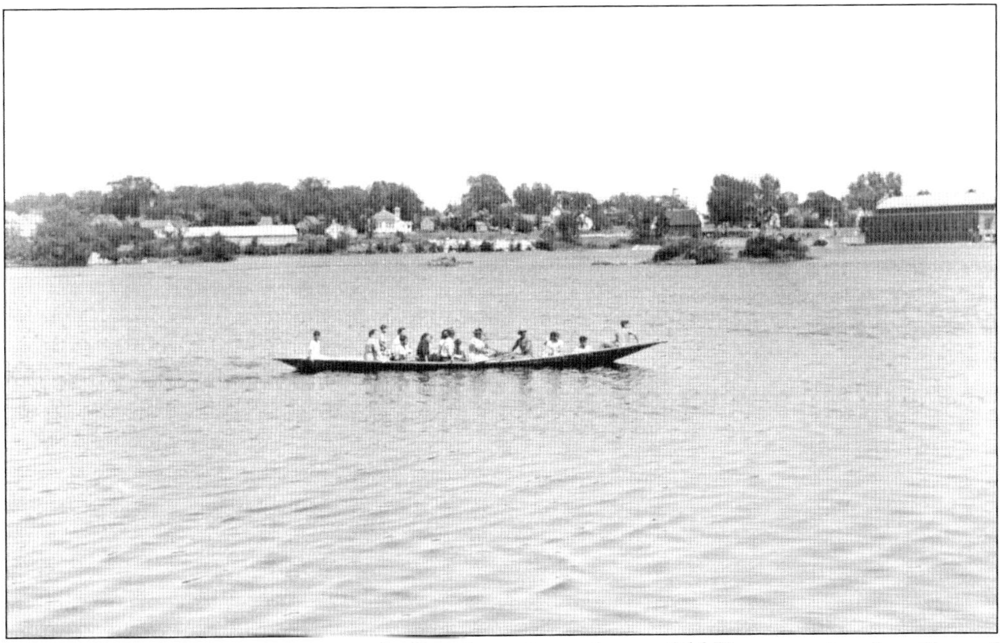

More than a dozen passengers cross the Penobscot River ferry to Old Town, passing the village of Milford in the background. Bateaux were built in various sizes for differing applications as ferries, on log drives, in the sawmills, and in the paper mills as well. (OTM.)

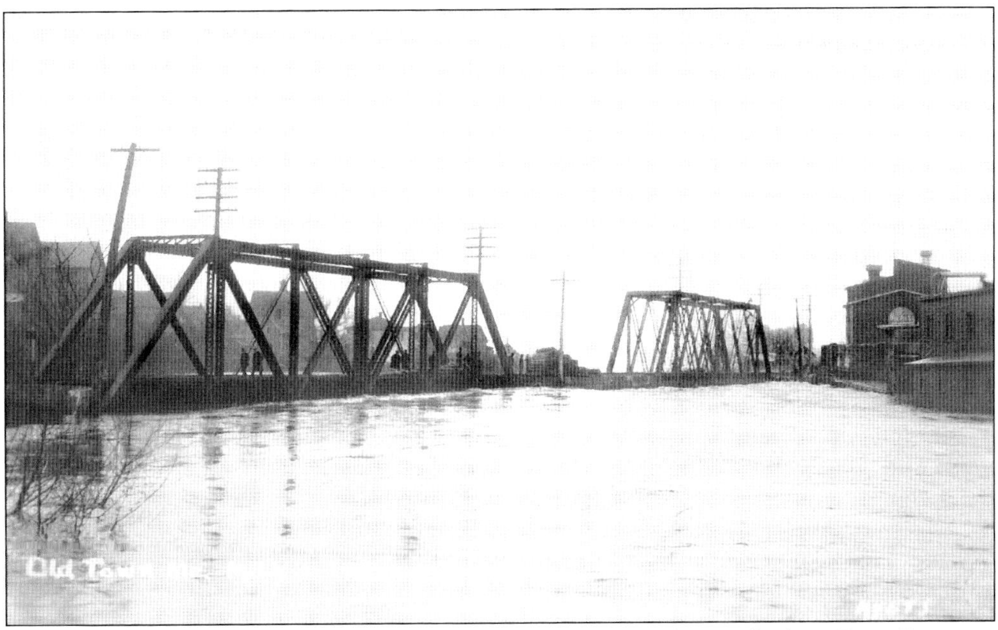

The Maine Central Railroad bridge splits the Penobscot River diagonally from Front Street on French Island to Water Street in Old Town on the right. Photographer Frank Myers took this image on May 1, 1923. The bridge may have been the only passable connecting structure. Water has climbed to the supports underneath, to a rise of about 15 feet. (OTM.)

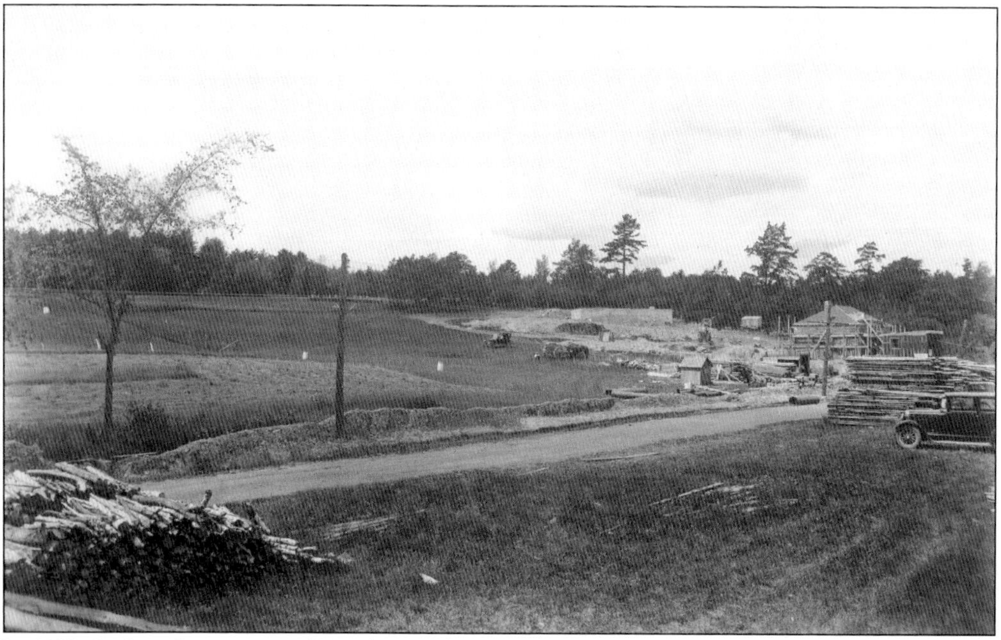

In 1929, the bucolic pastures of North Fourth Street and Gilman Falls Avenue were punctuated by the construction of the Old Town Water Company buildings on the site of the old Gray shingle mill. Land of Lucy A. Bachelder, an abutter, was taken by eminent domain for the pumping station, which was built by the Barrington Company of Boston, Massachusetts. (OTM.)

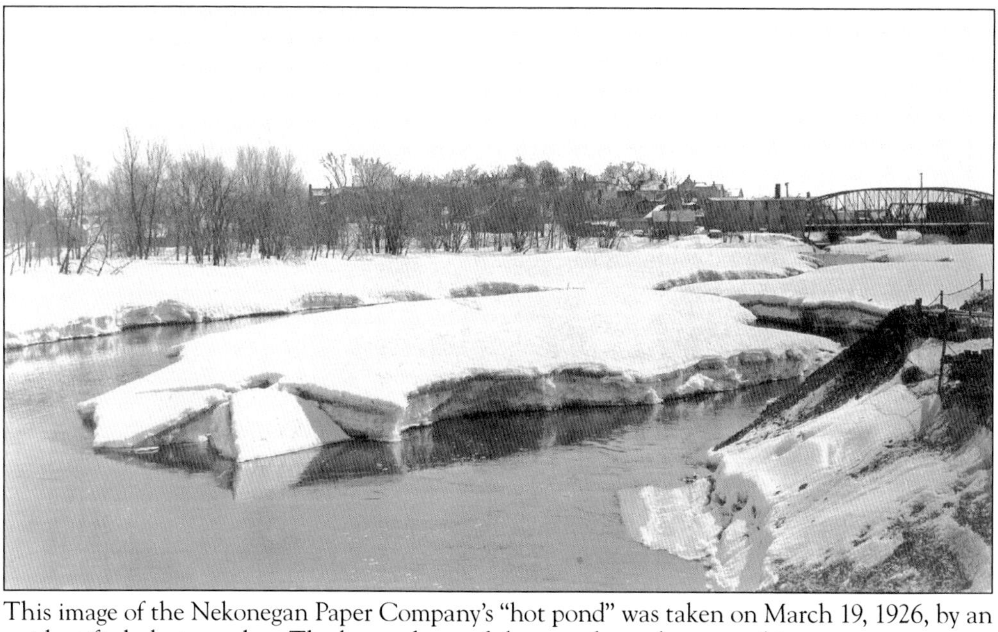

This image of the Nekonegan Paper Company's "hot pond" was taken on March 19, 1926, by an unidentified photographer. The by-products of the superheated papermaking process were not allowed to cool before being discharged directly into the Penobscot River. As a result, ice was prevented from forming where the hot water mixture entered the river. (OTPL.)

Six

People

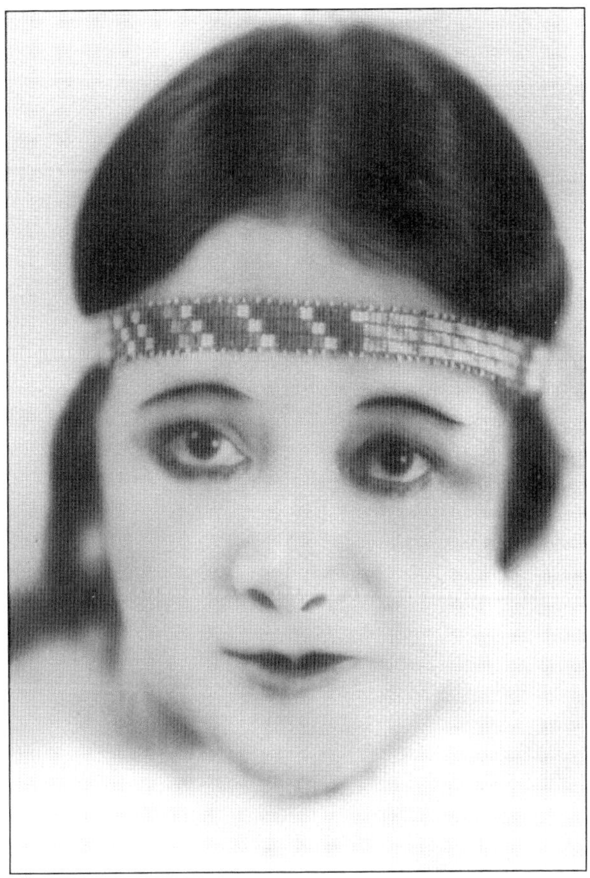

Lucy Nicolar, descended from the French Baron de Castin and Chief Josef Orono of the Penobscot Nation, displayed extraordinary talent as a young singer and interpreter of her people to the world outside her island. This image of Lucy was taken as she left Indian Island to seek her way in the entertainment industry. Known as Princess Watahwaso, Lucy toured on the Redpath Chautauqua Circuit for several years. The Penobscot Nation produced many widely known people: entertainer Molly Spotted Elk, Joe Attien (Henry David Thoreau's guide), Joe Polis, Molly Molasses, sports figures Louis Socklexis and Andrew Sockalexis, author-historian Joseph Nicolar, and his grandson, Charles Norman Shay, recipient of the French Legion of Honor in 2007. (CNS.)

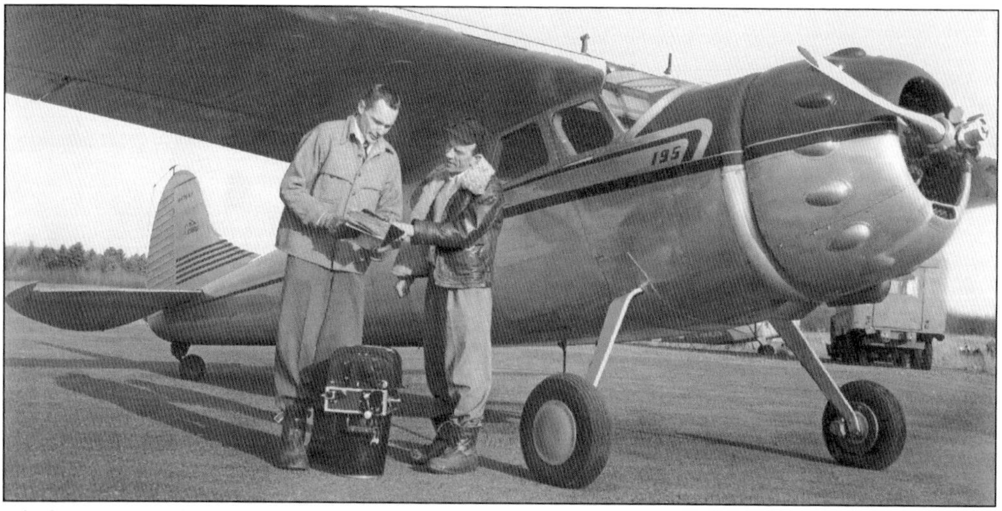

Clark Young Sr. (left) began as a forester with the James W. Sewall Company and moved up to vice president. He once piloted a twin-engine Apache airplane to Anchorage, Alaska. Fellow pilot Charles St. Lawrence (right) was also an aerial photographer. He was once deemed lost in a blinding snowstorm but turned up safely in what was called a "thousand-to-one" shot. (CLW.)

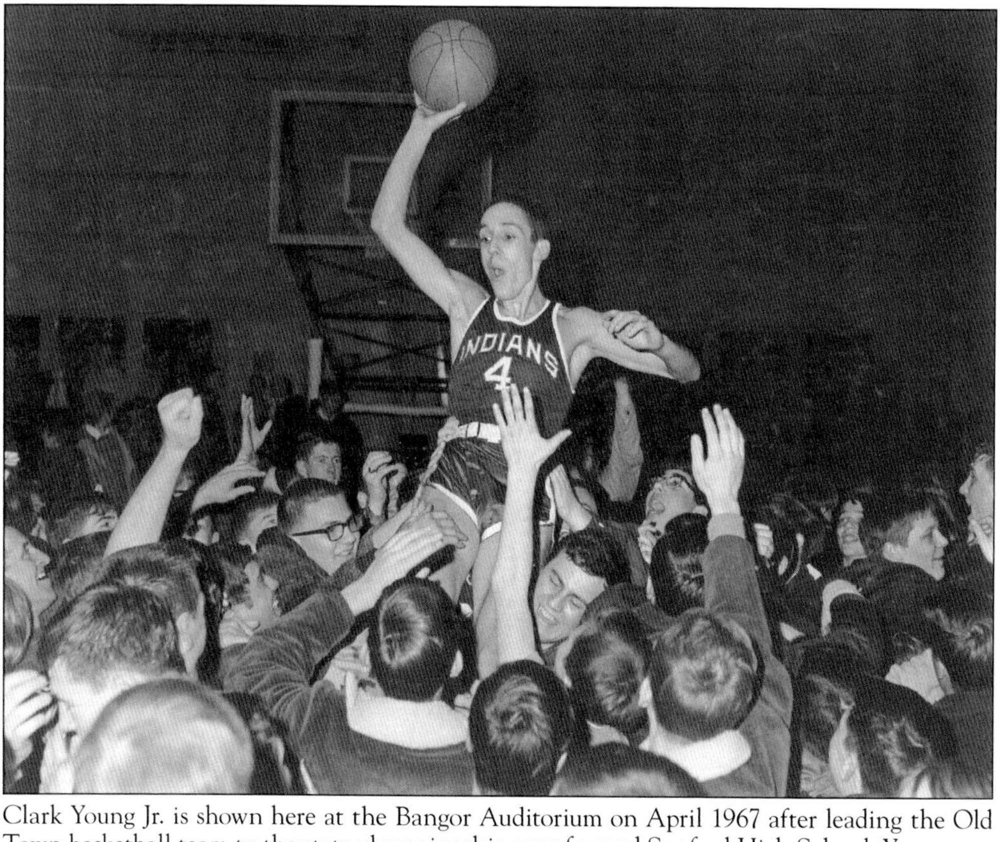

Clark Young Jr. is shown here at the Bangor Auditorium on April 1967 after leading the Old Town basketball team to the state championship over favored Sanford High School. Young was selected to the all-state basketball team both in 1967 and 1968. Young and his backcourt mate, Kevin Baker, remain legendary in Maine sports circles. (CAY.)

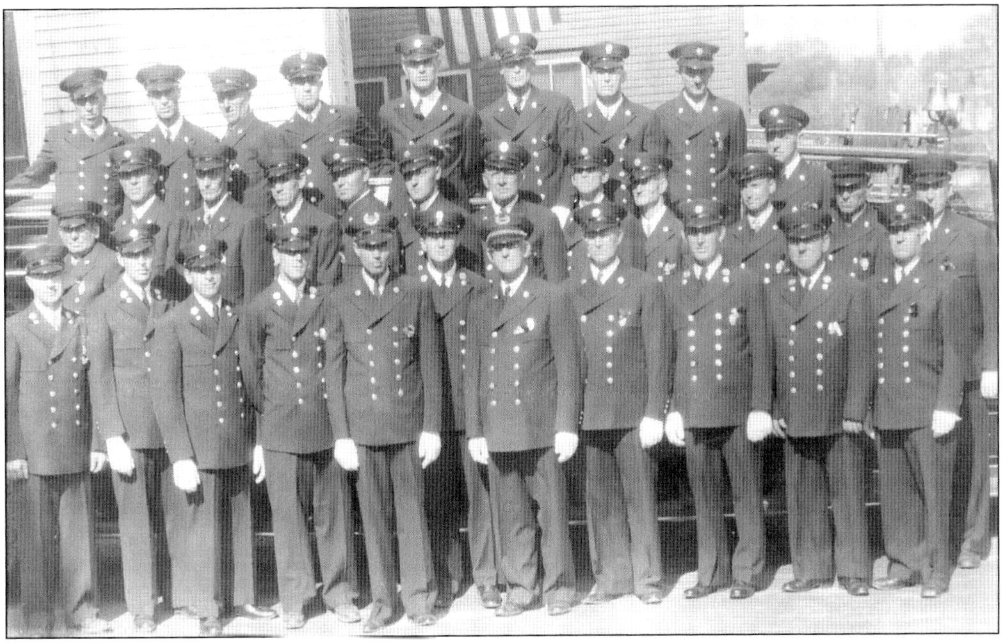

In 1938, the Old Town's Fire Department featured, from left to right, (first row) Merle Mitchell, George Cook, Walter LeBretton, Ed Savoy, Bryan Sibley, Charles Lowell, Walter Hellenbrand, L. Shirland, David Simon, Emile Landry, and Albert Fournier; (second row) Cleve Cyr, M. Collette, John Lawson, Edward Cote, Edmund Voter, Mark Gilman, Alexis Nadeau, Belonie Duplessis, Angus Richards, Gerard Morin, Archie Richard, and Claude Lovely; (third row) Alphonse Seymour, E. King, Noah Pelletier, Ray White, Andrew Bosse, Mervyn Gilman, Ralph Daigle, George Braley, and Chauncey Miller. (OTM.)

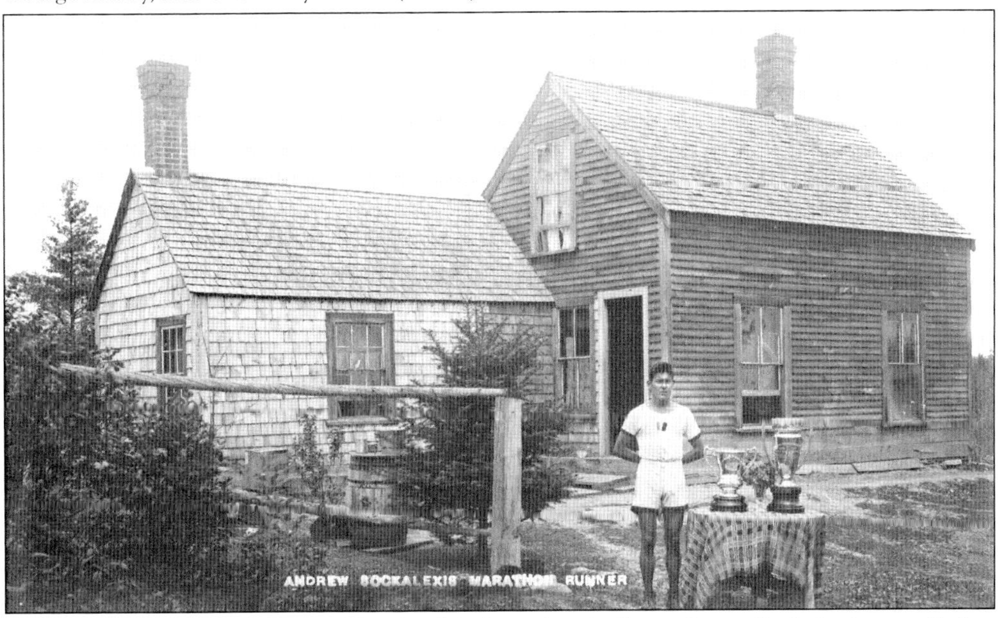

Andrew Sockalexis, cousin to Cleveland Indians baseball star Louis Sockalexis, excelled at running, finishing second in the Boston Marathon in 1912 and 1913 and fourth in the marathon at the Olympic Games in Stockholm in 1912. (MHPC.)

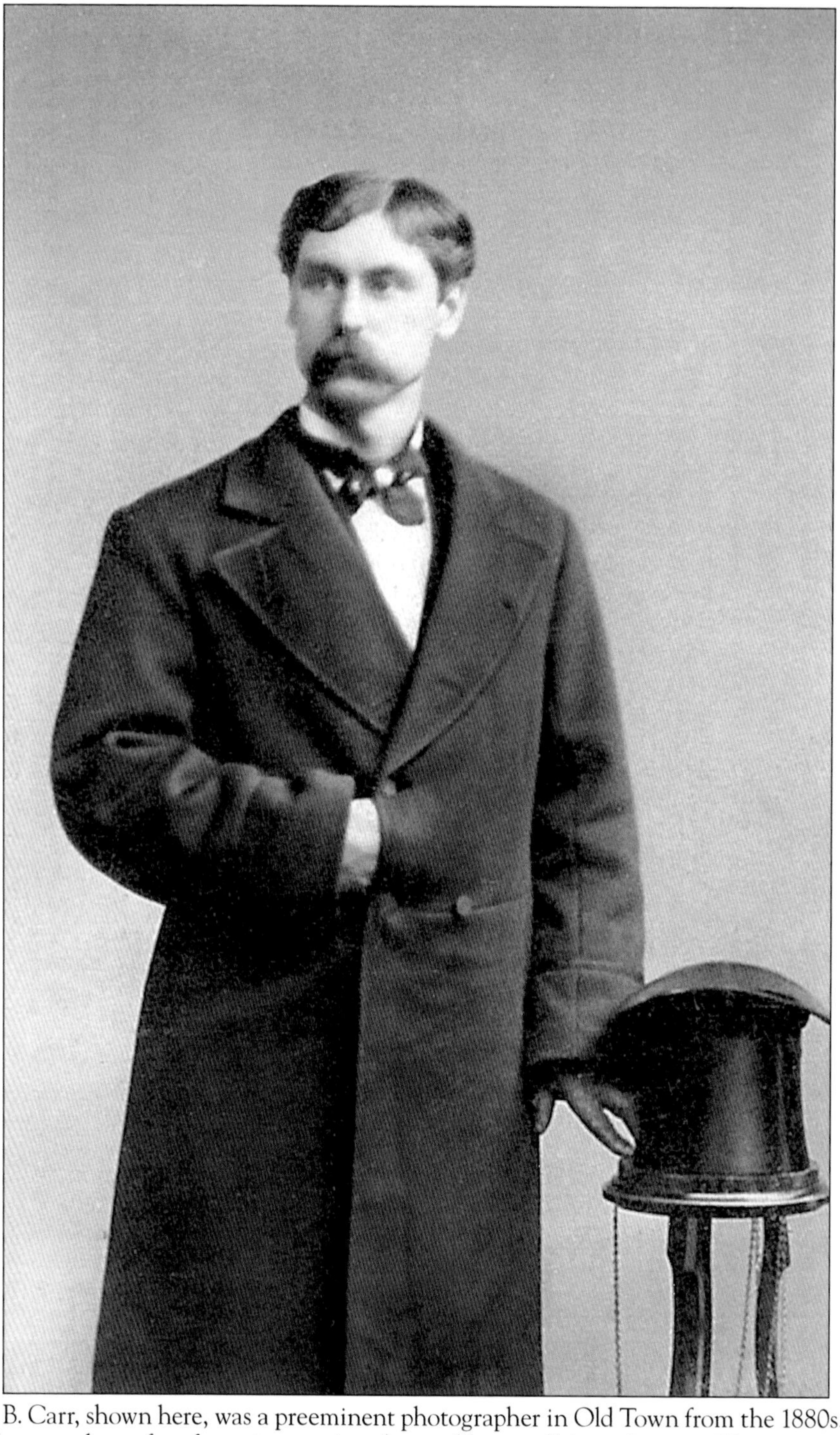

Almon B. Carr, shown here, was a preeminent photographer in Old Town from the 1880s. Many of his photographs surface from time to time, but no library of his work exists. The same is true of other talented area photographers, with the partial exception of M.G. Gilmore, who published a noteworthy souvenir booklet of the Old Town Orono area in 1894. The dozens of images contained therein provide priceless glimpses of the way life used to be. (OTM.)

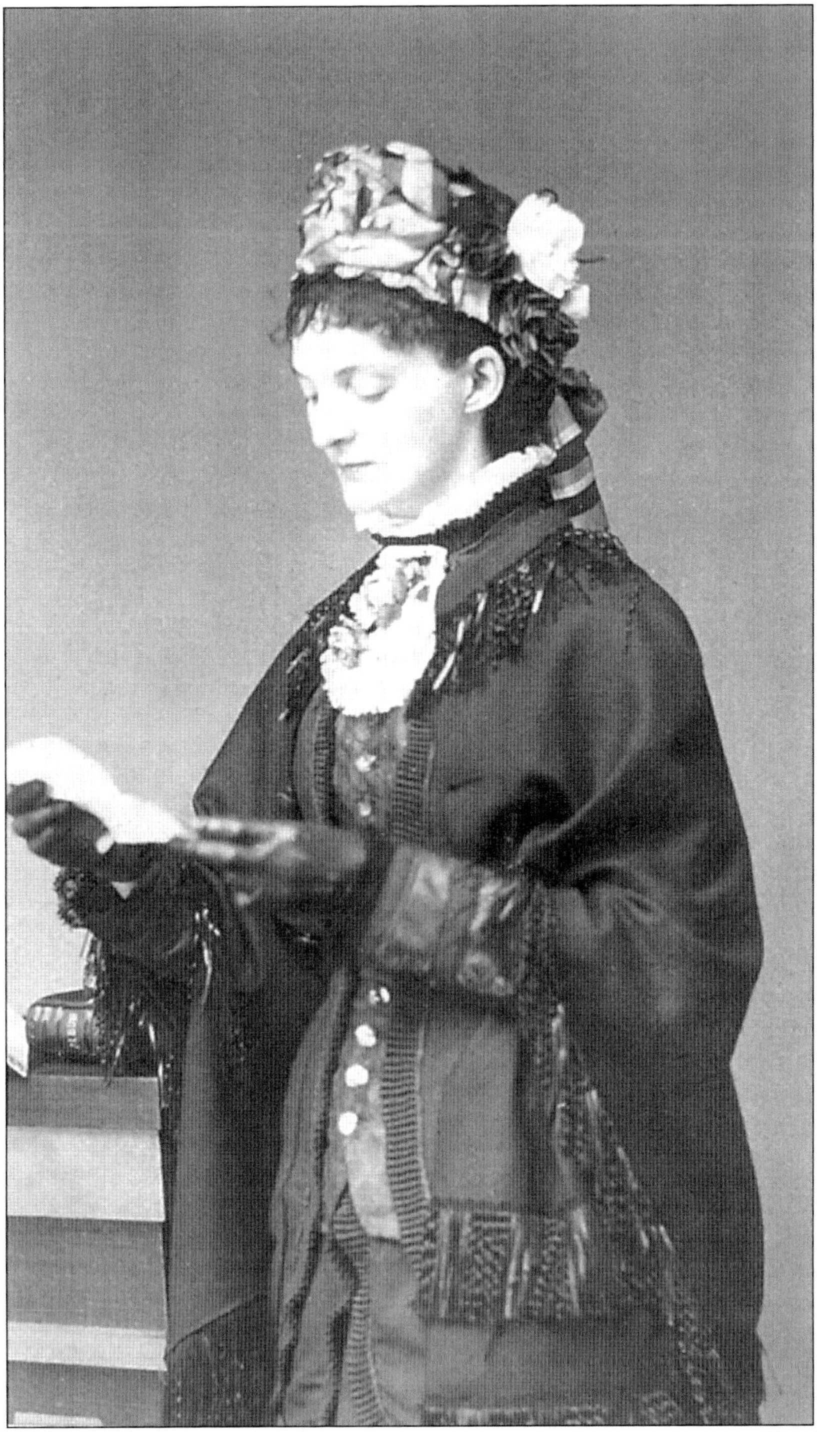

Amelia L. Carr is shown here in a rare image complementing the preceding image of her husband. Old Town photographers often advertised their services in the local newspaper and high school yearbook but managed to keep their names from local news articles. Images by R.M. Howe and Charles F. Rhodes can be found at the Maine Historic Preservation Commission. (OTM.)

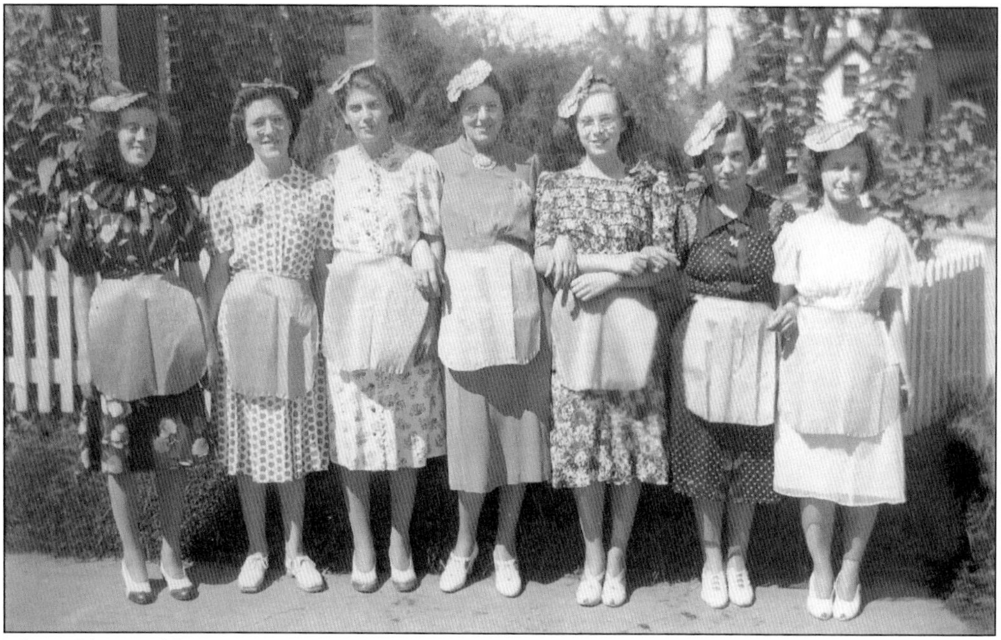

The golden wedding anniversary of Charles and Sophie Dubay, at their home on Hayes Street on French Island in 1939, provided this image. Serving as waitresses were, from left to right, Phoebe Sirois, Thelma Richard, Lorraine Dubay, Florence Dubay, Frances Sirois, Louise Richard, and Eva Brilliant. Phoebe, Frances, and Lorraine were granddaughters, and Florence was a daughter-in-law. (BHP.)

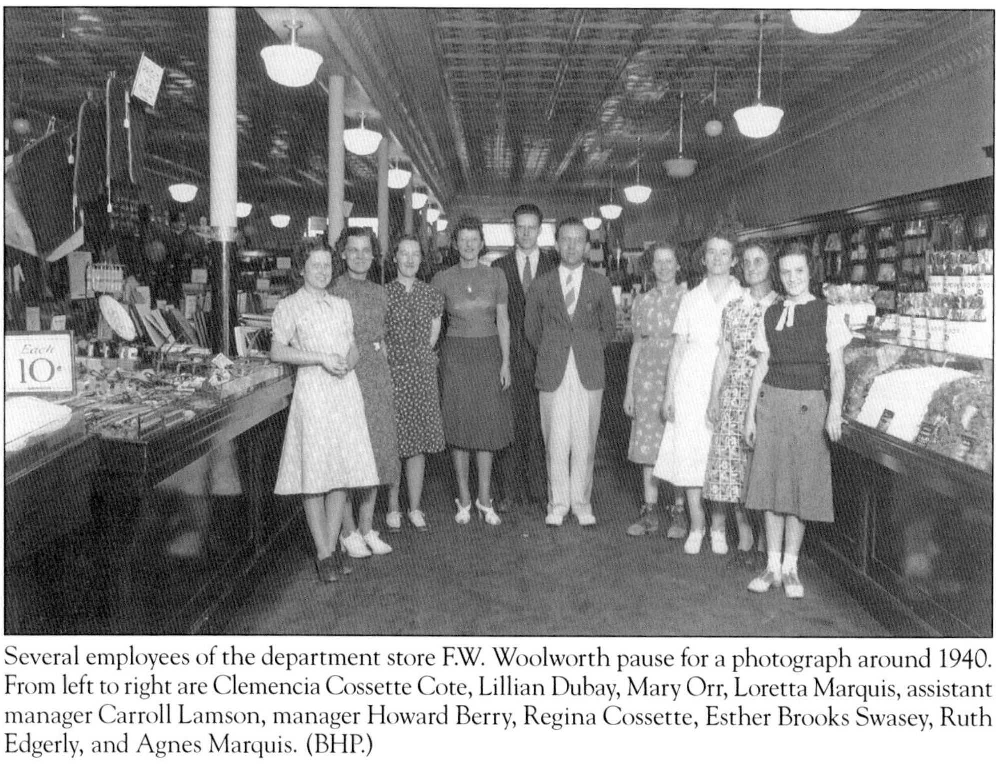

Several employees of the department store F.W. Woolworth pause for a photograph around 1940. From left to right are Clemencia Cossette Cote, Lillian Dubay, Mary Orr, Loretta Marquis, assistant manager Carroll Lamson, manager Howard Berry, Regina Cossette, Esther Brooks Swasey, Ruth Edgerly, and Agnes Marquis. (BHP.)

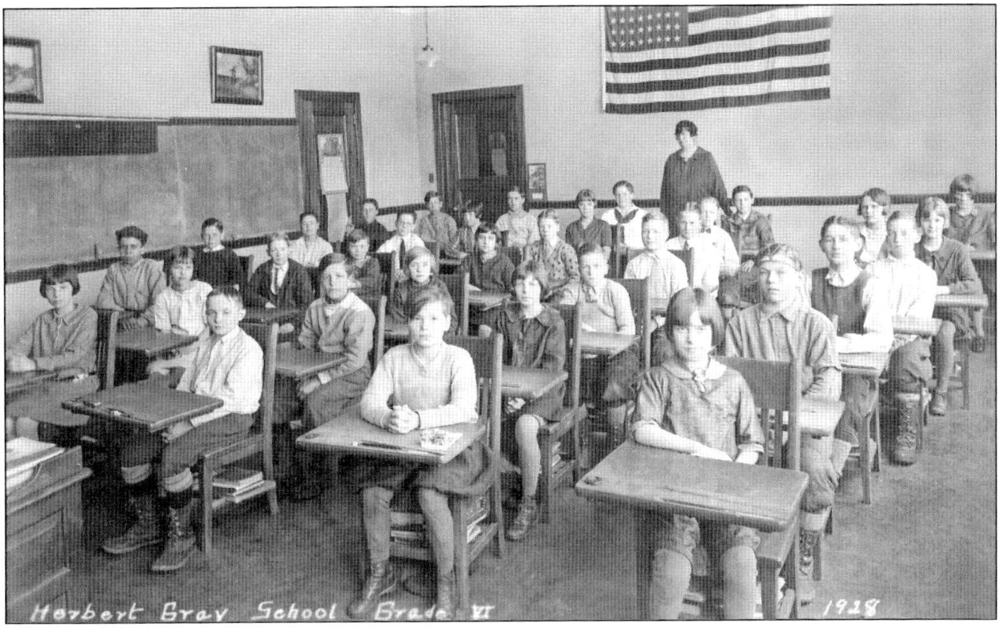

Shown here in 1928 is a class at the Herbert Gray School. Pictured, from front to back, are (far left row) George Thibodeau, Laurence Severence, Kenneth Ashe, Preston Way, and Clayton Boyington; (second row from left) Pauline Darveau, Sarah Hinckley, Charles Bowley, Marguerite Davis, Alfred Craig, Ruth Ward, and Clarence McLeod; (third row from left) Moses Lord, Stanley Baranska, Priscilla Folsom, Rose Sklar, Prentiss Markle, Mabel Mayhew, and Ruth Gray; (second row from the right) Phyllis Lancaster, Thelma Murray, Clinton Cormier, Jackson Higgins, Penn Hussey, Donald Mann, and Arthur Rowe; (far right row) Bernice Bressette, Freeman Thibodeau, Fred Martin, Irvin Young, Eleanor Tibbetts, Eleanor Buck, and Pauline Bradford. The teacher is Isabel Conant. (CLM.)

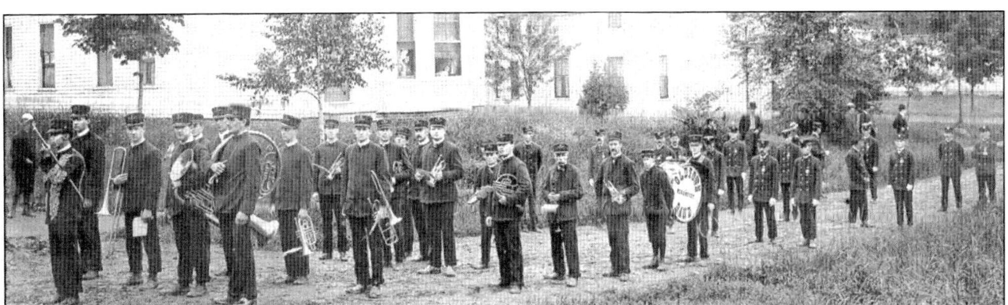

The Old Town Volunteer Band waits in the staging area for the Fourth of July parade to begin in 1906. (OTPL.)

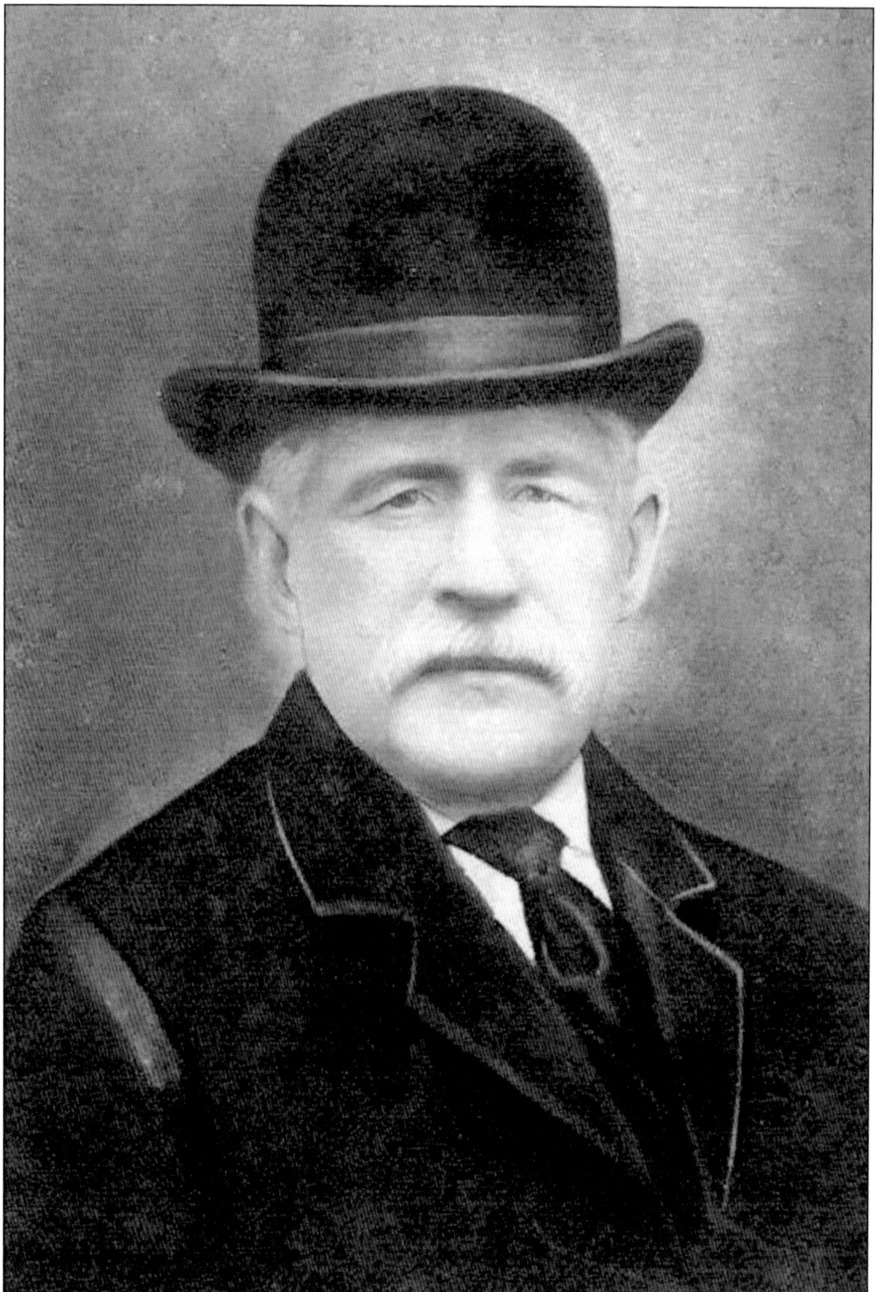

Herbert W. Gray was a driving business force in Old Town for decades. Besides supporting the development of the Old Town Canoe Company and the Bickmore Gall Cure Company, Gray brought the Old Town Woolen Company to North Main Street in 1888. He was one of the city's early mayors and the one who cleaned up its many saloons. He expanded his woolen mills holdings to include similar businesses in Guilford and Sangerville, Maine. Following the McKinley School fire in 1917, he and his nephew, Samuel Braley Gray, convinced the town to accept that rebuilding the popular school in the same location would be folly. The school erected on Stillwater Avenue in 1920 was named for him. (OTM.)

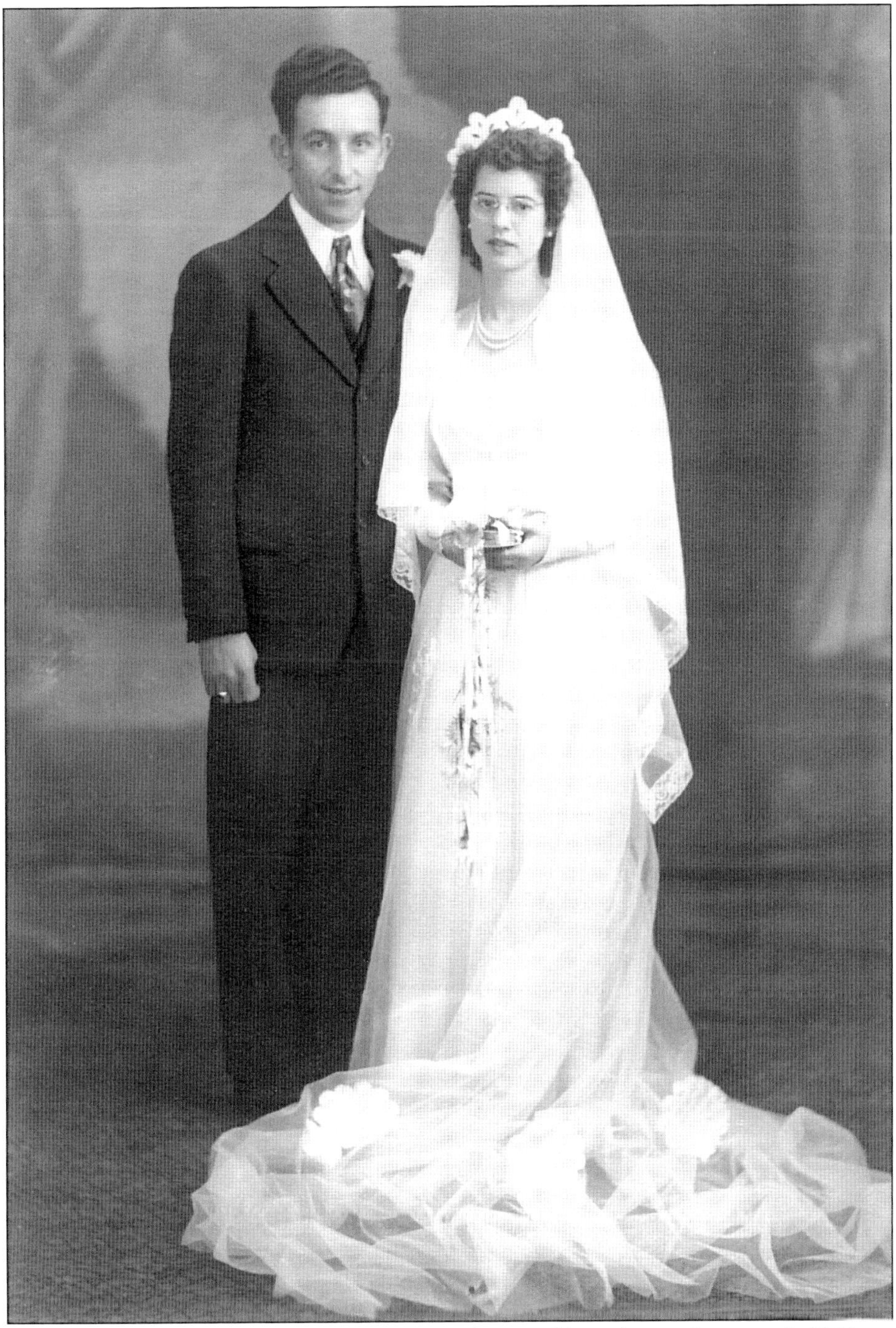

Mr. and Mrs. Clifford Doucette are shown on their wedding day on January 5, 1946, in St. Joseph's Catholic Church. They were better known as Dewey and Rita and had been engaged in September 1942 while Dewey was waiting to be called into the US Coast Guard. He was absent from Old Town for years at a time while serving his country. Rita remained close to both his and her families until he returned. Following their marriage, they made their home for a time with her parents on Hayes Street on French Island. (PRS.)

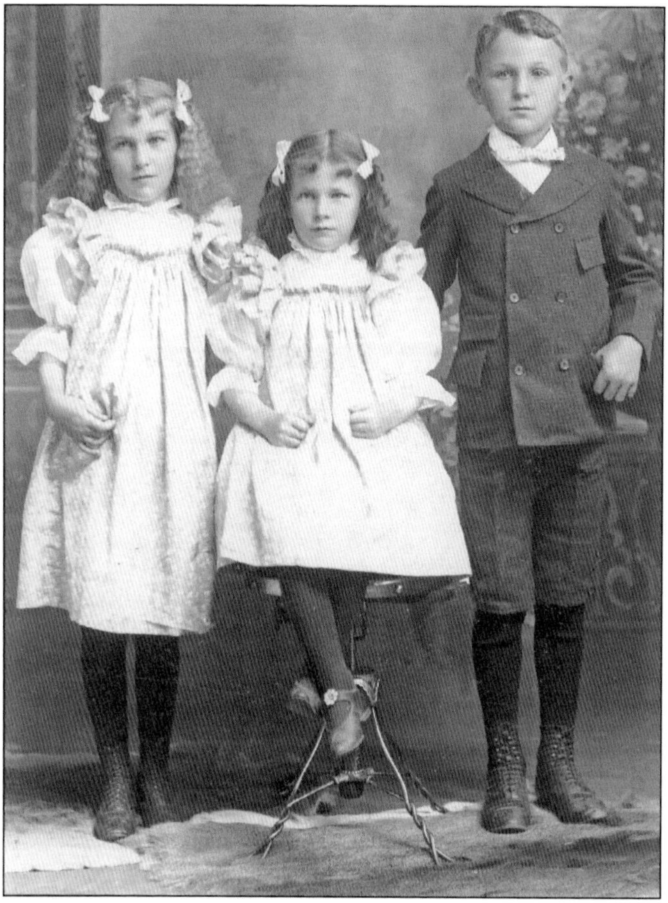

Edson Rand, of Alton, Maine, and his wife, Joanna C. Neally, hired Old Town photographer C.F. Rhodes to photograph their three youngest children, twins Hilma (left) and Harold and younger sister Hazel (center). The twins were born in 1889, and Hazel followed in 1891. (PRS.)

Carnation Day was held by various women's service clubs in town during the early 20th century. In 1916, the Our Neighborhood Club raised money for the junior high school. By 1926, the Neeburban Club had been selling the flowers for several years; during this year, the flowers were sold to benefit the public nurse fund. The image below is from 1915. (OTPL.)

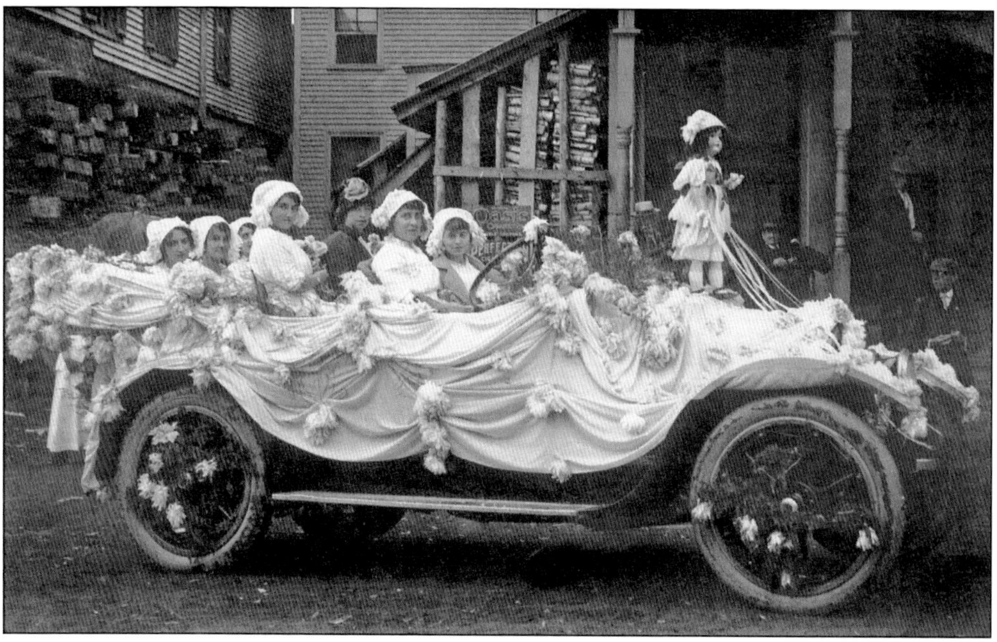

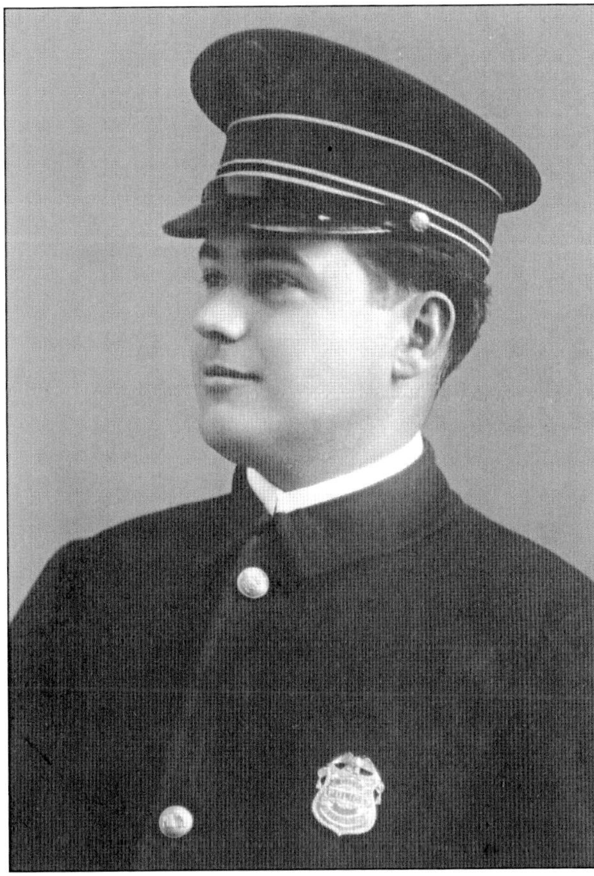

City marshal L. Phillip Tremblay occupied a position of public trust when he gave a false name during a police check in Aroostook County in 1920. An ongoing investigation revealed an illegal still at his home. He was suspended by the city council and later resigned. Tremblay moved to Boston, where he ran a successful liquor business once Prohibition ended. (PAD.)

Kiowa Indian Bruce Poolaw married Penobscot Lucy Nicholar, who was known as Princess Watahwaso during her singing career. Once ending their Redpath Chautauqua Circuit tour, they returned to Indian Island, where Chief Poolaw's Teepee became a big tourist draw. Lucy advocated for her people, successfully fighting for her people to vote and for a steel bridge to the mainland. (PRS.)

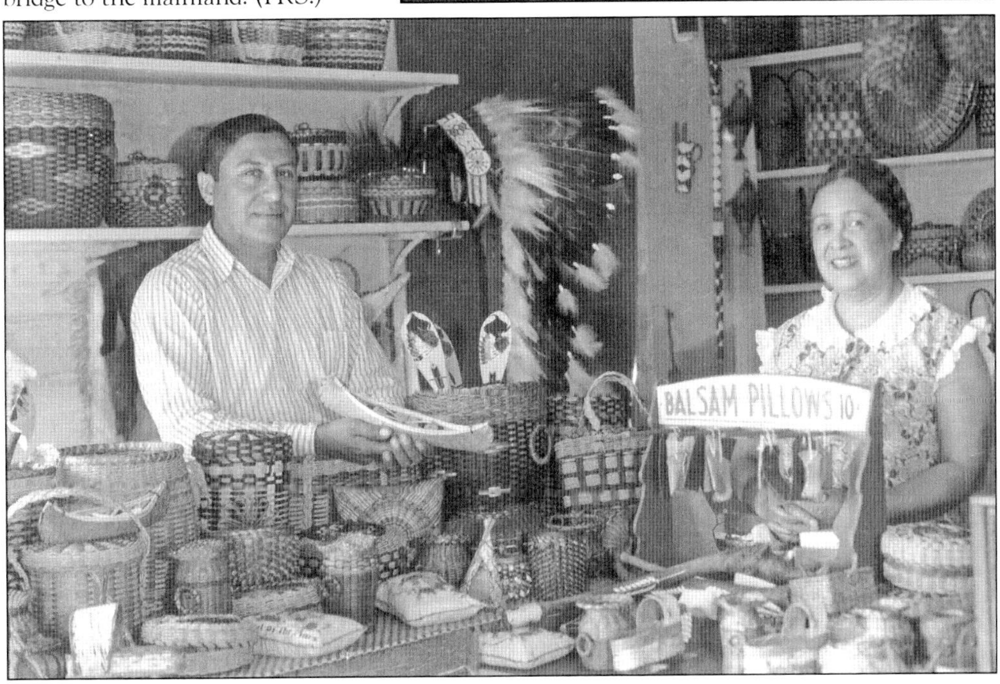

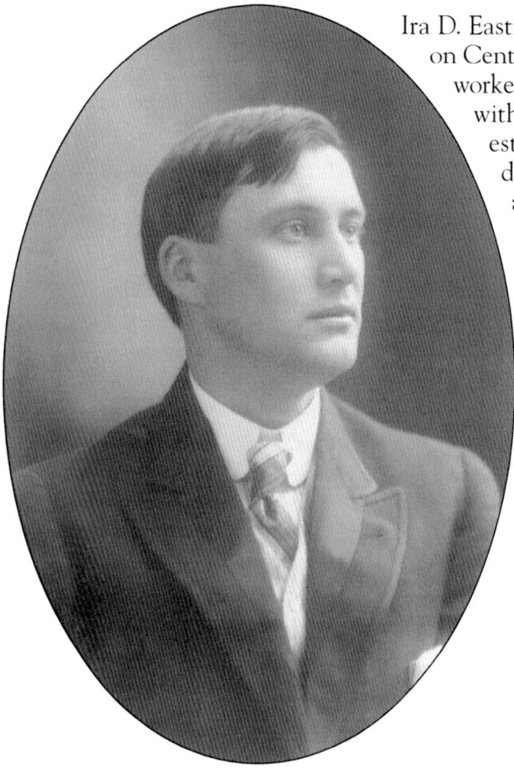

Ira D. Eastman hired A.J. Sampson to build Three Gates on Center Street in 1906. Eastman was a surveyor who worked with the State of Maine on its wildlands and with the James W. Sewall Company as well. A real estate dealer, Eastman lost much of his fortune during the stock market crash of October 1929 and died a few days later, never recovering from his loss. (DRP.)

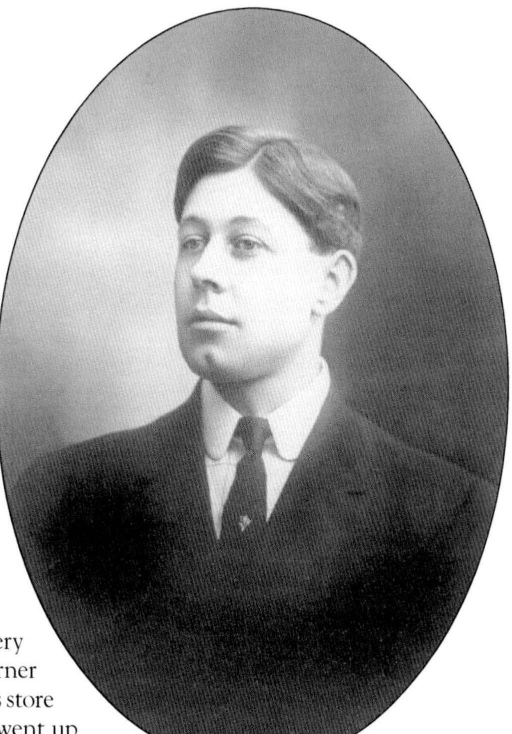

Chester M. Stevens was the proprietor of a grocery store in the Richardson-Kennedy Block at the corner of North Main Street and Stillwater Avenue. His store was one of many that burned when the block went up in flames in 1924. (DRP.)

Dr. Martin C. Maddan was a graduate of Bowdoin College School of Medicine in 1891 and practiced in Old Town for nearly half a century. When he retired in the late 1940s, the city proclaimed a "Dr. Maddan Day." Maddan was given a huge reception, and residents heaped upon him their admiration for all he had done. Maurice Gray was in charge of the festivities. (OTM.)

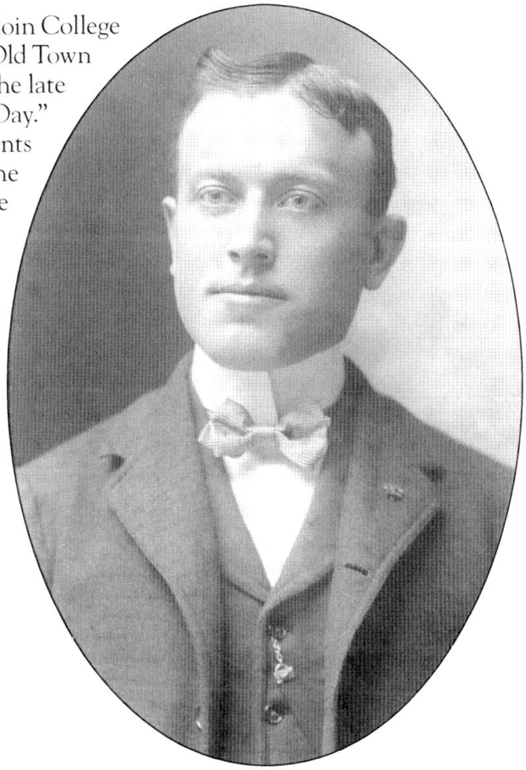

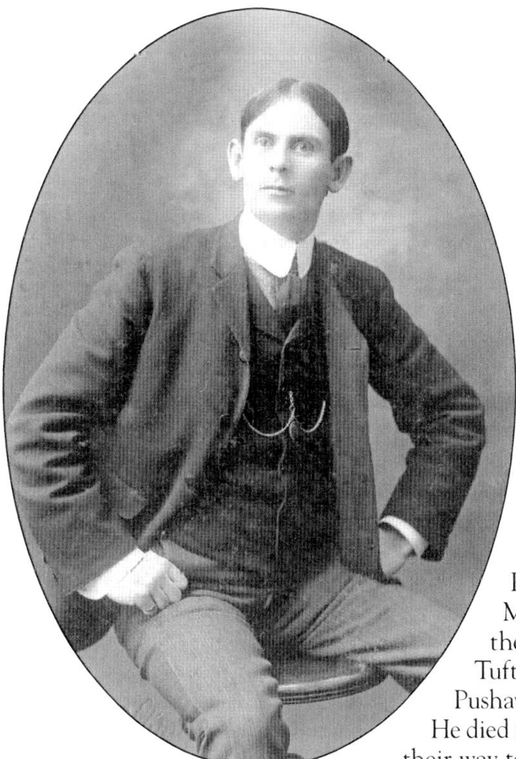

H.C. Mason, DDS, was a native of Ellsworth, Maine, who set up his dentistry practice in the Folsom Block in 1910. He was a graduate of Tufts Dental College. Mason owned a cottage at Pushaw Lake to enjoy during his 35 years of practice. He died in 1946, and eventually, his dental tools found their way to the Old Town Museum. (OTM.)

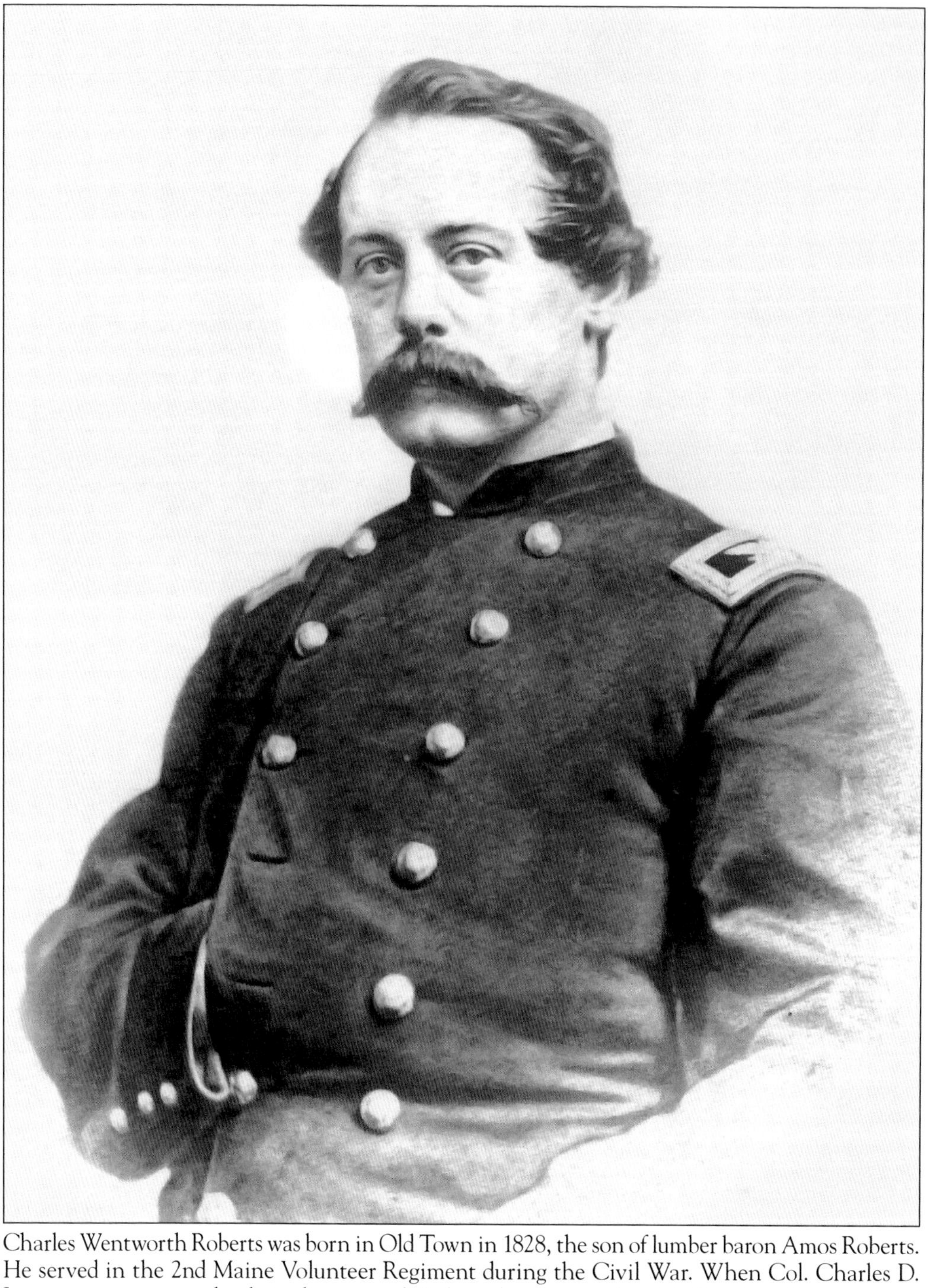

Charles Wentworth Roberts was born in Old Town in 1828, the son of lumber baron Amos Roberts. He served in the 2nd Maine Volunteer Regiment during the Civil War. When Col. Charles D. Jameson was promoted to brigadier general, Roberts became a colonel in his place. Seeing action as commander at the Battle of Second Bull Run, Roberts had his horse shot from beneath him but escaped without injury. He also led his troops at the Battle of Antietam. Roberts resigned his commission due to ill health and built a house on State Street in Bangor, which is now in the National Register of Historic Places. (PRS.)

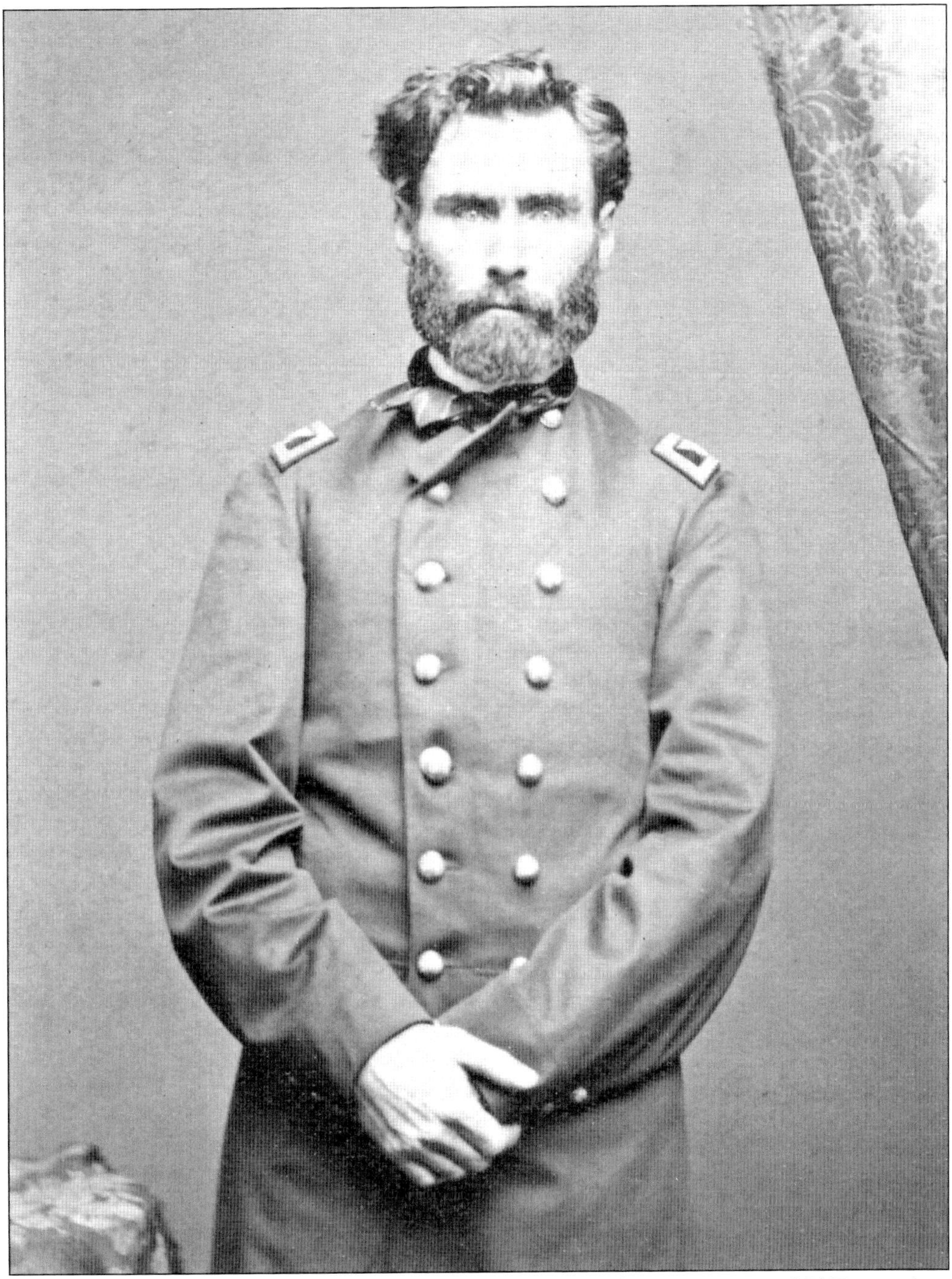

The lumber industry attracted the Jameson family from Gorham, Maine, to Old Town when Gen. Charles Davis Jameson was but a child. At the Civil War's commence, Jameson was elected colonel by his unit, the 2nd Maine Volunteer Regiment. Shipped to battle early in the war, the regiment saw immediate action in the First Battle of Bull Run. Jameson was made brigadier general of volunteers. He ran for governor of Maine on a pro-war platform as a Democrat but was defeated by Israel Washburn from Orono. Returning to battle, Jameson caught "camp fever" and was returned to Old Town, dying on route. (OTM.)

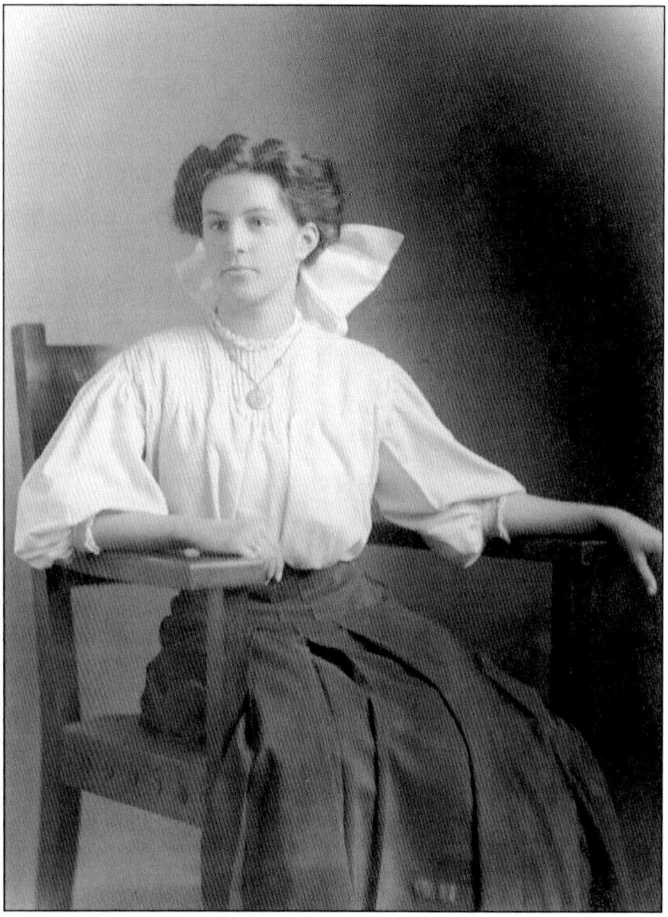

Edith Bussell graduated from the University of Maine in 1902 with a bachelor of science degree. She was hired immediately by the Old Town school system and taught biology (sometimes called "bugolgy" by her students) and retired in 1940 after 38 years of teaching. Originally from Old Town, she lived in neighboring Milford during much of her teaching career. (OTM.)

Penobscot Nation chief Joseph Nicholar—father of Lucy, Florence, and Emma—shakes hands with an unidentified official in 1920, perhaps the Indian agent or a representative of the Penobscot Lumber Association. Lucy became Princess Watahwaso, Florence built the Baptist church on Indian Island, and tribal advocate Emma married Joseph Ranco, a noted Penobscot canoe builder. (OTPL.)

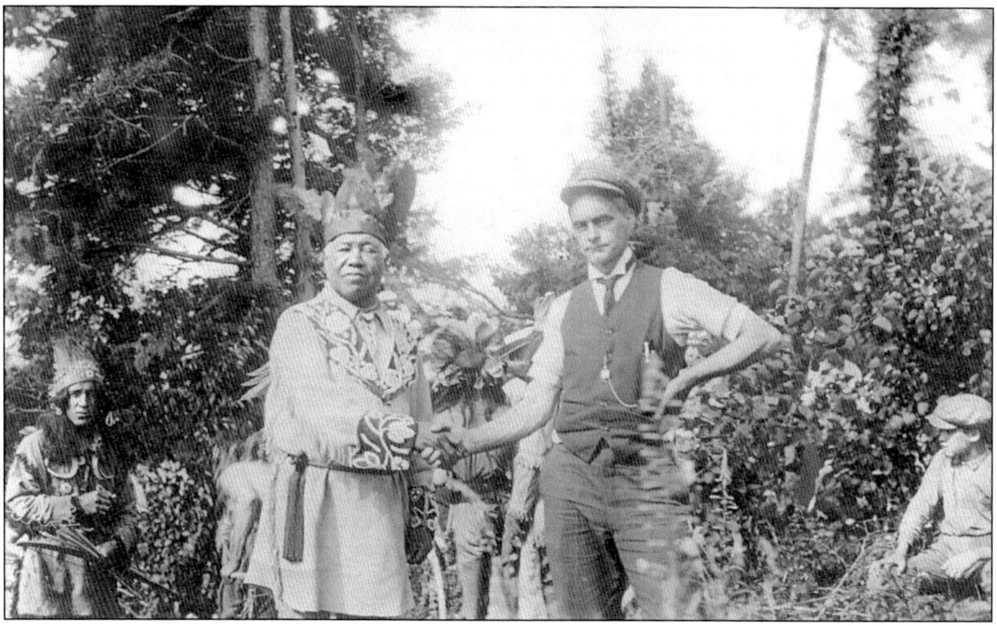

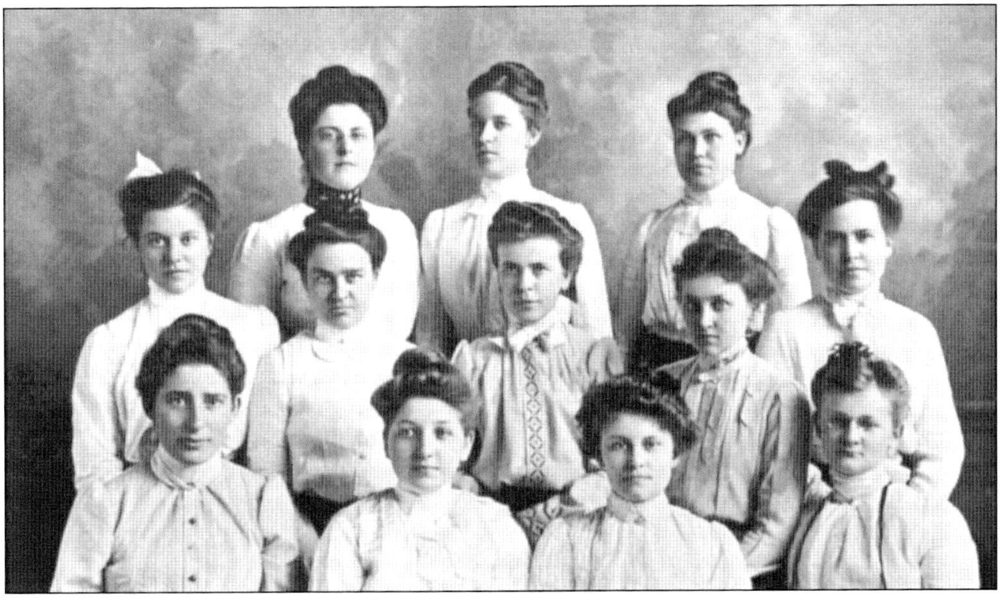

Cleora Carr (center), the daughter of David and Mary Carr, was a 1903 graduate of the University of Maine. She was devoted to the affairs of the Alpha Omicron Pi fraternity. In November 1920, her mother died. Her father, a former city councilor, died a year later. Cleora, suffering from a long-term illness, died on December 23, 1921. (PRS.)

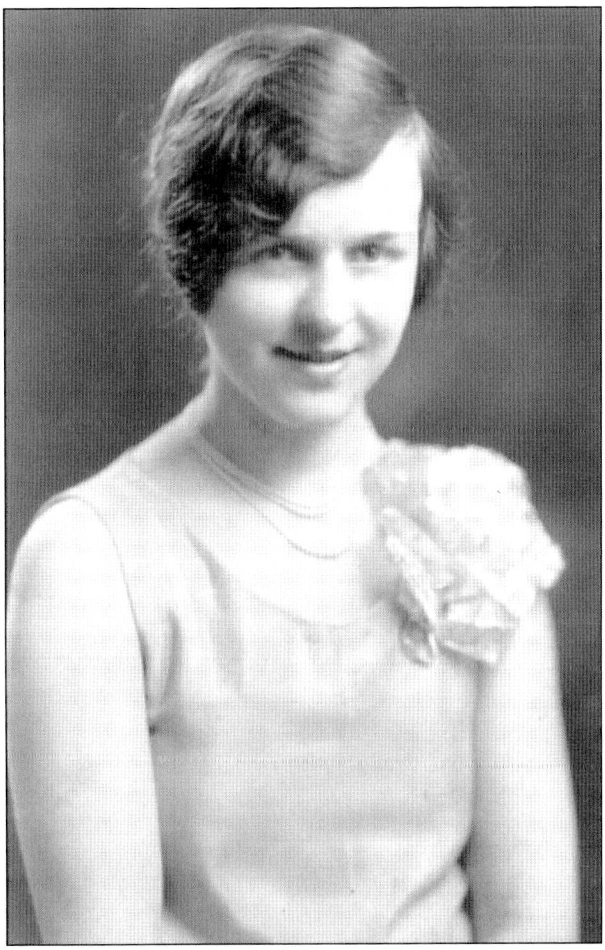

Following her graduation in 1919, Lillian Leveille worked briefly at Gray's Hardware but soon took another job, with the Maine Central Railroad in Bangor. She developed appendicitis and recovered successfully from emergency surgery. Leveille was a pitcher for the Penobscot Chemical Fibre's softball team, an actress in local plays, and a stenographer. (OTM.)

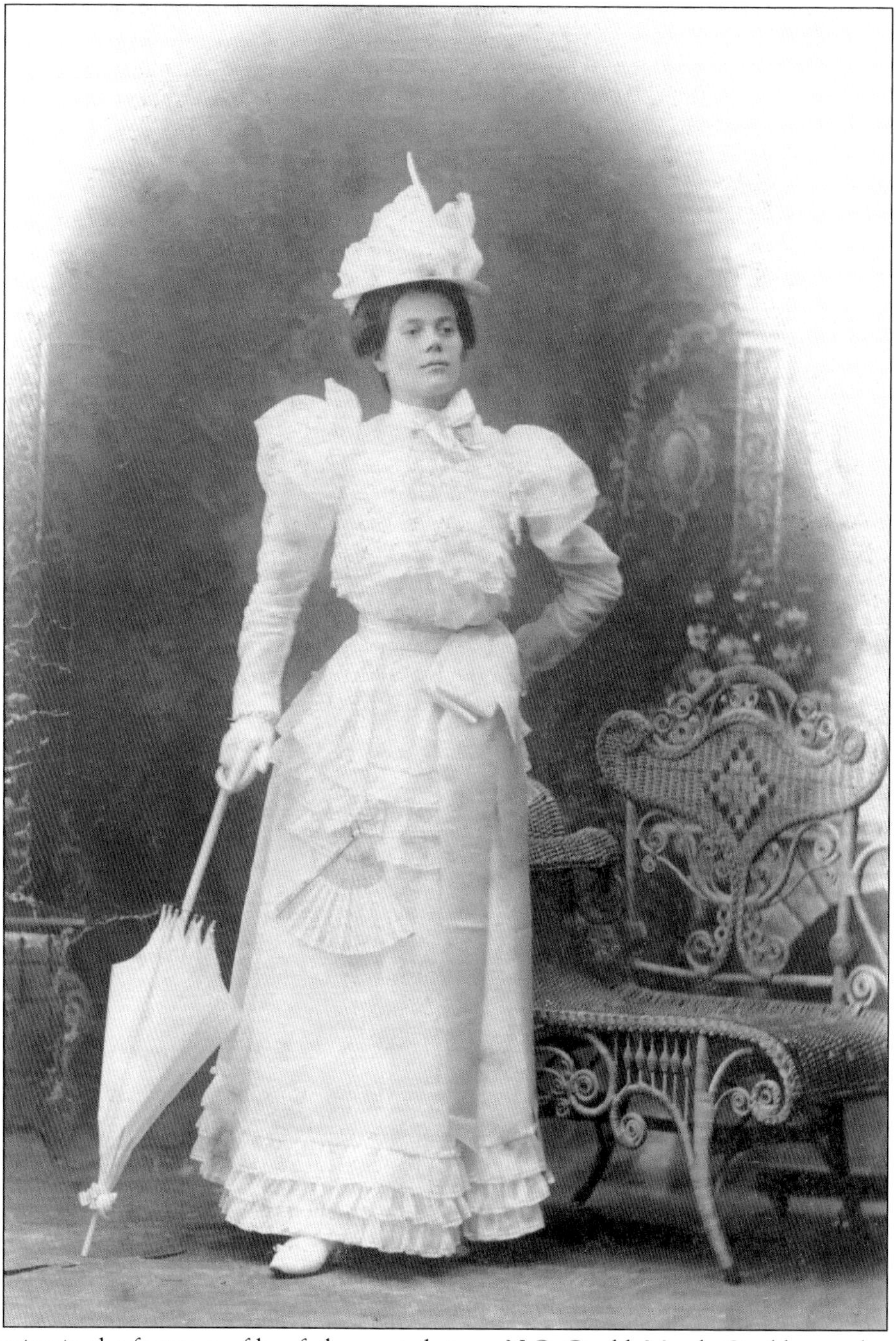

Following in the footsteps of her father, noted singer N.G. Gould, Maude Gould, a graduate of the Eastman School of Music in Rochester, New York, embraced a career in music. Instructing young people from Orono, Milford, and Old Town from the 1890s, she was also in demand as an entertainer. She found her calling with the Old Town school system in 1909, first as a certified voice and piano teacher and then as supervisor of music. Gould delighted in combining singers, orchestras, and even gymnastics in her public performances. During the 1930s, she pioneered group singing on WLBZ radio with her students. (OTM.)

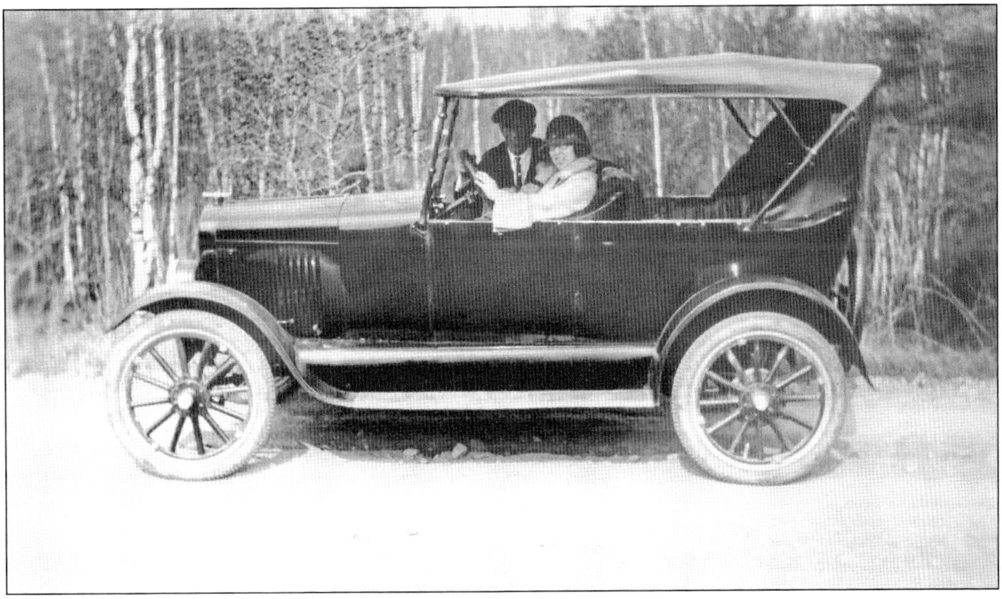

Lillian Roy sits at the wheel of an automobile while Victor Leveille looks on from the passenger seat. In 1903, there were about 125 autos in Maine, with half of them in the Portland area. As early as 1911, the *Old Town Enterprise* was lamenting the condition of the city's roads in the spring, noting that the automobile was here to stay. (OTM.)

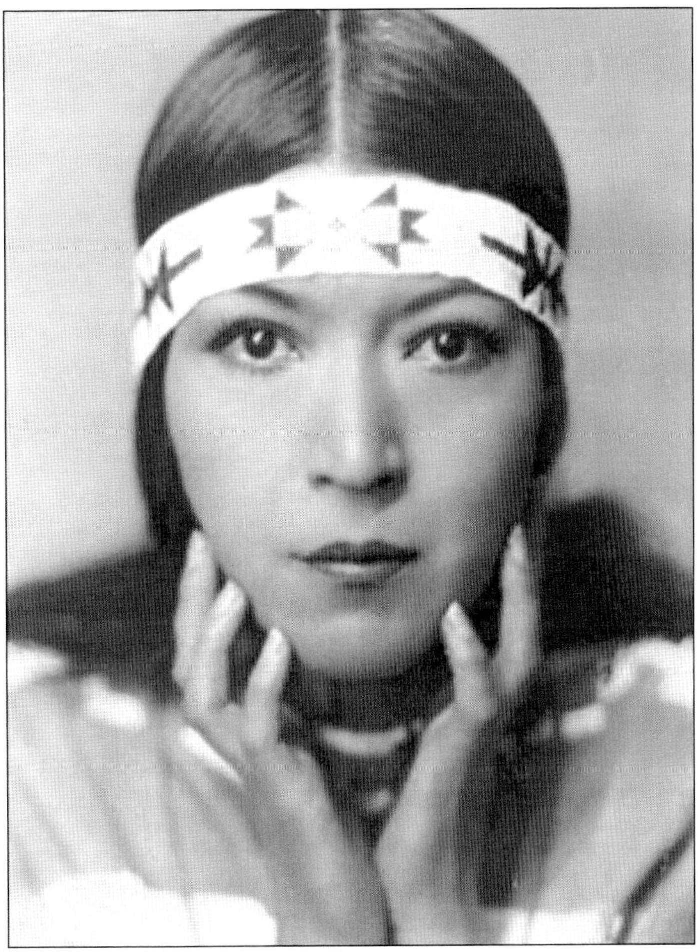

Molly Spotted Elk, born Mary Alice Nelson, was a member of the Penobscot Nation who became an internationally recognized entertainer as a dancer initially but as a film actress later. While a teenager, she moved into the household of Frank Speck, a noted anthropologist who wrote the classic ethnographical work *Penobscot Man* in 1940. (PRS.)

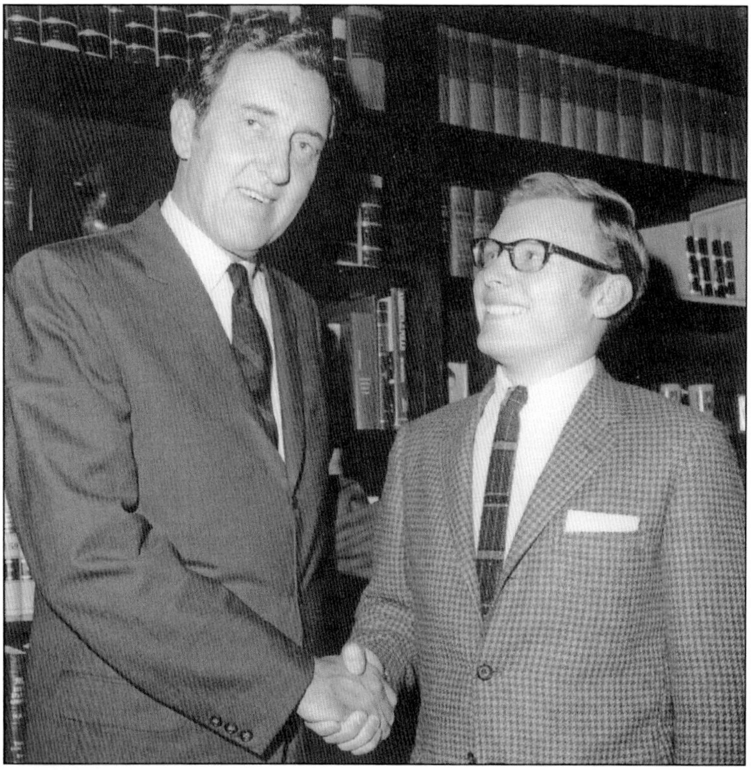

Gary Thorne (right) was a well-rounded scholar when he graduated from Old Town High School in the class of 1966. Shown here as an intern for Maine senator Edmund S. Muskie in the 1970s, Thorne earned a law degree and became a sports announcer for the New York Mets, the Baltimore Orioles, Major League Baseball, and the National Hockey League. (GAT.)

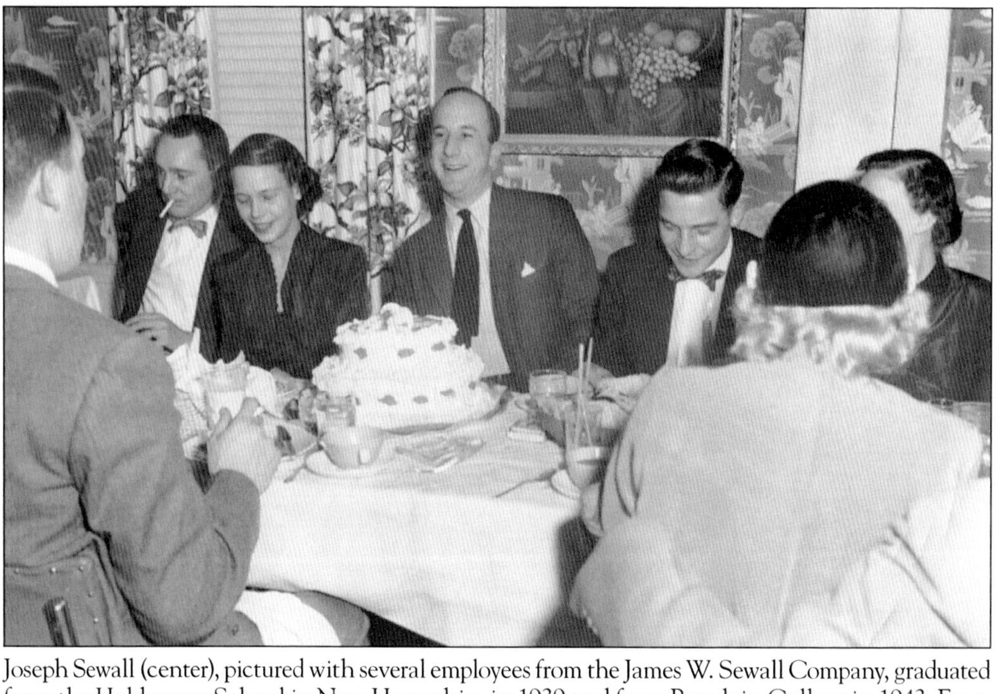

Joseph Sewall (center), pictured with several employees from the James W. Sewall Company, graduated from the Holderness School in New Hampshire in 1939 and from Bowdoin College in 1943. From 1946 to his retirement, he increased the number of employees fifteenfold. Elected a state senator four times, Sewall chaired the legislature's powerful Appropriations Committee. (CLW.)

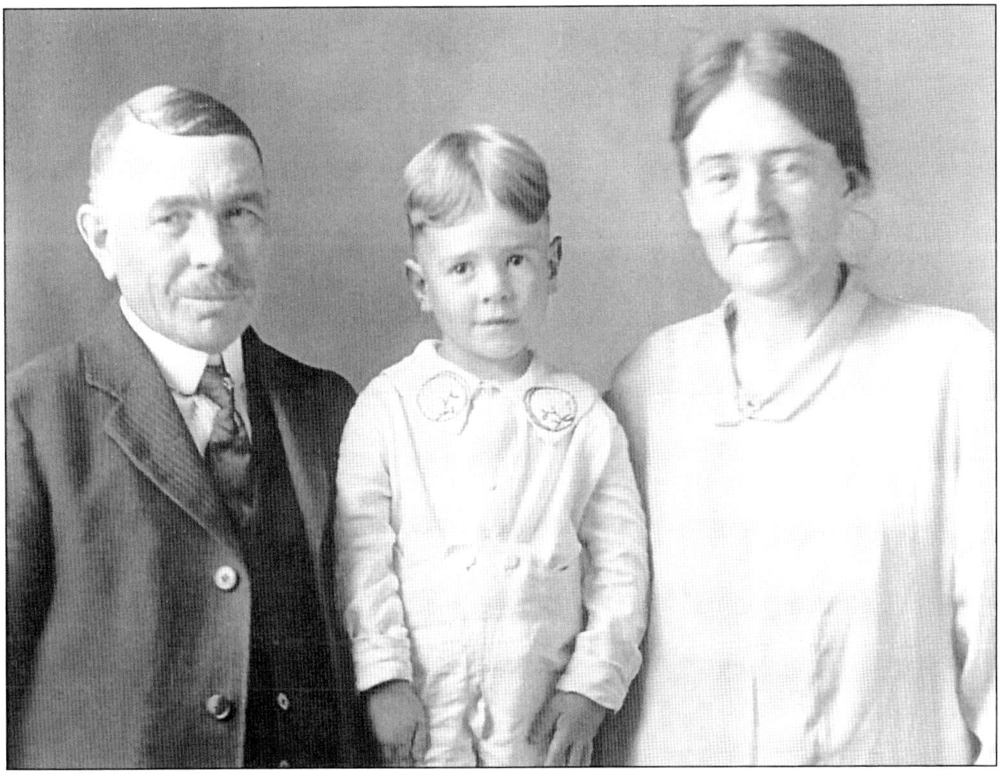

From left to right are Hamuel Carr, Hamuel Carr Jr., and Ina Carr, members of a large family of Carrs who migrated to the Pea Cove section of Old Town from the Fredericton, New Brunswick, area in the 1890s. Hamuel and Ina were cooks in the lumber camps in Pea Cove. Young Hamuel Carr died in 1949 while in the military. (RJV.)

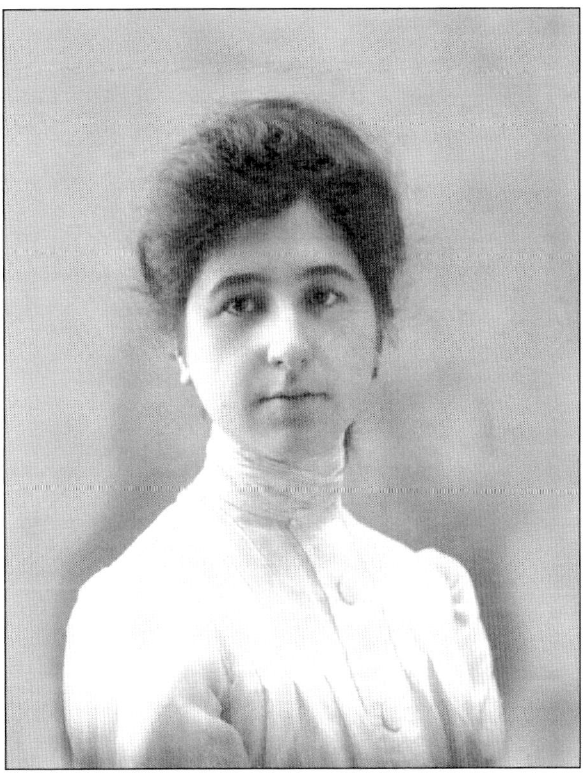

Louise Gray was the daughter of Old Town Canoe founder George A. Gray. She married James W. Sewall Jr., son of the founder of the James W. Sewall Company, in 1908, thus merging two noted Old Town families. One of their children was Joseph Sewall, who not only succeeded his father but became president of the Maine Senate from 1975 to 1982. (OTM.)

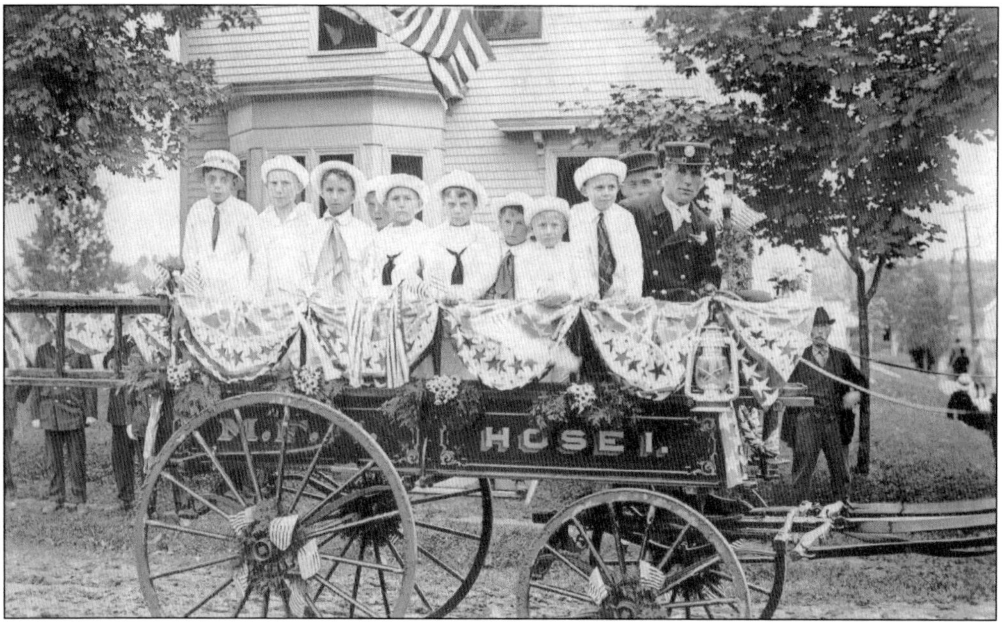

A group of boys joins firemen from the neighboring Milford Fire Department in this image from the 1920s. (CLM.)

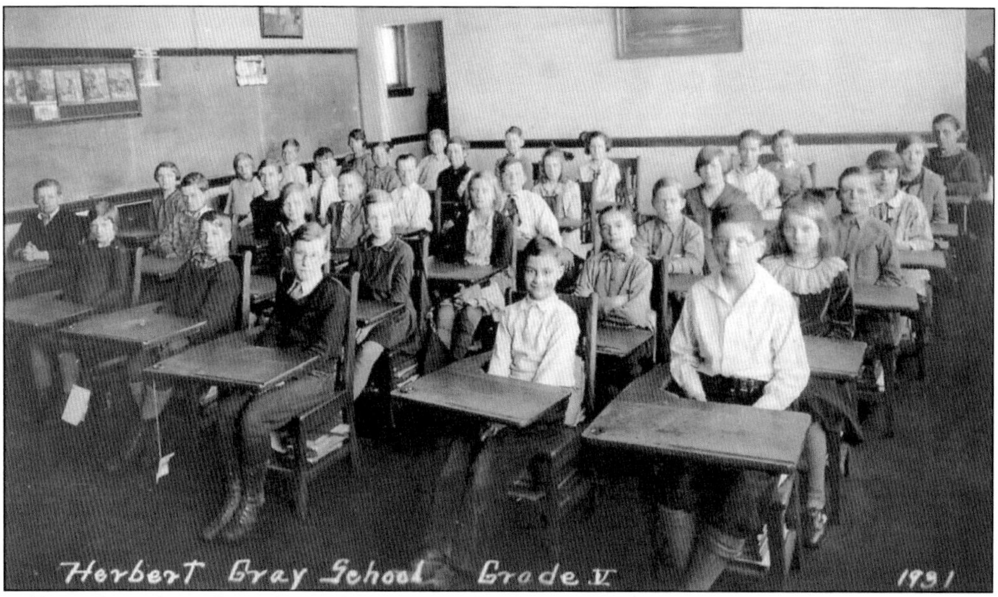

Fifth-grade students from the Herbert Gray School are pictured here in 1931. They are, from front to back, (far left row) Ellison Coffin, Freda Cates, Ethel Kennedy, Percy Young, and Margaret Way; (second row from left) Lois Tripp, Clayton Gilman, Hazel Campbell, Howard Merrill, Otis Butler, and Lynwood Rand; (third row from left) Edward Veazie, Grace Treadwell, Kenneth Fields, James Kennedy, Roy Whitlock, and Paul Danforth; (fourth row from left) Lynwood Dolan, Florence Cousins, Phyliss Hutchinson, George Cunningham, Virginia Stevens, and Helen Mehann; (second row from right) Orman Fernandez, Wesley Gray, Walter Mayhew, Esther Boynton, Harold Thibodeau, and John Davidson; (far right row) Joe Sewall, Helen Foley, Everett Fields, Katherine Fayles, Paula Goodwin, and Leo Levasseur. (CLM.)

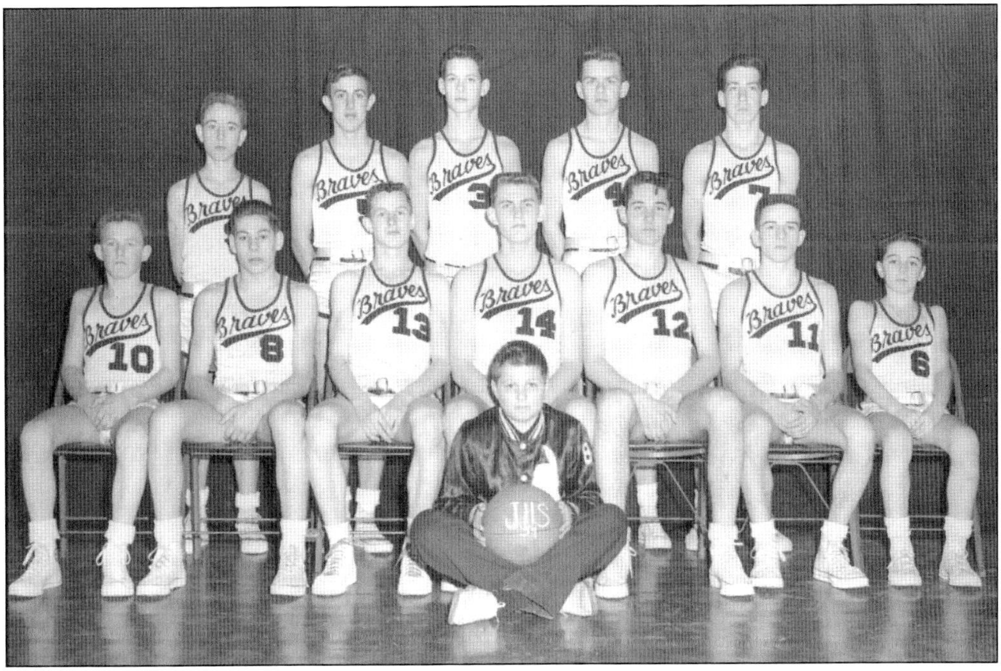

The Old Town Braves enjoyed an undefeated season in 1957–1958. From left to right are (first row) Robert Moores, Ron Thiboudeau, Tim Smart, Doug Thibault, Bob Fields, Bernard LaPlante, and Frank Commeau; (second row) John Hall, Ron Cote, George McCrum, Wayne Petrie, and Floyd McLaughlin. Manager Jim Willey is holding the ball. (OTM.)

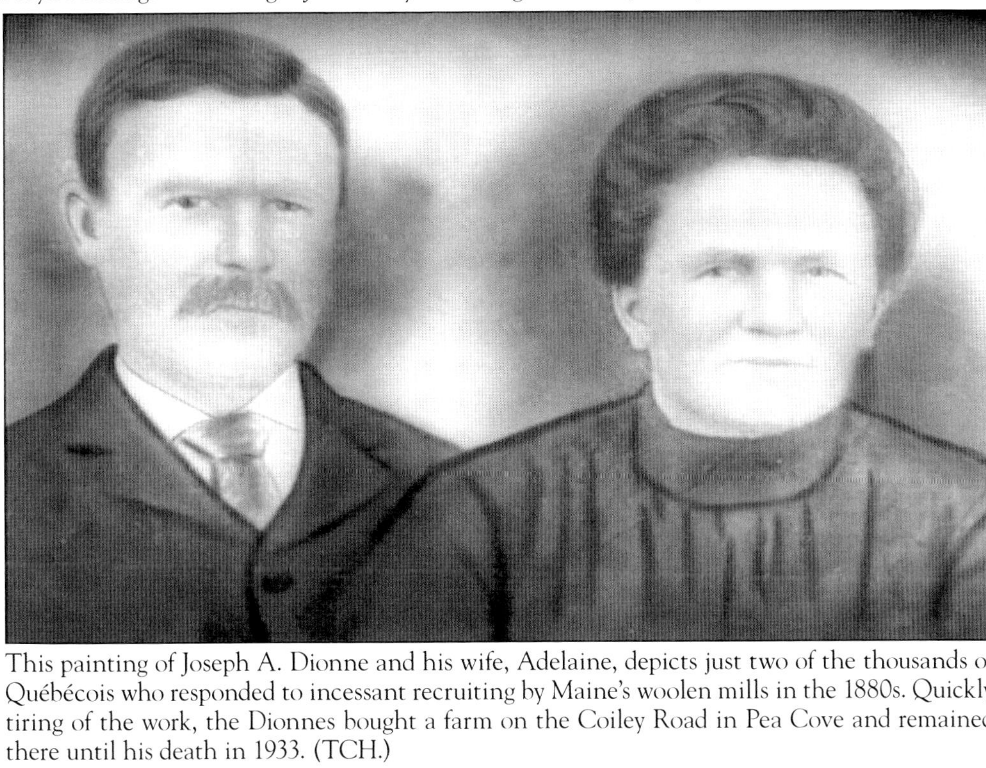

This painting of Joseph A. Dionne and his wife, Adelaine, depicts just two of the thousands of Québécois who responded to incessant recruiting by Maine's woolen mills in the 1880s. Quickly tiring of the work, the Dionnes bought a farm on the Coiley Road in Pea Cove and remained there until his death in 1933. (TCH.)

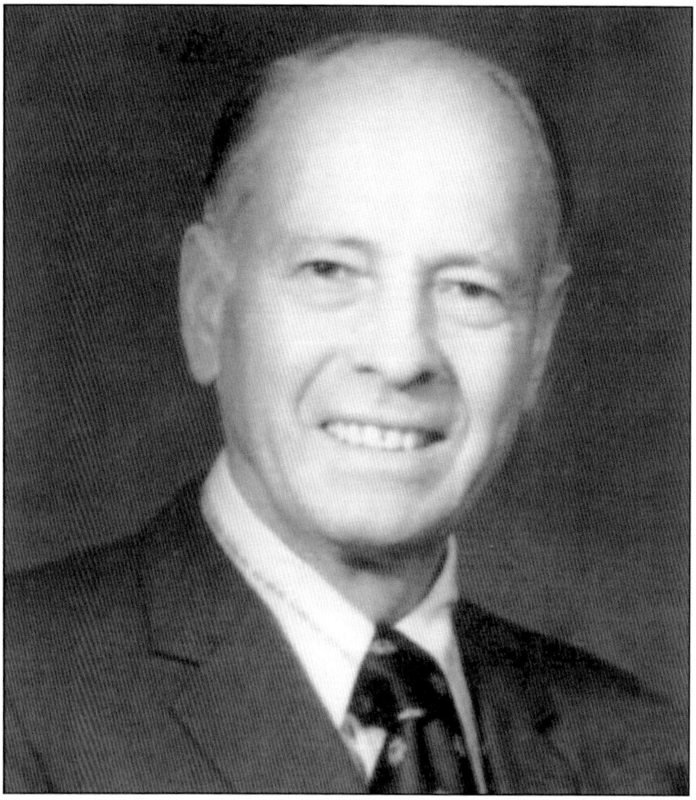

Herbert E. Sargent was born in 1906 and lived a full century. In the meantime, he became a civil engineer and went on to form one of the largest construction companies in Maine. Known for his lifelong community involvement, Sargent was instrumental in expanding the YMCA in Old Town and was a founding member of the Maine Community Development Foundation. (OTM.)

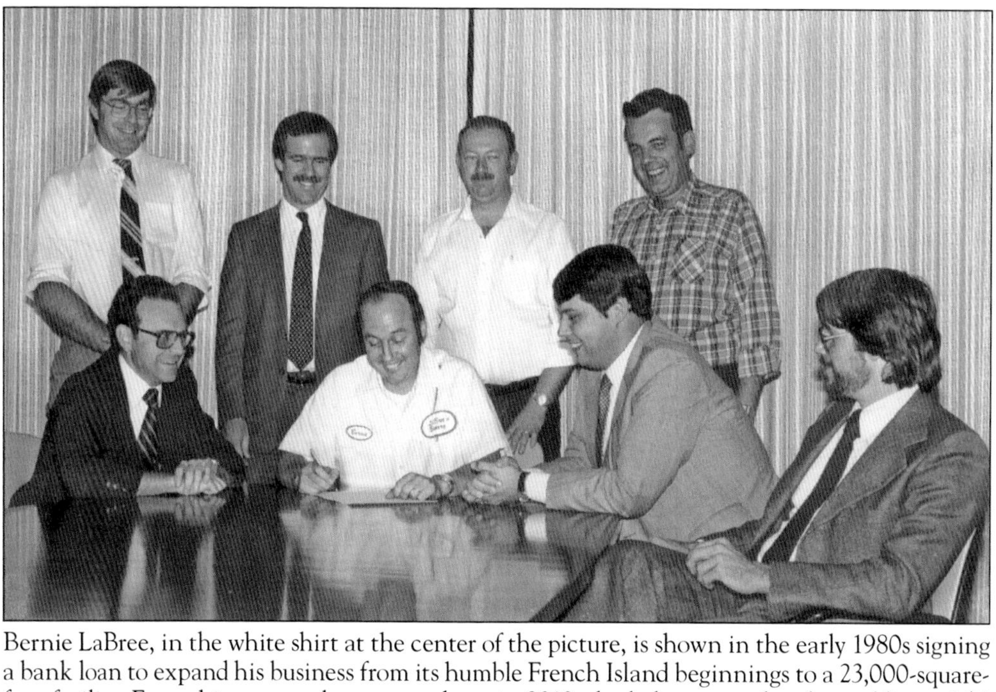

Bernie LaBree, in the white shirt at the center of the picture, is shown in the early 1980s signing a bank loan to expand his business from its humble French Island beginnings to a 23,000-square-foot facility. Even this was not large enough, as in 2010, the bakery completed an additional $5 million expansion. (BLB.)

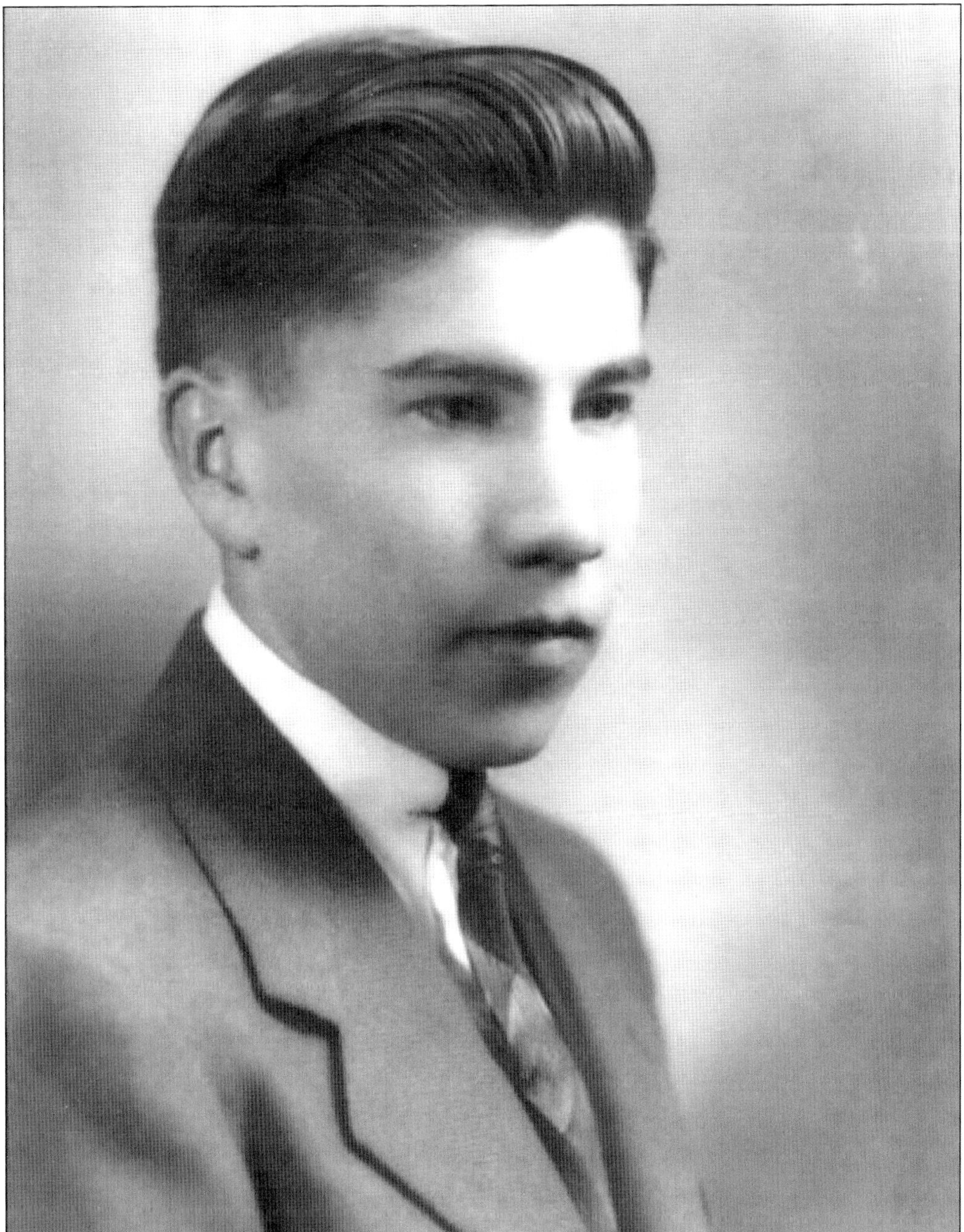

Descended from the Baron de Castin of France and Chief Orono's daughter, Charles Norman Shay's grandfather was Joseph Nicolar, whose seminal 1893 book *Life and Traditions of the Red Man* is still read today. Shay was born in Connecticut in 1924, but his parents were from Indian Island. A 1942 graduate of Old Town High School, he became a medic on Omaha Beach on June 6, 1944. During his service, he received the Bronze Star and the Silver Star and was briefly a prisoner of war. In 2007, Shay was made a Chevalier de la Légion d'honneur by Pres. Nicolas Sarkozy of France for his distinguished service. Since then, Shay has penned a touching autobiography called *Project Omaha Beach*, mostly in the form a personal letter to his late wife, Lilli. (CNS.)